MERN Projects for Beginners

Create Five Social Web Apps Using MongoDB, Express.js, React, and Node

Nabendu Biswas

Apress®

MERN Projects for Beginners: Create Five Social Web Apps Using MongoDB, Express.js, React, and Node

Nabendu Biswas
Bhopal, India

ISBN-13 (pbk): 978-1-4842-7137-7 ISBN-13 (electronic): 978-1-4842-7138-4
https://doi.org/10.1007/978-1-4842-7138-4

Managing Director, Apress Media LLC: Welmoed Spahr
Acquisitions Editor: Louise Corrigan
Development Editor: James Markham
Coordinating Editor: Jessica Vakili

Distributed to the book trade worldwide by Springer Science+Business Media New York, 1 NY Plaza, New York, NY 10014. Phone 1-800-SPRINGER, fax (201) 348-4505, e-mail orders-ny@springer-sbm.com, or visit www.springeronline.com. Apress Media, LLC is a California LLC and the sole member (owner) is Springer Science + Business Media Finance Inc (SSBM Finance Inc). SSBM Finance Inc is a **Delaware** corporation.

For information on translations, please e-mail booktranslations@springernature.com; for reprint, paperback, or audio rights, please e-mail bookpermissions@springernature.com.

Apress titles may be purchased in bulk for academic, corporate, or promotional use. eBook versions and licenses are also available for most titles. For more information, reference our Print and eBook Bulk Sales web page at http://www.apress.com/bulk-sales.

Any source code or other supplementary material referenced by the author in this book is available to readers on GitHub via the book's product page, located at www.apress.com/978-1-4842-7137-7. For more detailed information, please visit http://www.apress.com/source-code.

Printed on acid-free paper

Table of Contents

About the Author

Nabendu Biswas is a full-stack JavaScript developer who has been working in the IT industry for the past 16 years. He has worked for some of the world's top development firms and investment banks. Nabendu is a tech blogger who publishes on DEV Community (dev.to), Medium (medium.com), and The Web Dev(TWD) (thewebdev. tech). He is an all-around nerd who is passionate about everything JavaScript, React, and Gatsby. You can find him on Twitter @nabendu82.

About the Technical Reviewer

Alexander Nnakwue is a self-taught software engineer with experience in back-end and full-stack engineering. With experience spanning more than four years, he loves to solve problems at scale. Currently, he is interested in startups, open source web development, and distributed systems. In his spare time, Alexander loves watching soccer and listening to all genres of music.

CHAPTER 1

MERN Deployment Setup

Welcome to *MERN Projects for Beginners*, where you learn to build awesome web apps using the MERN (MongoDB, Express, React, Node.js) framework. This stack is in high demand in the startup sector because you can make a fully functional web app using it. A front-end engineer who knows HTML, CSS, and React can quickly learn Node.js and MongoDB and build a fully production-ready web app.

In this book, you learn how to host a back end using Node.js code in Heroku. The front-end site uses React code and Firebase hosting. It is also hosted through a cloud database called MongoDB Atlas. Most of the hosting setups are the same in the next five chapters, so it won't be repeated in most chapters.

The MERN Stack at a Glance

Before installing Firebase, let's discuss the basics of the technologies involved in the MERN stack.

- **MongoDB** is an open source document based on the NoSQL database. It is different from traditional relational databases that store data in tables. It stores data in JSON-like documents. It is highly scalable and performance-oriented and thus suited for modern-day web apps.

- **React** is the most popular open source JavaScript library for building a website's or web app's front end or user interface. It is developed and maintained by Facebook.

- **Node.js** lets developers write server-side code using JavaScript. It integrates very well with React or Angular at the front end and with MongoDB for databases.

- **Express** is a framework of Node.js, and through it, you can create API endpoints, which are the basis of any back-end server-side code.

© Nabendu Biswas 2021
N. Biswas, *MERN Projects for Beginners*, https://doi.org/10.1007/978-1-4842-7138-4_1

Firebase Hosting Initial Setup

You need a Google account to work with Firebase. Go to `https://firebase.google.com`
and click **Go to console** in the top-right corner. You must be logged in to your Google
account to do so, as seen in Figure 1-1.

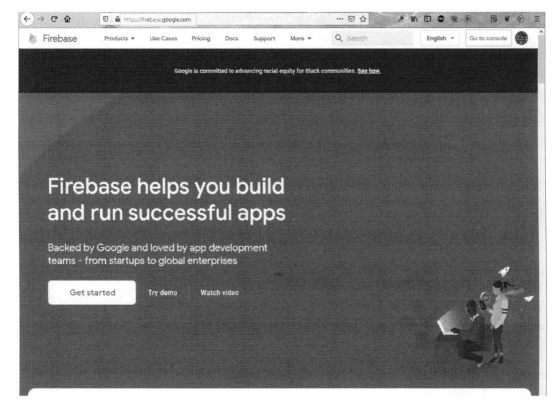

Figure 1-1. *Firebase console caption*

Click the **Add project** link on the page, as seen in Figure 1-2.

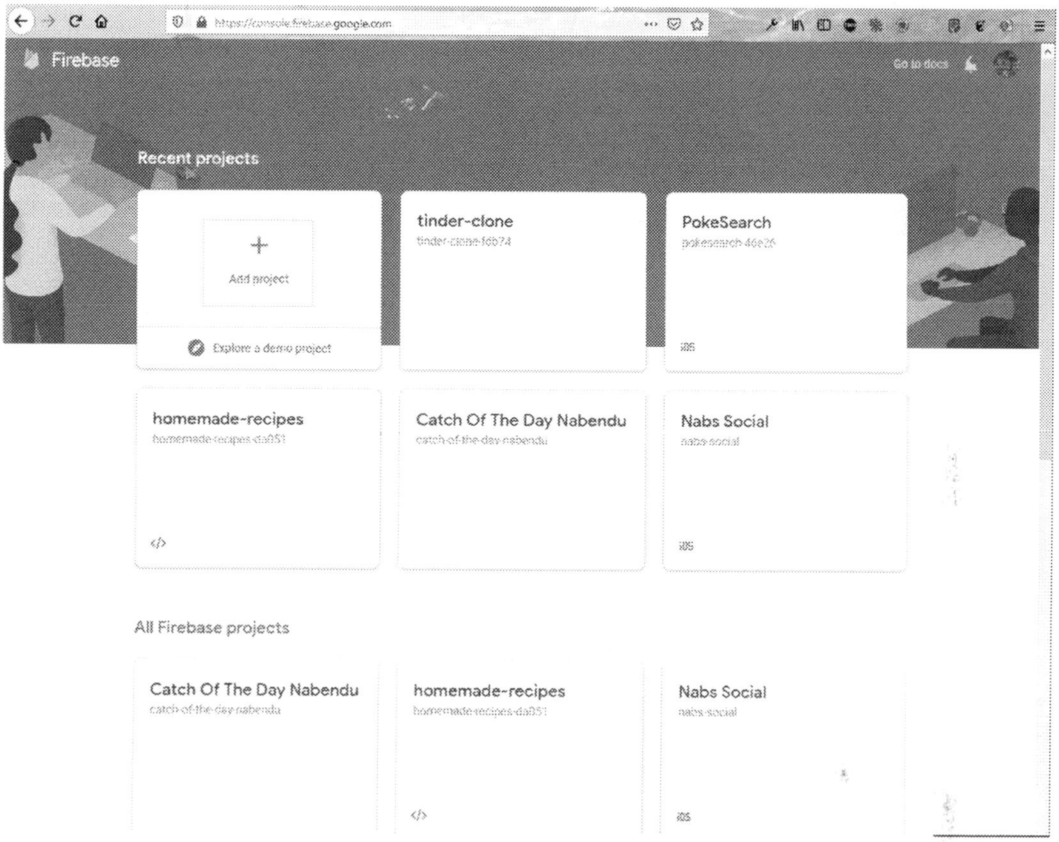

Figure 1-2. *Add project*

On this page, name the project **dating-app-mern**, and then click the **Continue** button, as seen in Figure 1-3. Note that this is just an installation instruction. You start building the app in the next chapter.

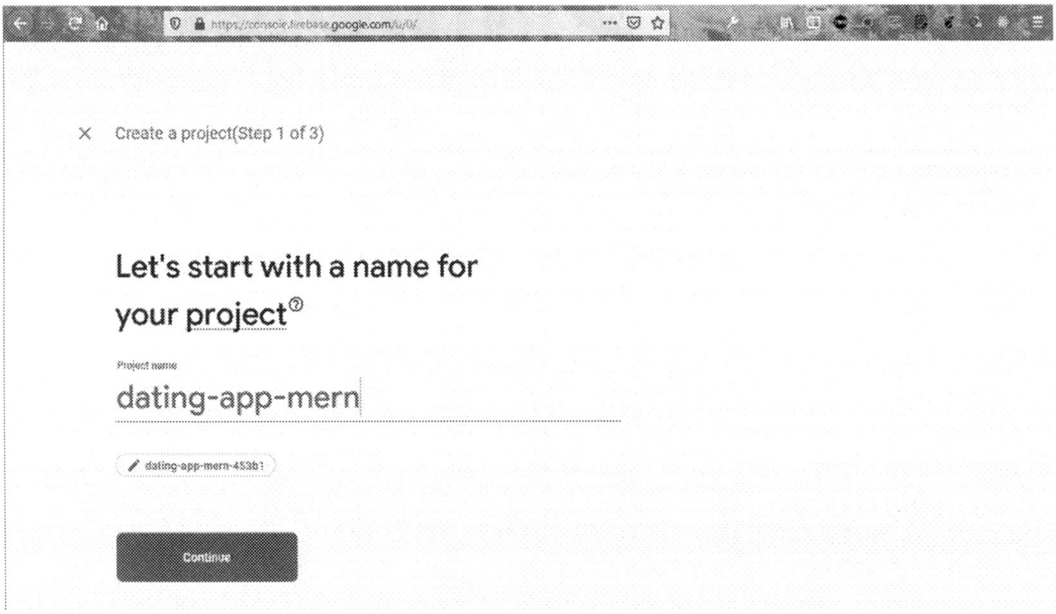

Figure 1-3. *App name*

On the next page, click the **Create project** button, as seen in Figure 1-4.

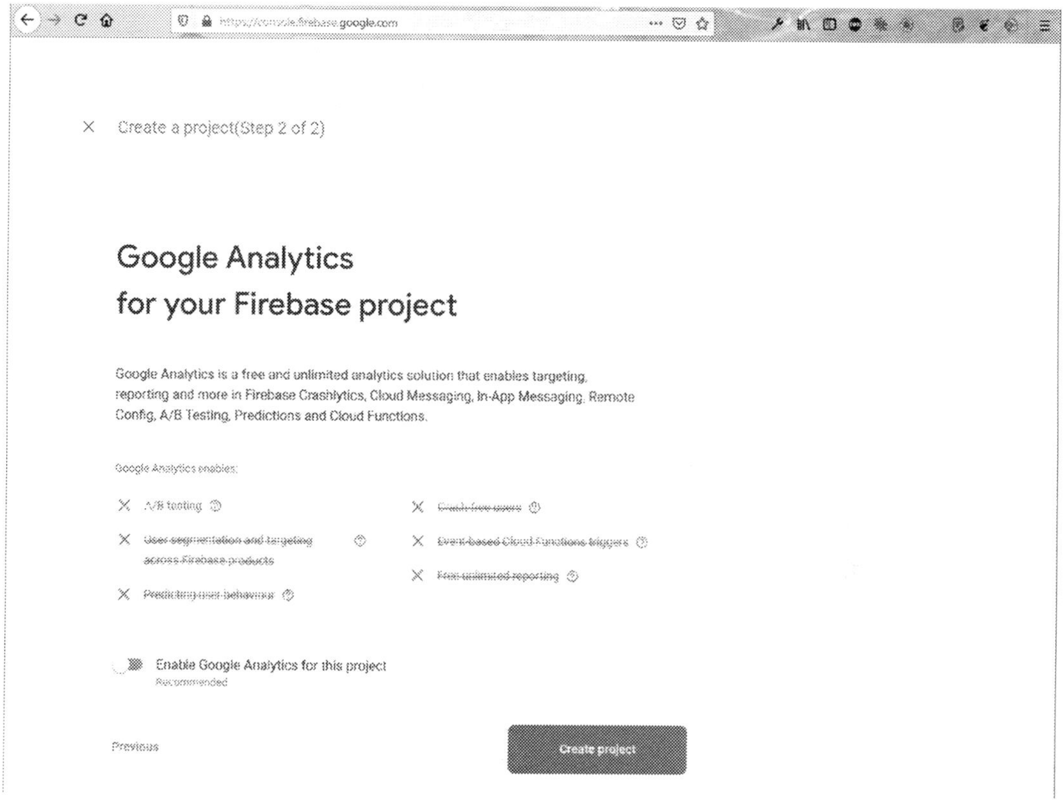

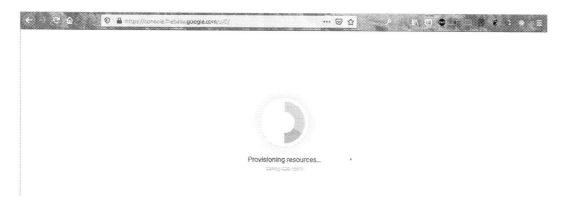

Figure 1-4. *Create project*

It takes some time to create the project, as seen in Figure 1-5.

Figure 1-5. *Project created*

MongoDB Setup

MongoDB is the database that you work with on the cloud. It is also known as MongoDB Atlas. This is easier to work with than setting up on a local machine. Go to www.mongodb.com and log in or create a new account.

Creating a New Project

After logging in, you see a screen similar to the one shown in Figure 1-6. Click the **New Project** button.

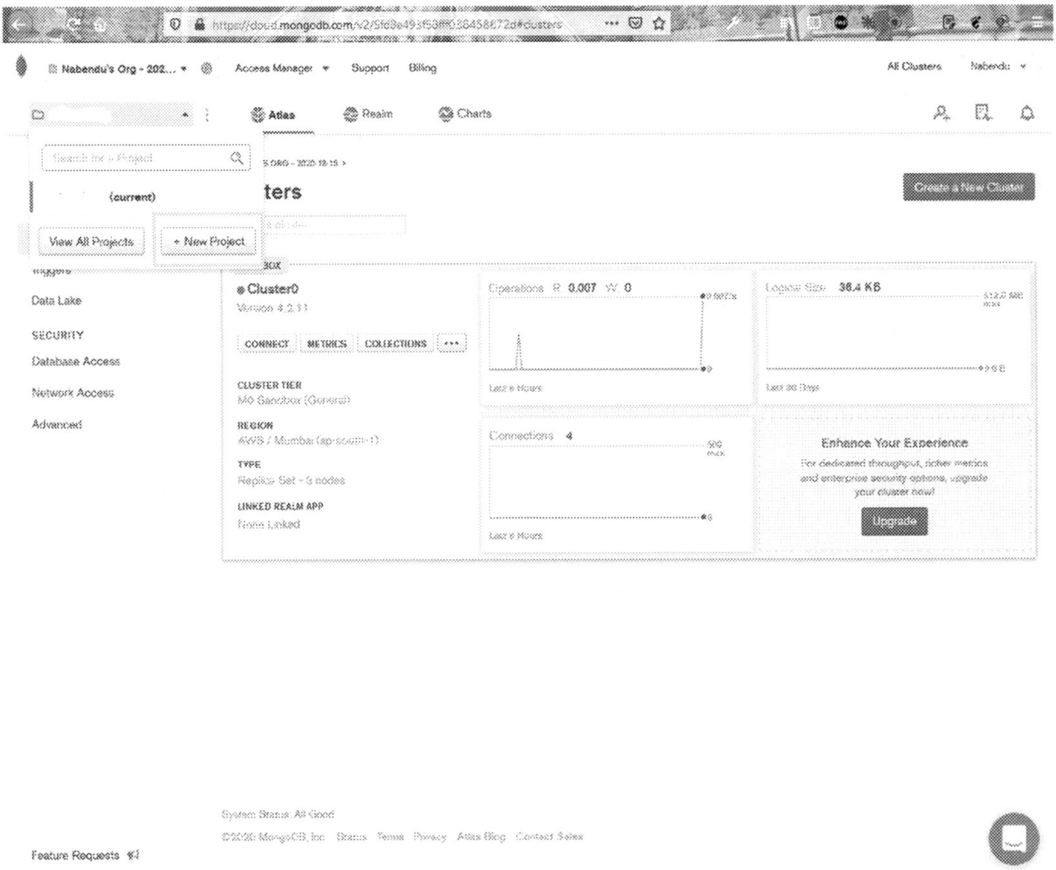

Figure 1-6. *MongoDB new project*

Name your project **dating-app-mern**, and then click the **Next** button, as seen in Figure 1-7.

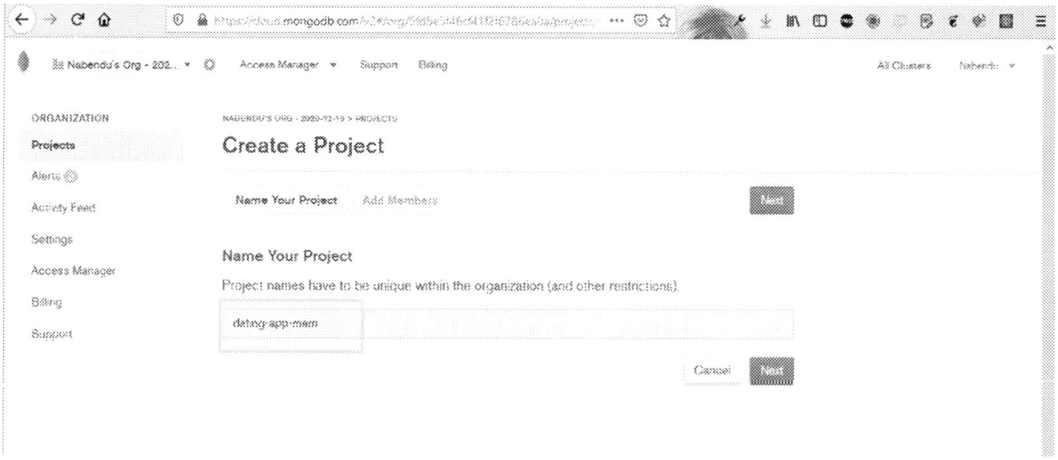

Figure 1-7. *Project name*

On the next screen, click the **Create Project** button, as seen in Figure 1-8.

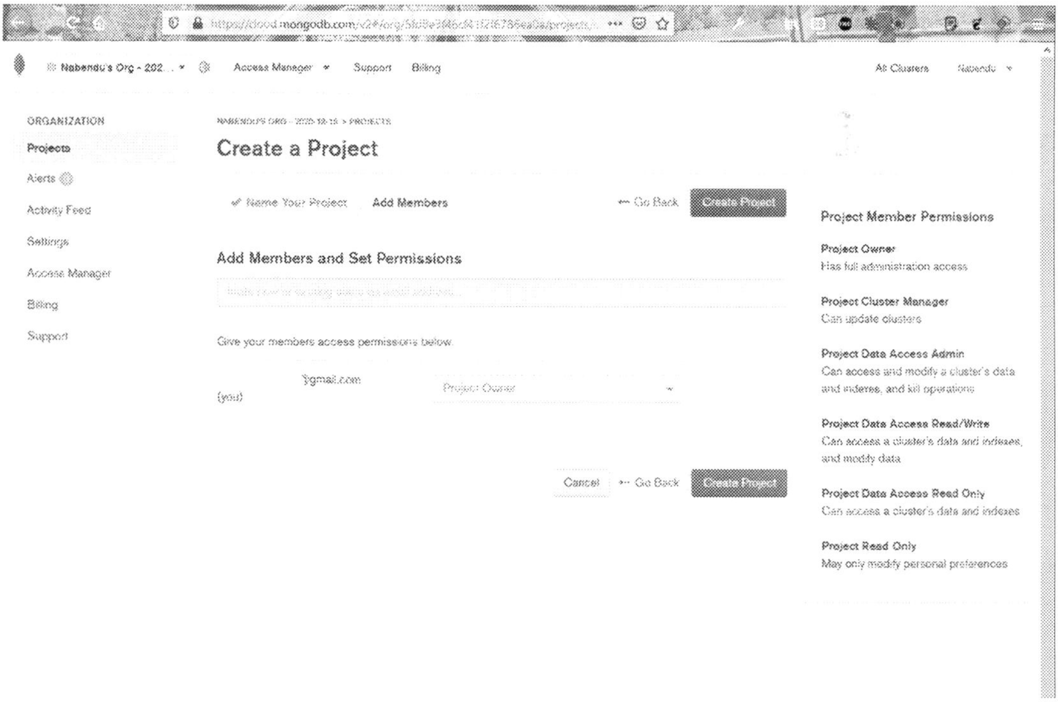

Figure 1-8. *MongoDB Create Project*

On the next screen, click the **Build a Cluster** button, as seen in Figure 1-9.

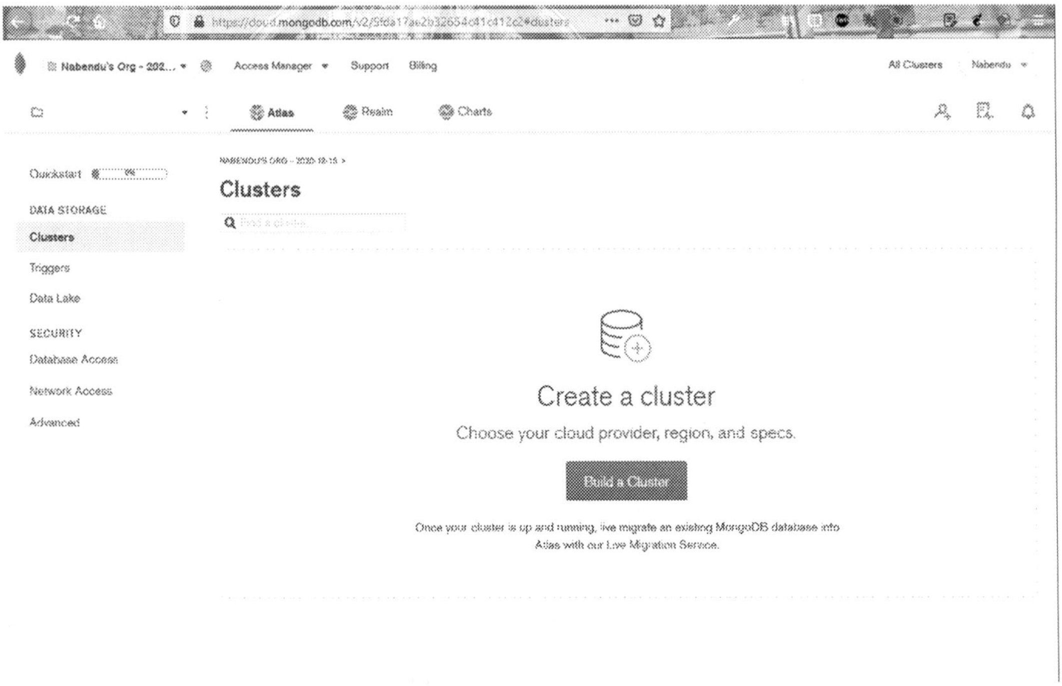

Figure 1-9. *Build a Cluster*

On the next screen, select the Free tier, as seen in Figure 1-10.

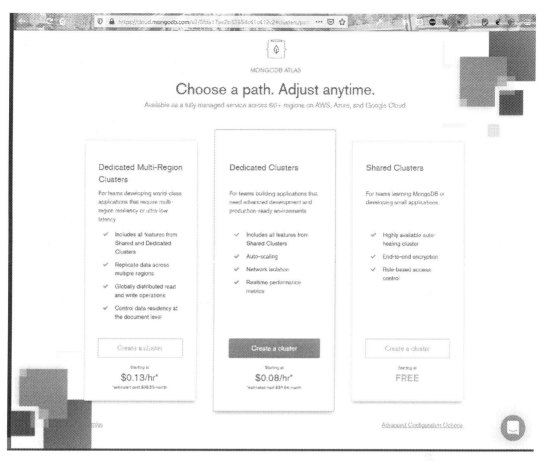

Figure 1-10. *Free tier*

On the next screen, you need to choose the AWS region in which to create the
database. (I chose Mumbai because I live in India, and this gives me low latency.)
Afterward, click the **Create Cluster** button, as seen in Figure 1-11.

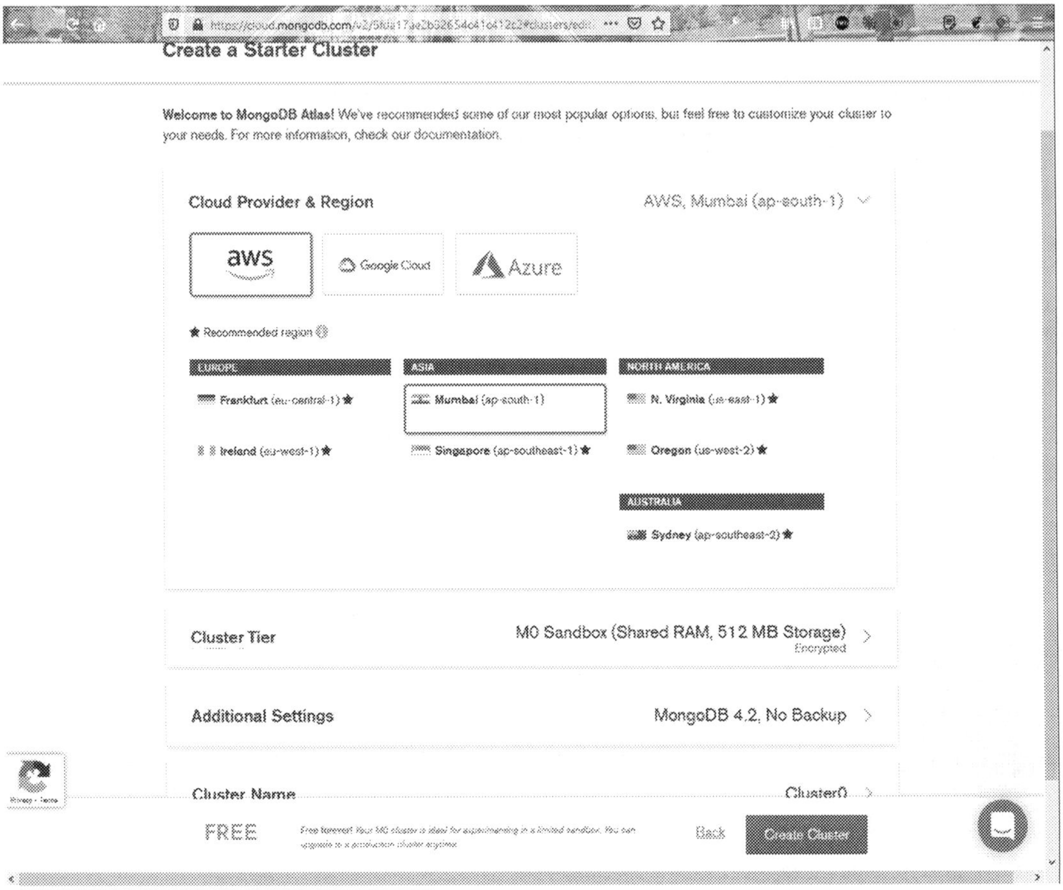

Figure 1-11. *Choose region*

The next screen shows that the cluster has been created, which takes time. You can go back and create your first API endpoint, as seen in Figure 1-12.

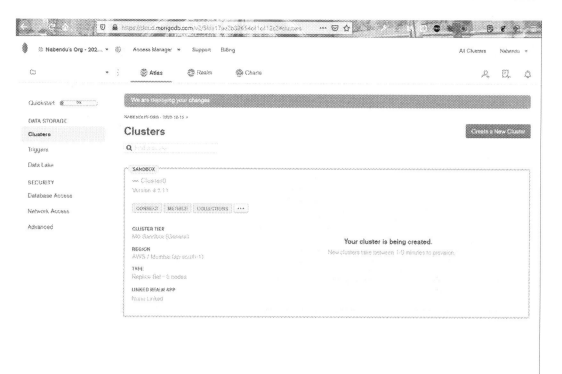

Figure 1-12. *Cluster created*

Database User and Network Access

To create a user in MongoDB, click the **Database Access** tab and then the **Add New Database User** button, as seen in Figure 1-13.

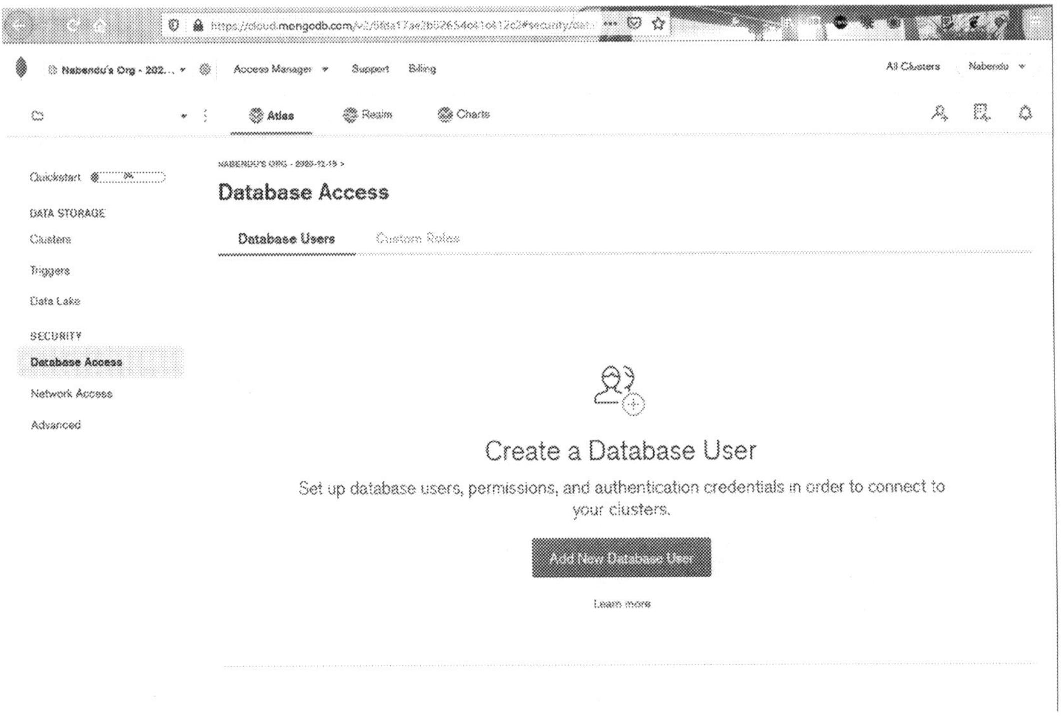

Figure 1-13. *Create database user*

On the next screen, you need to enter a username and a password, as seen in Figure 1-14. You must remember both. Next, scroll down and click the **Add User** button.

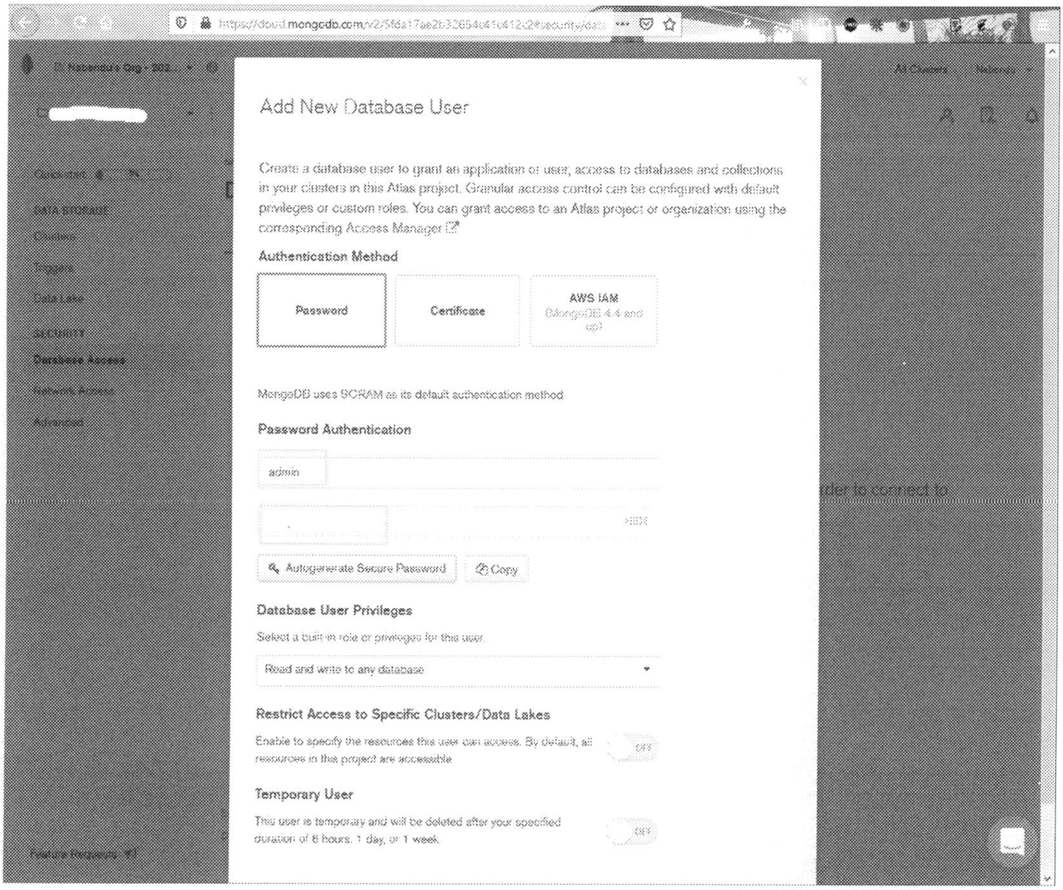

Figure 1-14. *Add user*

Next, go to the **Network Access** tab and click the **Add IP Address** button, as seen in Figure 1-15.

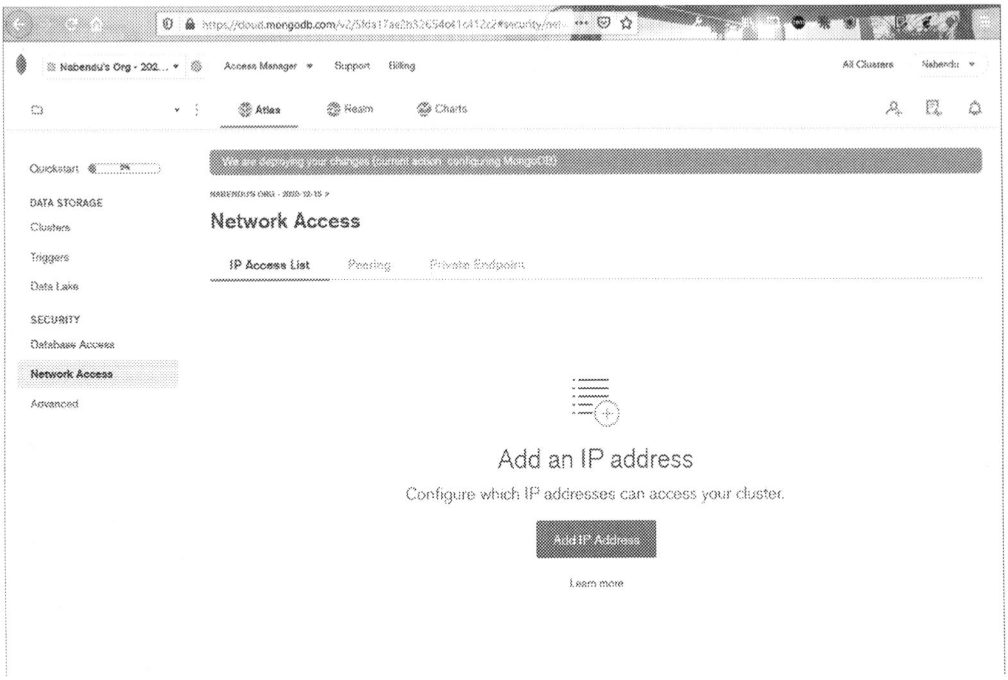

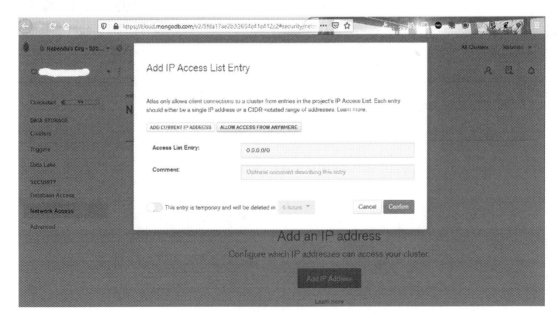

Figure 1-15. *Network access*

In the popup window, click the **ALLOW ACCESS FROM ANYWHERE** button and then click the **Confirm** button, as seen in Figure 1-16.

Figure 1-16. *Allow access*

Next, return to the **Cluster** tab and click the **CONNECT** button, which opens the popup window shown in Figure 1-17. Click the **Connect your application** tab.

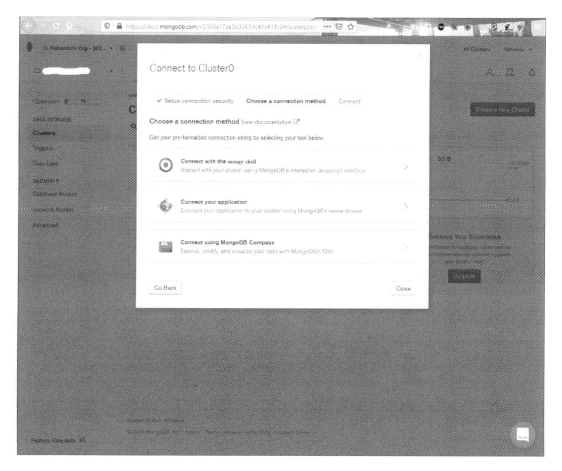

Figure 1-17. *Connect your application*

Copy the connection URL by clicking the **Copy** button, as seen in Figure 1-18.

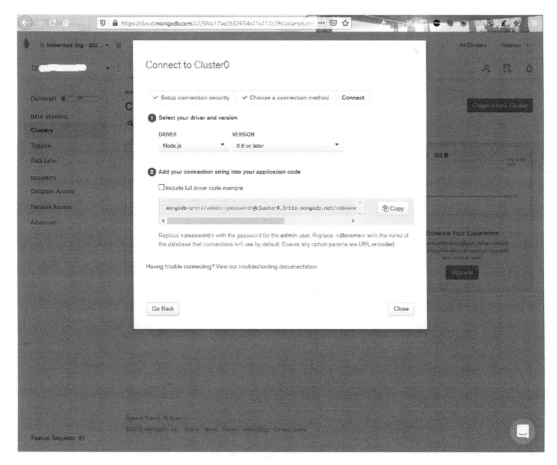

Figure 1-18. *Connection string*

Deploying the Back End to Heroku

Once you complete the back-end code, go to www.heroku.com to deploy the back end.
Log in to your Heroku account, click the **New** drop-down menu, and then click the
Create new app button, as seen in Figure 1-19. You can also do this from the command
line using the Heroku CLI, but that is not covered here.

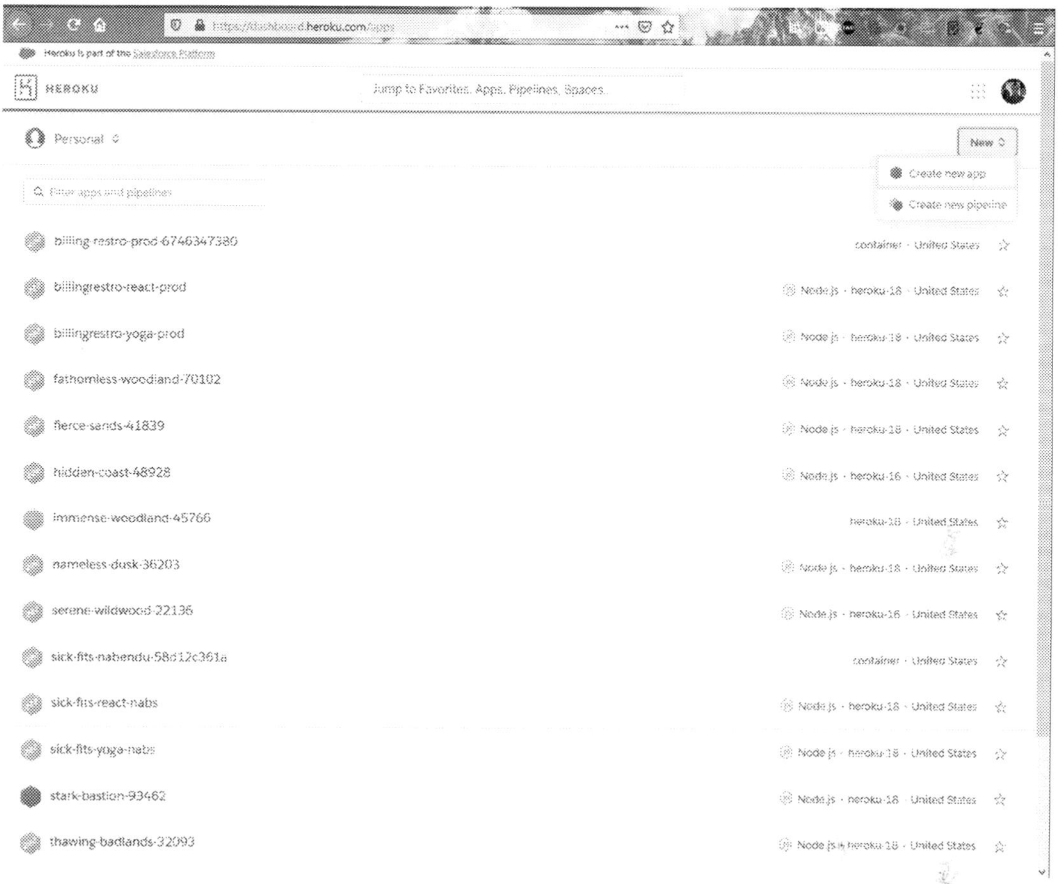

Figure 1-19. *Heroku login*

Next, name the app and click the **Create app** button, as seen in Figure 1-20.

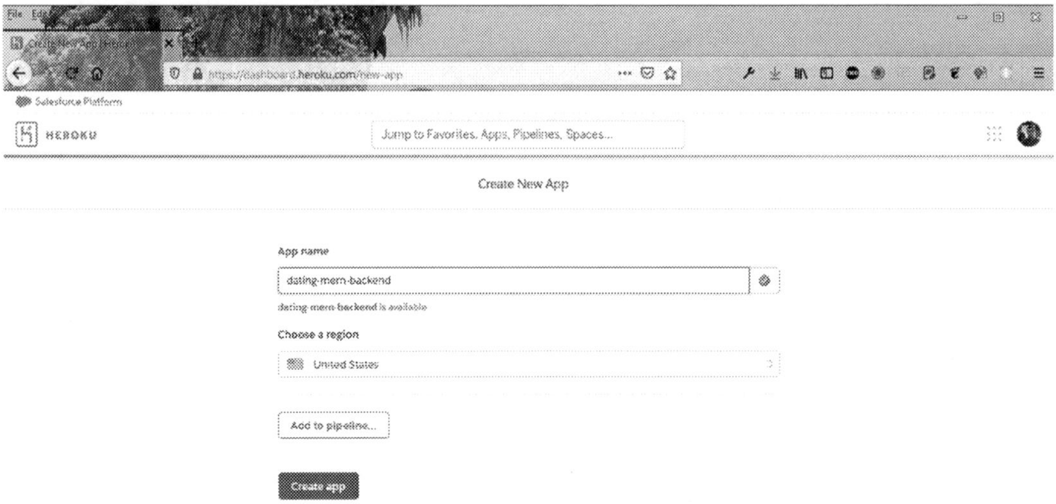

Figure 1-20. *Heroku app name*

The next screen shows all the commands to deploy your app, but you need the Heroku CLI. Click the link and follow the instructions to install it on your operating system, as seen in Figure 1-21.

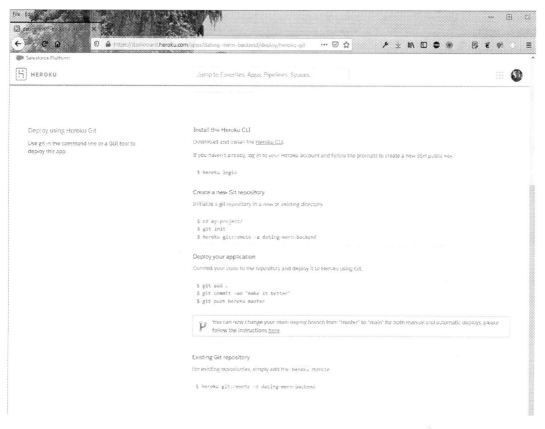

Figure 1-21. *Heroku instructions*

Run the `heroku login` command in the `backend` folder. You are asked for permission to open the browser. This command asks you to press any key to open in the browser.

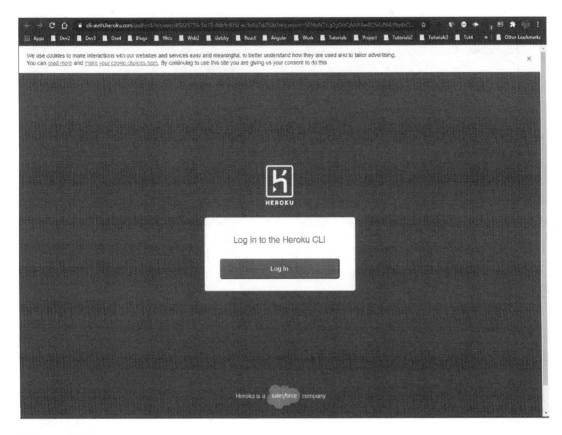

Figure 1-22.

Here, you can log in with your credentials, as seen in Figure 1-23.

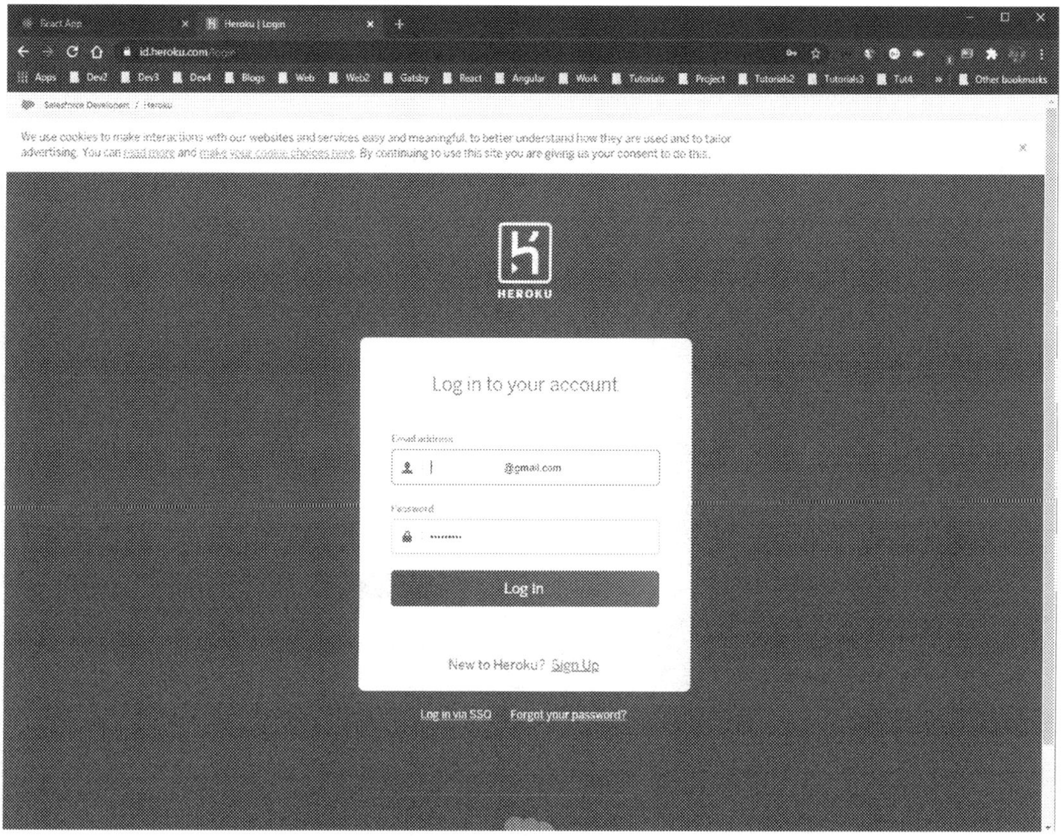

Figure 1-23. *Login credentials*

After successfully logging in, you see the page shown in Figure 1-24, which you need to close.

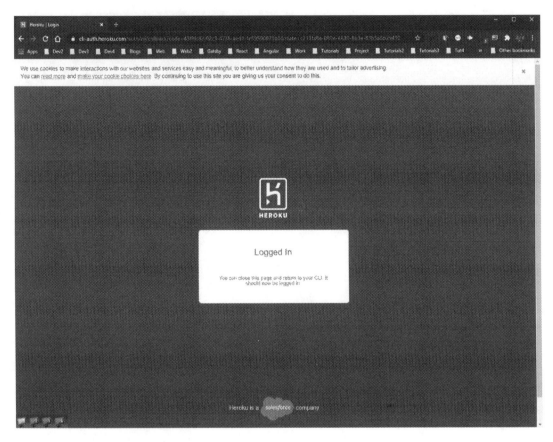

Figure 1-24. *Close popup*

You need to push the code from your local machine to the Heroku repository. Now that you are logged in to your account, you can run the following command to connect to Heroku Git.

```
heroku git:remote -a dating-mern-backend
```

Next, let's run the familiar `git` command to commit the code. Now, Git is software that tracks changes in a file; it is a must in software development. The following commands add code to the staging area, then commits it. The `push` command pushes it to remote Heroku servers.

```
git add .
git commit -m "backend code complete"
git push heroku master
```

After the installation is done, click the **Open app** button, which takes you to the deploy site, as seen in Figure 1-25.

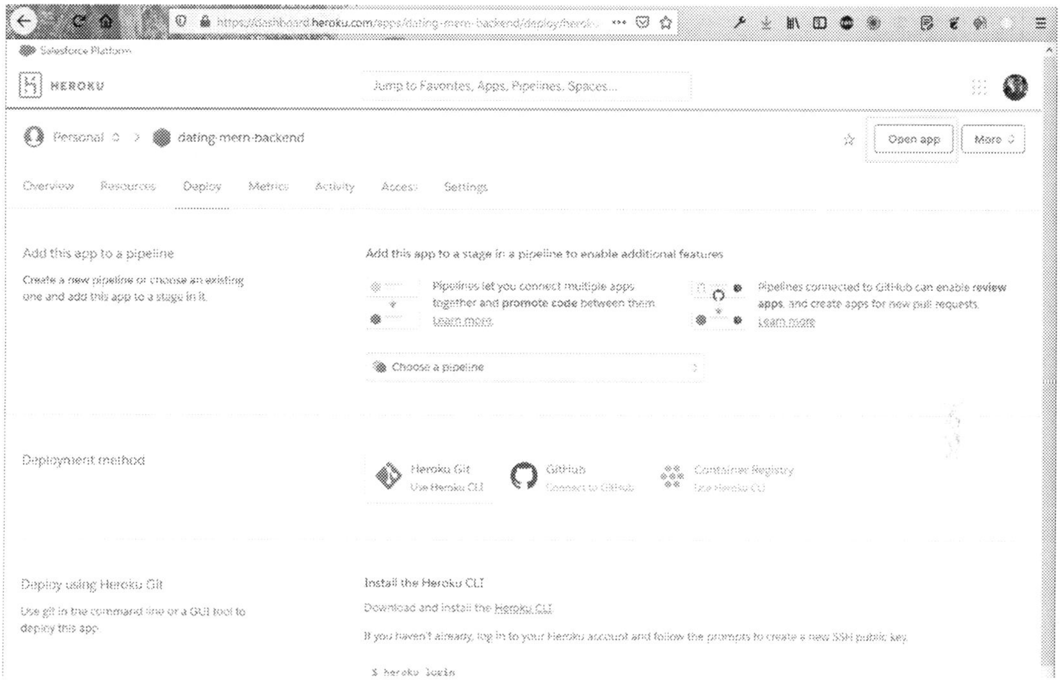

Figure 1-25. *Open back-end app*

Deploying the Front End to Firebase

After the front-end project is complete (in an upcoming chapter), you can deploy it in Firebase. Go to the `frontend` folder and run the `firebase login` command in the terminal. If you are running it for the first time, a popup window opens. Next, run the `firebase init` command. Type **Y** to proceed.

```
firebase login
firebase init
```

Use the down arrow key to go to **Hosting**, as seen in Figure 1-26. Press the spacebar to select it, and then press the Enter key.

```
? Are you ready to proceed? Yes
? Which Firebase CLI features do you want to set up for this folder? Press Space to select features, then Enter to confirm your choices.

 ( ) Database: Configure Firebase Realtime Database and deploy rules
 ( ) Firestore: Deploy rules and create indexes for Firestore
 ( ) Functions: Configure and deploy Cloud Functions
>(*) Hosting: Configure and deploy Firebase Hosting sites
 ( ) Storage: Deploy Cloud Storage security rules
 ( ) Emulators: Set up local emulators for Firebase features
 ( ) Remote Config: Get, deploy, and rollback configurations for Remote Config
```

Figure 1-26. *Configure*

Select **Use an existing project**, as seen in Figure 1-27, and press the Enter key.

```
? Please select an option: (Use arrow keys)
> Use an existing project
  Create a new project
  Add Firebase to an existing Google Cloud Platform project
  Don't set up a default project
```

Figure 1-27. *Existing project*

Next, select the correct project, which is **dating-app-mern-453b1** in my case, as seen in Figure 1-28.

```
? Please select an option: Use an existing project
? Select a default Firebase project for this directory:
  career-firebase-app (career-firebase-app)
  covid-19-tracker-dc20a (covid-19-tracker)
> dating-app-mern-453b1 (dating-app-mern)
  facebook-clone-mern-aa5a3 (facebook-clone-mern)
  facebook-firebase-clone (facebook-firebase-clone)
  final-space-react-c84fa (final-space-react)
  homemade-recipes-da051 (homemade-recipes)
(Move up and down to reveal more choices)
```

Figure 1-28. *Correct project*

Next, choose the public directory, which is build. The following question asks about a single-page app; answer **Yes**. The next question is about GitHub deploys; answer **No**, as seen in Figure 1-29.

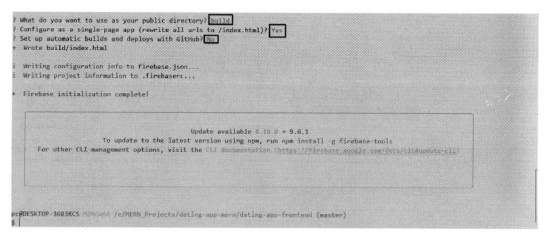

Figure 1-29. Build

Next, run npm run build in the frontend folder for an optimal production build. The final command, firebase deploy, deploys the project to Firebase. If successful, the site is now live, which is shown in upcoming chapters.

Install Node.js and npm

Let's go over installing Node.js and npm (node package manager) if they are not already installed on your system. Most of the code in this book requires Node.js and npm. The React front-end code also requires Node.js. Through npm, you can install many small open sourced programs, which adds functionality to both React and Node.js.

When you install Node.js, npm is also automatically installed on your system. The following instructions are for a Windows-based system, although macOS users can find a similar guide on the Internet.

In your web browser, enter **https://nodejs.org/en/download/** and click Windows Installer, as seen in Figure 1-30. Again, it also installs npm.

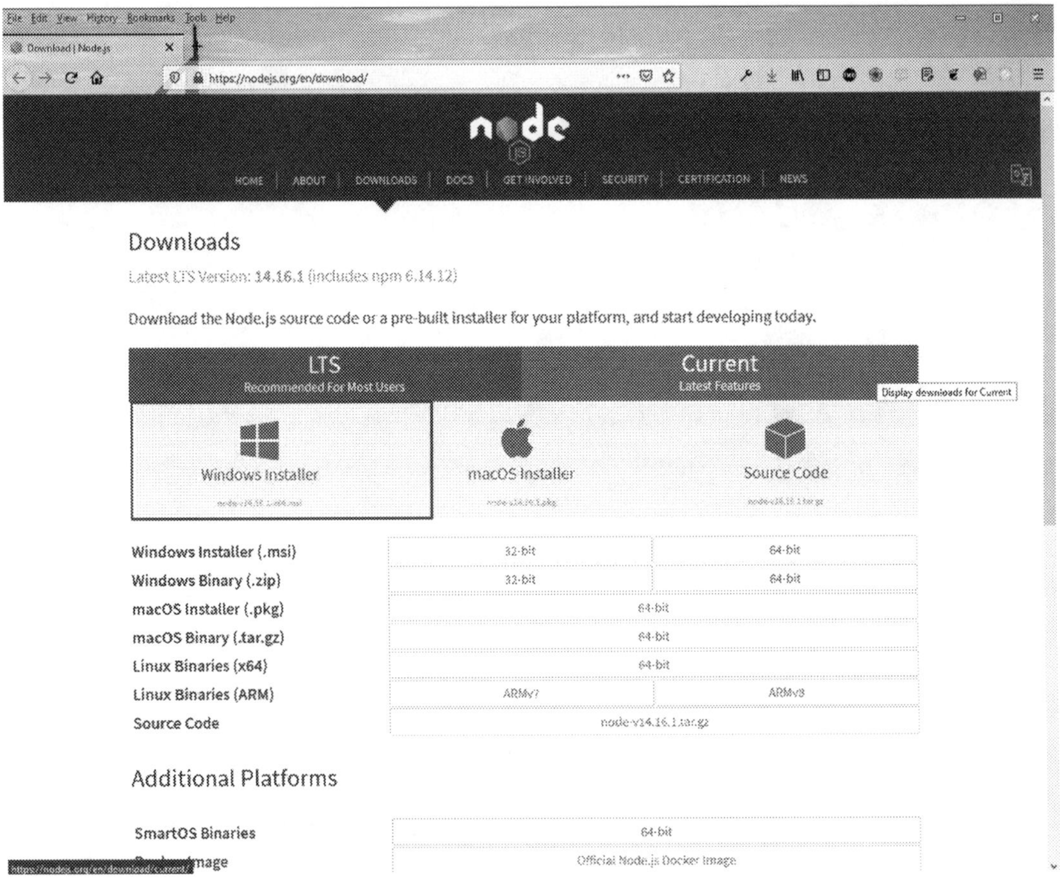

Figure 1-30. *Node.js installer*

The downloaded file is installed in your Download folder by default. Click it, and then click the **Run** button, as seen in Figure 1-31.

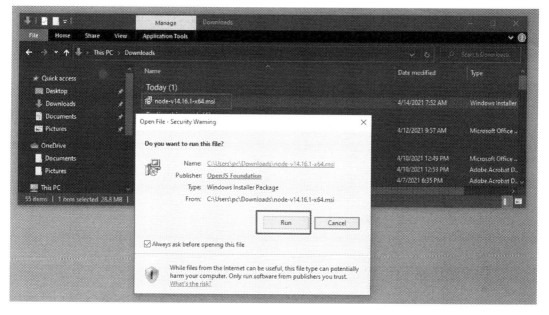

Figure 1-31. *Run button*

In the Node.js installation popup window, click the **Next** button, as seen in Figure 1-32.

Figure 1-32. *Node.js welcome*

Click to accept the end-user license agreement, and then click the **Next** button, as seen in Figure 1-33.

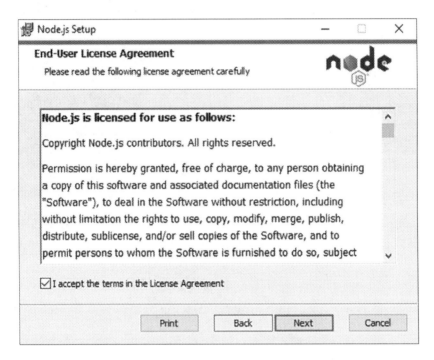

Figure 1-33. *Agreement*

Next, I advise that you use the installation location shown in Figure 1-34.

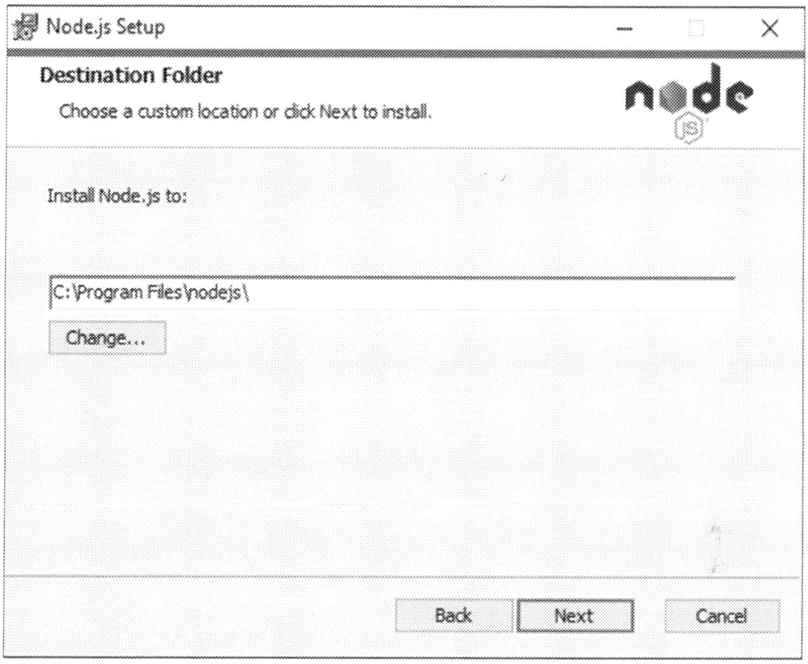

Figure 1-34. *Installation location*

The wizard asks you to choose a package. Keep the defaults, as seen in Figure 1-35.

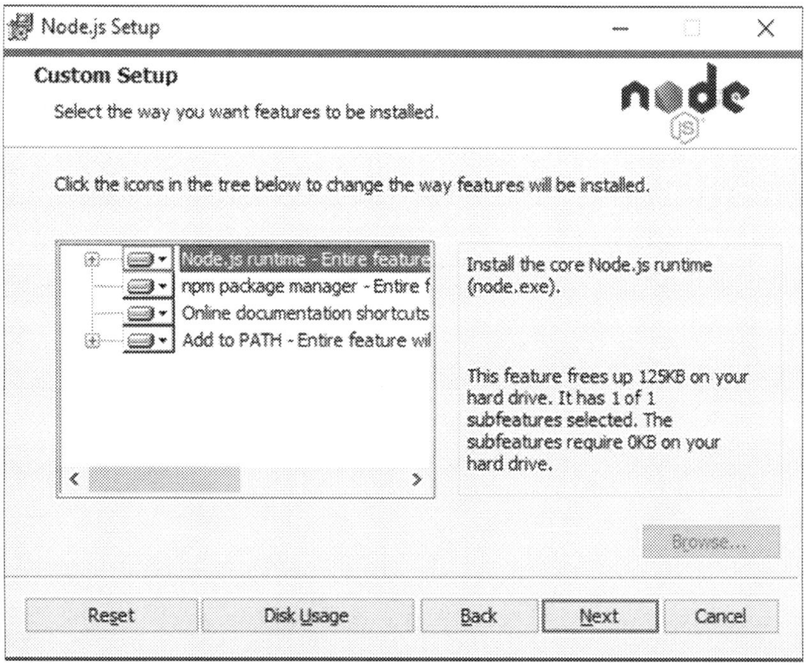

Figure 1-35. *Default packages*

Next, click the check box and then the **Next** button, as seen in Figure 1-36.

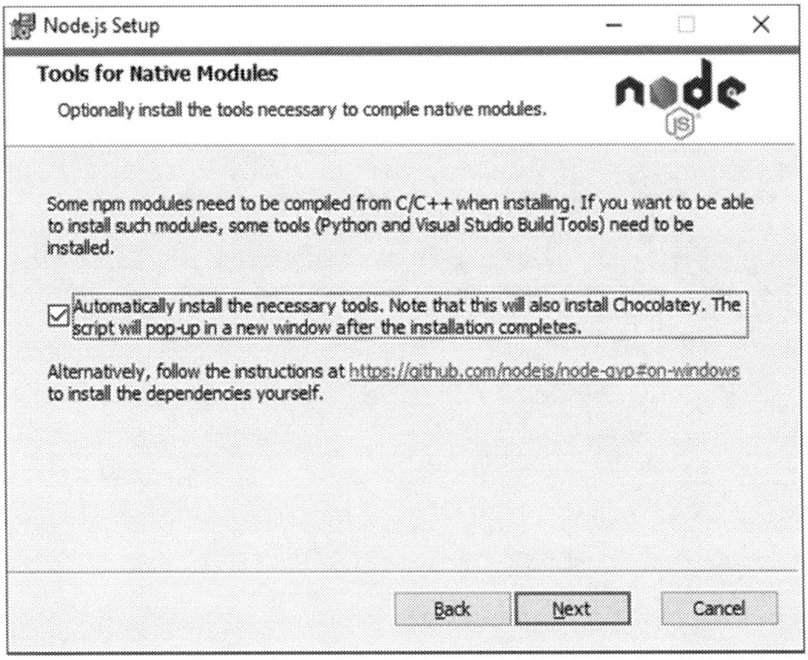

Figure 1-36. *Dependencies*

Then, click the **Install** button, as seen in Figure 1-37.

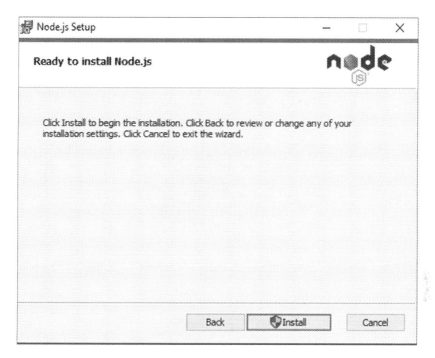

Figure 1-37. *Install*

Once the installation is done, run the following commands to check the versions and verify that everything is right.

```
node -v
npm -v
```

Summary

In this chapter, we have learnt about all the different technologies to create a MERN(MongoDB, Express, ReactJS, NodeJS) project. We have also learnt how to deploy them in different environments and we will be using them in the next chapters.

CHAPTER 2

Building a Dating App with MERN

Welcome to Chapter 2, where you build a dating app using the MERN (MongoDB, Express, React, Node.js) framework. The back end is hosted in Heroku, and the front-end site uses Firebase hosting. The icons in the project come from Material-UI.

The web app has simple functionality and is the first MERN stack project. A screenshot of the finished app, which is deployed in Firebase, is shown in Figure 2-1. All the data comes from a MongoDB database, with API endpoints set in Node.js.

Figure 2-1. *Finished app*

© Nabendu Biswas 2021
N. Biswas, *MERN Projects for Beginners*, https://doi.org/10.1007/978-1-4842-7138-4_2

Let's review the React front end and then move to the back end. Open your terminal and create a `dating-app-mern` folder. Inside it, use **create-react-app** to create a new app called **dating-app-frontend**. The following are the commands to do this.

```
mkdir dating-app-mern
cd dating-app-mern
npx create-react-app dating-app-frontend
```

Firebase Hosting Initial Setup

Since the front-end site is hosted through Firebase, let's create the basic setting while create-react-app creates the React app. Following the same setup instructions in Chapter 1, I created dating-app-mern in the Firebase console.

React Basic Setup

Return to the React project and `cd` to the `dating-app-frontend` directory. Start the React app with `npm start`.

```
cd dating-app-frontend
npm start
```

Next, let's delete some of the files that you don't need. Figure 2-2 shows how the app looks on localhost.

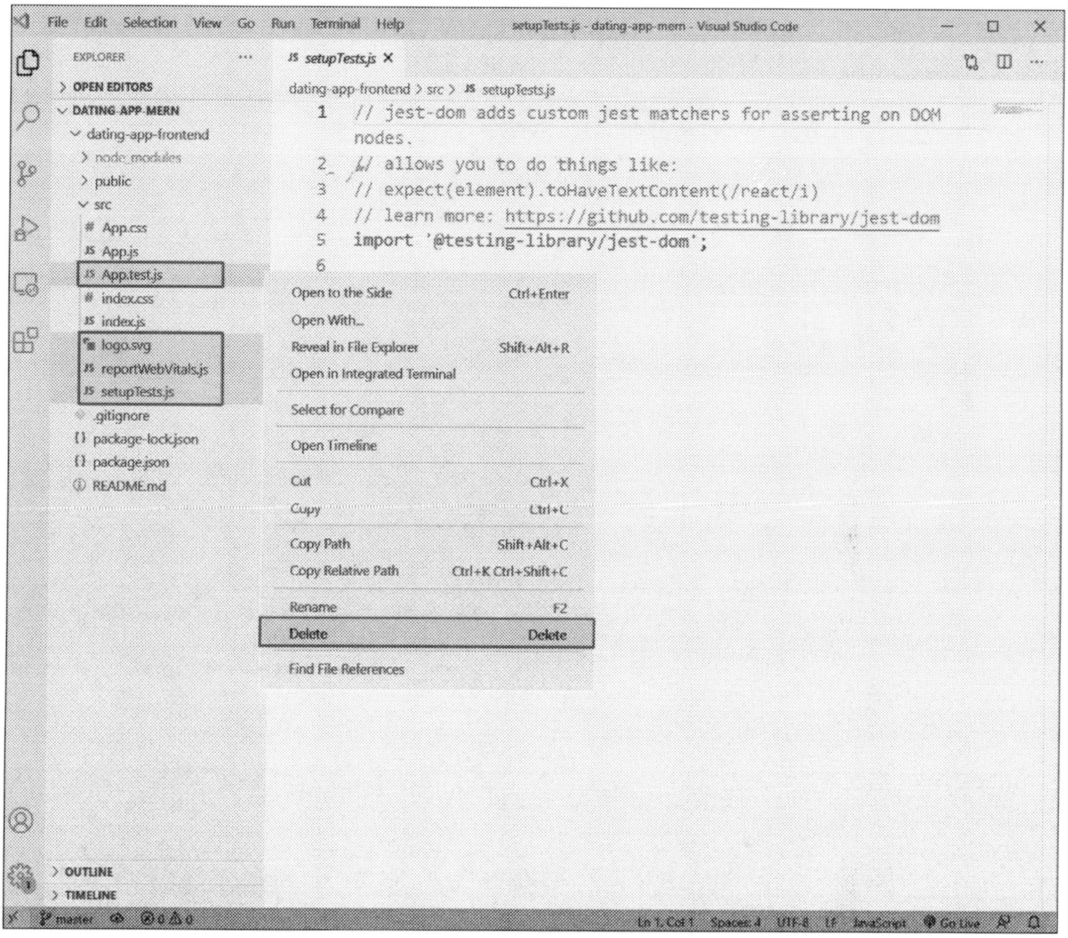

Figure 2-2. *Delete files*

Let's remove all the unnecessary boilerplate code. The index.js file should look like the following.

```
import React from 'react';
import ReactDOM from 'react-dom';
import './index.css';
import App from './App';
ReactDOM.render(
  <React.StrictMode>
    <App />
  </React.StrictMode>,
  document.getElementById('root')
);
```

App.js contains only the text **Dating App MERN**. All the content from the App.css file has been removed.

```
import './App.css';

function App() {
  return (
    <div className="app">
      <h1>Dating App MERN </h1>
    </div>
  );
}

export default App;
```

In index.css, update the CSS to have margin: 0 at the top.

```
* {
    margin: 0;
}
```

Figure 2-3 shows how the app looks on localhost.

Dating App MERN

Figure 2-3. *Initial app*

Creating a Header Component

Let's create a header component. First, you must install Material-UI (https://material-ui.com), which provides the icons. You need to do two npm installs, as per the Material-UI documentation. Install the core through the integrated terminal in the dating-app-frontend folder.

```
npm i @material-ui/core @material-ui/icons
```

Next, create a components folder inside the src folder. Create two files—Header.js and Header.css—inside the components folder. Header.js has three things: a person icon, a logo, and a forum icon. The logo is taken from the project's public directory, which contains the React logo by default.

The following is the Header.js file's content.

```
import React from 'react'
import './Header.css'
import PersonIcon from '@material-ui/icons/Person'
import IconButton from '@material-ui/core/IconButton'
import ForumIcon from '@material-ui/icons/Forum'

const Header = () => {
    return (
        <div className="header">
            <IconButton>
                <PersonIcon fontSize="large" className="header__icon" />
            </IconButton>
            <img className="header__logo" src="logo192.png" alt="header" />
            <IconButton>
                <ForumIcon fontSize="large" className="header__icon" />
            </IconButton>
        </div>
    )
}

export default Header
```

Include the Header component in the App.js file and on localhost. The updated code is marked in bold.

```
import './App.css';
import Header from './components/Header';

function App() {
  return (
```

```
    <div className="app">
      <Header />
    </div>
  );
}

export default App;
```

The Header.css file contains the following content, including simple styles, which completes the header.

```
.header{
    display: flex;
    align-items: center;
    justify-content: space-between;
    z-index: 100;
    border-bottom: 1px solid #f9f9f9;
}

.header__logo{
    object-fit: contain;
    height: 40px;
}

.header__icon{
    padding: 20px;
}
```

Figure 2-4 shows how the app looks now on localhost.

Figure 2-4. *Header component*

Creating the Dating Cards Component

Let's now work on the second component. Create two files—DatingCards.js and DatingCards.css—inside the components folder. Then include the DatingCards component in the App.js file. The updated code is marked in bold.

```
import './App.css';
import Header from './components/Header';
import DatingCards from './components/DatingCards';

function App() {
  return (
    <div className="app">
      <Header  />
      < DatingCards />
    </div>
  );
}

export default App;
```

Before moving forward, you need to install a react-tinder-card package. This package has a feature that provides the swipe effect.

```
npm i react-tinder-card
```

Next, put the content in DatingCards.js. Here, inside a people state variable, you store the name and images of four people. Next, import DatingCard and use it as a component. Here, you use the props mentioned in the react-tinder-card documentation.

The swiped and outOfFrame functions are required. When looping through each person, use the imgUrl background image and display the name in the h3 tag.

```
import React, { useState } from 'react'
import DatingCard from 'react-tinder-card'
import './DatingCards.css'

const DatingCards = () => {
    const [people, setPeople] = useState([
```

```
  { name: "Random Guy", imgUrl: "https://images.unsplash.com/photo-
  1520409364224-63400afe26e5?ixid=MnwxMjA3fDB8MHxwaG90by1wYWdlfHx8fGVu
  fDB8fHx8&ixlib=rb-1.2.1&auto=format&fit=crop&w=658&q=80" },

  { name: "Another Guy", imgUrl: "https://images.unsplash.com/photo-
  1519085360753-af0119f7cbe7?ixid=MnwxMjA3fDB8MHxwaG90b
  y1wYWdlfHx8fGVufDB8fHx8&auto=format&fit=crop&w=634&q=80" },

  { name: "Random Girl", imgUrl: "https://images.unsplash.com/photo-
  1494790108377-be9c29b29330?ixid=MnwxMjA3fDB8MHxwaG90b
  y1wYWdlfHx8fGVufDB8fHx8&auto=format&fit=crop&w=634&q=80" },

  { name: "Another Girl", imgUrl: "https://images.unsplash.com/photo-
  1529626455594-4ff0802cfb7e?ixid=MnwxMjA3fDB8MHxwaG90by1wYWdlfHx8fGVu
  fDB8fHx8&ixlib=rb-1.2.1&auto=format&fit=crop&w=634&q=80" }

])
  const swiped = (direction, nameToDelete) => {
      console.log("receiving " + nameToDelete)
  }
  const outOfFrame = (name) => {
      console.log(name + " left the screen!!")
  }
  return (
      <div className="datingCards">
          <div className="datingCards__container">
              {people.map((person) => (
                  <DatingCard
                      className="swipe"
                      key={person.name}
                      preventSwipe={['up', 'down']}
                      onSwipe={(dir) => swiped(dir, person.name)}
                      onCardLeftScreen={() => outOfFrame(person.name)} >
                      <div style={{ backgroundImage: `url(${person.
                      imgUrl})`}} className="card">
                          <h3>{person.name}</h3>
```

```
                </div>
              </DatingCard>
          ))}
        </div>
      </div>
    )
}

export default DatingCards
```

Localhost shows four "people," as seen in Figure 2-5, but you need to style everything.

Figure 2-5. *All people*

Add the first styles in the DatingCards.css file, and make datingCards__container a flexbox. Next, style each card to contain the image and other things. Note that you are setting position: relative for each card, which offsets the element relative to itself and provides width and height.

```
.datingCards__container{
    display: flex;
    justify-content: center;
    margin-top: 10vh;
}

.card{
    position: relative;
    background-color: white;
    width: 600px;
    padding: 20px;
```

41

```
    max-width: 85vw;
    height: 50vh;
    box-shadow: 0px 18px 53px 0px rgba(0, 0, 0, 0.3);
    border-radius: 20px;
    background-size: cover;
    background-position: center;
}
```

Figure 2-6 shows how this looks on localhost.

Figure 2-6. *Images appear*

Let's add three more styles, and out of this swipe is a class within the card class. Use position: absolute to create the magic of the swipe effect. Add the following content in the DatingCards.css file.

```
.swipe{
    position: absolute;
}
```

```
.cardContent{
    width: 100%;
    height: 100%;
}
.card h3{
    position: absolute;
    bottom: 0;
    margin: 10px;
    color: white;
}
```

The front end is almost complete, as seen in Figure 2-7. It contains the right swipe and left swipe functionality. Everything is done except the footer, which contains the swipe buttons.

Figure 2-7. *Almost complete*

Creating the Swipe Buttons Component

Let's now create the SwipeButtons component, which are the buttons in the footer. These buttons add to the app's styling. They won't be functional since it's a simple app. Create two files—SwipeButtons.js and SwipeButtons.css—inside the components folder. You also need to include it in the App.js file.

The updated content is marked in bold.

```
import './App.css';
import Header from './components/Header';
import DatingCards from './components/DatingCards';
import SwipeButtons from './components/SwipeButtons';

function App() {
  return (
    <div className="app">
      <Header  />
      < DatingCards />
      < SwipeButtons />
    </div>
  );
}
export default App;
```

The content of the SwipeButtons.js file is straightforward. There are five icons from Material-UI wrapped inside IconButton.

```
import React from 'react'
import './SwipeButtons.css'
import ReplayIcon from '@material-ui/icons/Replay'
import CloseIcon from '@material-ui/icons/Close'
import StarRateIcon from '@material-ui/icons/StarRate'
import FavoriteIcon from '@material-ui/icons/Favorite'
import FlashOnIcon from '@material-ui/icons/FlashOn'
import IconButton from '@material-ui/core/IconButton'
const SwipeButtons = () => {
```

```
    return (
        <div className="swipeButtons">
            <IconButton className="swipeButtons__repeat">
                <ReplayIcon fontSize="large" />
            </IconButton>
            <IconButton className="swipeButtons__left">
                <CloseIcon fontSize="large" />
            </IconButton>
            <IconButton className="swipeButtons__star">
                <StarRateIcon fontSize="large" />
            </IconButton>
            <IconButton className="swipeButtons__right">
                <FavoriteIcon fontSize="large" />
            </IconButton>
            <IconButton className="swipeButtons__lightning">
                <FlashOnIcon fontSize="large" />
            </IconButton>
        </div>
    )
}
export default SwipeButtons
```

Next, style the buttons in the SwipeButtons.css file. First, style the swipeButtons class and make it flex with position: fixed. In a fixed position, an element remains attached where stated (at the bottom in this case), even as the user scrolls. You are also styling the MuiIconButton-root class, which was created by the package.

In the SwipeButtons.css file, style each button with a different color.

```
.swipeButtons{
    position: fixed;
    bottom: 10vh;
    display: flex;
    width: 100%;
    justify-content: space-evenly;
}
```

```
.swipeButtons .MuiIconButton-root{
    background-color: white;
    box-shadow: 0px 10px 53px 0px rgba(0, 0, 0, 0.3) !important;
}

.swipeButtons__repeat{
    padding: 3vw !important;
    color: #f5b748 !important;
}

.swipeButtons__left{
    padding: 3vw !important;
    color: #ec5e6f !important;
}

.swipeButtons__star{
    padding: 3vw !important;
    color: #62b4f9 !important;
}

.swipeButtons__right{
    padding: 3vw !important;
    color: #76e2b3 !important;
}

.swipeButtons__lightning{
    padding: 3vw !important;
    color: #915dd1 !important;
}
```

Figure 2-8 shows the project on localhost.

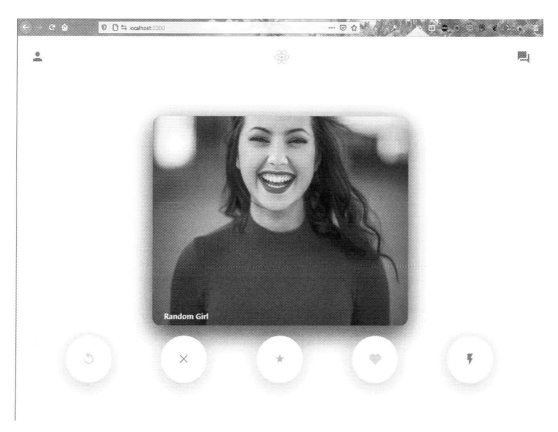

Figure 2-8. *Front end complete*

Initial Back-End Setup

Let's move to the back end by starting with the Node.js code. Open a new terminal window and create a new `dating-app-backend` folder in the root directory. Enter `git init` because it is required later for Heroku.

```
mkdir dating-app-backend
cd dating-app-backend
git init
```

Next, create a `package.json` file by entering the `npm init` command in the terminal. You are asked several questions; for most of them, press the Enter key. You can enter a **description** and the **author**, but it is not mandatory. You can generally make the entry point at `server.js` because it is the standard (see Figure 2-9).

47

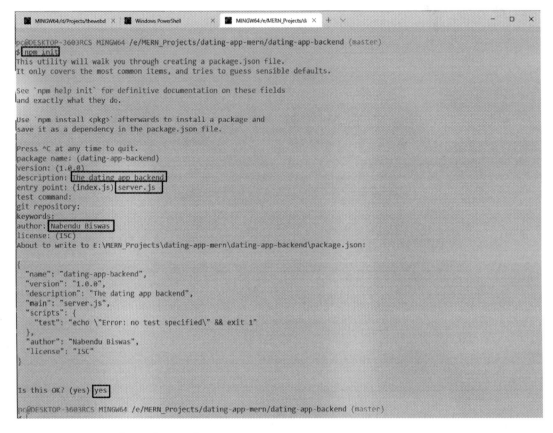

Figure 2-9. *Back-end initial setup*

Once `package.json` is created, you need to create the `.gitignore` file with `node_modules` in it since you don't want to push `node_modules` to Heroku later. The following is the content of the `.gitignore` file.

```
node_modules
```

Next, open `package.json`. The line `"type": "module"` is required to have React-like imports enabled in Node.js. These modules are known as ECMA modules. The initial modules with require statements are known as CommonJS modules. You can read more about it at `https://blog.logrocket.com/how-to-use-ecmascript-modules-with-node-js/`.

You also need to include a start script to run the `server.js` file. The updated content is marked in bold.

```json
{
  "name": "dating-app-backend",
  "version": "1.0.0",
  "description": "The dating app backend",
  "main": "server.js",
  "type": "module",
  "scripts": {
    "test": "echo \"Error: no test specified\" && exit 1",
    "start": "node server.js"
  },
  "author": "Nabendu Biswas",
  "license": "ISC"
}
```

You need to install two packages before starting. Open the terminal and install Express and Mongoose in the dating-app-backend folder.

```
npm i express mongoose
```

MongoDB Setup

The MongoDB setup is the same as described in Chapter 1. You need to follow it and create a new project named **dating-app-mern**.

Before moving forward, install nodemon in the dating-app-backend folder. Whenever you make any changes to the code in the server.js file, the Node server restarts instantaneously.

```
npm i nodemon
```

Initial Route Setup

Let's create the initial route, which generally checks whether everything is set up correctly. The Express package in Node.js allows you to create routes, which is how most of the Internet works. Most back-end languages like Node.js, Java offer capabilities to create these routes, which interact with the databases. The initial route doesn't interact with the database and simply returns a text when you go to it, using a GET request.

Create a `server.js` file in the `dating-app-backend` folder. Here, you import the Express and the Mongoose packages first. Next, use Express to create a `port` variable to run on port 8001.

The first API endpoint is a simple GET request created by `app.get()`, which shows **Hello TheWebDev** text if successful.

Then you listen on port 8001 with `app.listen()`.

```
import express from 'express'
import mongoose from 'mongoose'

//App Config
const app = express()
const port = process.env.PORT || 8001

//Middleware

//DB Config

//API Endpoints
app.get("/", (req, res) => res.status(200).send("Hello TheWebDev"))

//Listener
app.listen(port, () => console.log(`Listening on localhost: ${port}`))
```

In the terminal, type **nodemon server.js**. You can see the **Listening on localhost: 8001** console log. To check that the route is working correctly, go to `http://localhost:8001/` to see the endpoint text (see Figure 2-10).

Hello TheWebDev

Figure 2-10. *Initial route*

Database User and Network Access

In MongoDB, you need to create a database user and provide network access. The process is the same as in Chapter 1. Follow those instructions and get the user credentials and connection URL.

In server.js, create a connection_url variable and paste the URL within the string that you got from MongoDB. Enter the password that you saved earlier and provide a database name. The updated code is marked in bold.

```
...
//App Config
const app = express()
const port = process.env.PORT || 8001
const connection_url = 'mongodb+srv://admin:yourpassword@cluster0.lggjc.
mongodb.net/datingDB?retryWrites=true&w=majority'

//Middleware

//DB Config
mongoose.connect(connection_url, {
    useNewUrlParser: true,
    useCreateIndex: true,
    useUnifiedTopology: true
})

//API Endpoints
app.get("/", (req, res) => res.status(200).send("Hello TheWebDev"))

...
```

MongoDB Schema and Routes

MongoDB stores data in a JSON format instead of the regular table structure found in a traditional database like Oracle. You create the schema file required by MongoDB. It tells you how fields are stored in MongoDB.

Here, cards is considered a collection name, and you store a value like cardSchema in the database. It consists of an object with a name and imgUrl keys. These are the names that you use in MongoDB. Create a dbCards.js file and put the following content in it.

```
import mongoose from 'mongoose'
const cardSchema = mongoose.Schema({
    name: String,
    imgUrl: String
})
```

```
export default mongoose.model('cards', cardSchema)
```

You now use the schema to create the endpoint that adds data to the database. The MVC pattern is followed here; it is the traditional flow of a web application. Read more about it at https://medium.com/createdd-notes/understanding-mvc-architecture-with-react-6cd38e91fefd.

Next, use a POST request that takes any data from the user and sends it to the database. You can use any endpoint. For example, if you write an article on Facebook and hit the POST button, your article is saved in the Facebook database once the POST request is made.

The GET endpoints fetch all the data from the database. Again, you can give any endpoint. For example, when you browse through the feed in Facebook, a GET request is sent to the endpoint, which in turn fetches all posts from the Facebook database.

In `server.js`, create a POST request to the `/dating/cards` endpoint. The load is in `req.body` to MongoDB. Then you use `create()` to send `dbCard`. If it's a success, you receive status 201; otherwise, you receive status 500. The updated content is marked in bold.

Next, create the GET endpoint to `/dating/cards` to get the data from the database. You are using `find()` here and receive a status 200 on success (otherwise, status 500). The updated content is marked in bold.

```
import express from 'express'
import mongoose from 'mongoose'
import Cards from './dbCards.js'

...

//API Endpoints
app.get("/", (req, res) => res.status(200).send("Hello TheWebDev"))

app.post('/dating/cards', (req, res) => {
    const dbCard = req.body
```

```
    Cards.create(dbCard, (err, data) => {
        if(err) {
            res.status(500).send(err)
        } else {
            res.status(201).send(data)
        }
    })
})

app.get('/dating/cards', (req, res) => {
    Cards.find((err, data) => {
        if(err) {
            res.status(500).send(err)
        } else {
            res.status(200).send(data)
        }
    })
})

//Listener
app.listen(port, () => console.log(`Listening on localhost: ${port}`))
```

To check the routes, let's use the Postman app. Download and install it.

Send a GET request to `http://localhost:8001` to check that it's working in Postman, as seen in Figure 2-11.

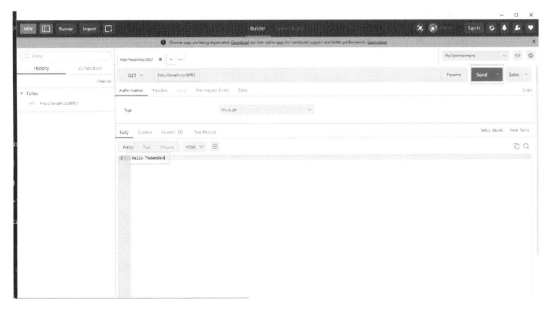

Figure 2-11. *Initial route check*

Before moving forward with the POST request, you need to complete two things. First, implement CORS; otherwise, you get cross-origin errors later when you deploy the app. CORS (Cross-Origin Resource Sharing) is the mechanism that restricts access from one domain to another. Suppose you are on `http://example.com` and want to access `http://mybank.com/accountdetails`. CORS won't allow you to do so. It is only allowed if `http://mybank.com` allows cross-origin sharing with `http://example.com`.

Open the terminal and install CORS in the `dating-app-backend` folder.

```
npm i cors
```

In `server.js`, import CORS and use it in with `app.use()`. You also need to use the `express.json()` middleware. It is required because you need it to parse the incoming JSON object from MongoDB to read the body.

The updated code is marked in bold.

```
import express from 'express'
import mongoose from 'mongoose'
import Cors from 'cors'
import Cards from './dbCards.js'

...
```

```
//Middleware
app.use(express.json())
app.use(Cors())
```

...

In Postman, change the request to POST, and then add the `http://localhost:8001/dating/cards` endpoint.

Next, click **Body** and select **raw**. Select **JSON(application/json)** from the drop-down menu. In the text editor, copy the data from `DatingCards.js` file. Make the data JSON by adding double quotes to the keys.

Next, click the **Send** button. If everything is correct, you get **Status: 201 Created** (see Figure 2-12).

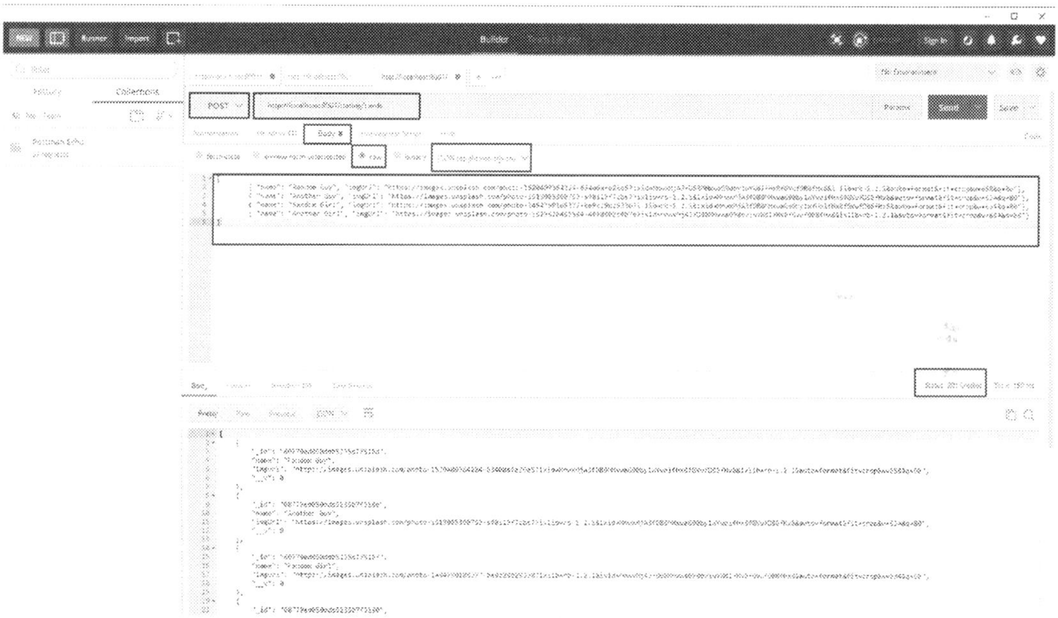

Figure 2-12. *POST route*

You need to test the GET endpoint. Change the request to GET and click the **Send** button. If everything is right, you get **Status: 200 OK** (see Figure 2-13).

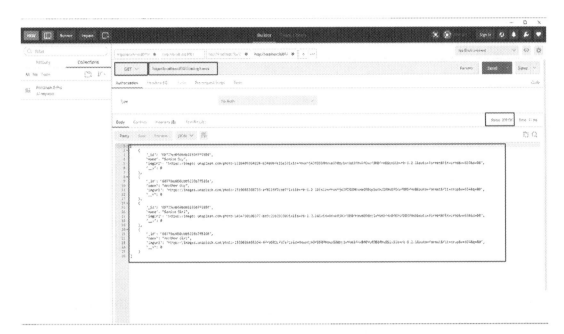

Figure 2-13. *GET route*

Integrating the Back End with the Front End

Let's hook the back end to the front end. Use the `axios` package to call from the front end. Axios is a JavaScript library that makes the API request to the REST endpoint. You just created two endpoints in the back end. To access them, you need Axios. Open the `dating-app-frontend` folder and install it.

```
npm i axios
```

Next, create a new `axios.js` file inside the `components` folder, and then create an instance of `axios`. The base URL is `http://localhost:8001`.

```
import axios from 'axios'
const instance = axios.create({
    baseURL: "http://localhost:8001"
})

export default instance
```

In DatingCards.js, get rid of the hard-coded stuff in the people state. Then import the local axios and use the useEffect hook to do the API call to the /dating/cards endpoint. Once you receive the data, reset it using the setPeople() function. The updated code is marked in bold.

```
import React, { useState, useEffect } from 'react'
import DatingCard from 'react-tinder-card'
import './DatingCards.css'
import axios from './axios'

const DatingCards = () => {
    const [people, setPeople] = useState([])
    useEffect(() => {
        async function fetchData() {
            const req = await axios.get("/dating/cards")
            setPeople(req.data)
        }
        fetchData()
    }, [])

    const swiped = (direction, nameToDelete) => {
        console.log("receiving " + nameToDelete)
    }
...
```

Go to http://localhost:3000/ to see the data. The app is now complete (see Figure 2-14).

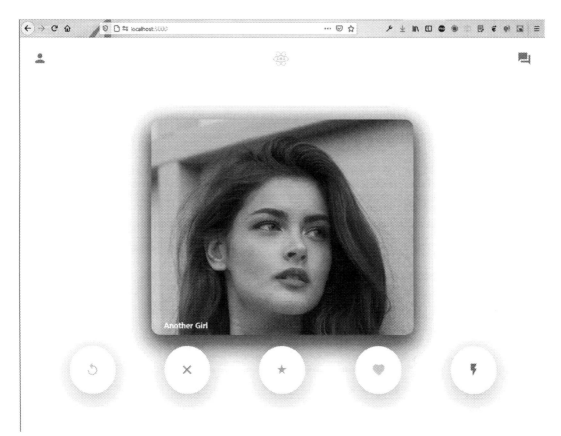

Figure 2-14. *App complete*

Deploying the Back End to Heroku

Go to www.heroku.com to deploy the back end. You followed the same procedure in Chapter 1 to create an app named dating-mern-backend.

Return to axios.js and change the endpoint to https://dating-mern-backend. herokuapp.com. If everything is working fine, your app should run.

```
import axios from 'axios'
const instance = axios.create({
    baseURL: https://dating-mern-backend.herokuapp.com
})

export default instance
```

Deploying the Front End to Firebase

It's time to deploy the front end in Firebase. Follow the same procedure that you did in Chapter 1. After this process, the site should be live and working properly, as seen in Figure 2-15.

Figure 2-15. *Deployed app*

Summary

In this chapter, we have created a dating app in MERN stack. We build the frontend in ReactJS and hosted it in Firebase. The backend was build in NodeJS and hosted in Heroku. The database was build in MongoDB.

CHAPTER 3

Building a Short Video App with MERN

Welcome to your next MERN project, where you build an awesome short video app using the MERN (MongoDB, Express, React, Node.js) framework. On the back end, it is hosted in Heroku, and the front-end site uses Firebase hosting. Material-UI (`https://material-ui.com`) supplies the icons in the project.

This web app shows short videos stored in MongoDB, which can be played by clicking on it. You can pause it by clicking it again. This web app also has very smooth vertical scrolling to show more videos. In Figure 3-1, you can see the final deployed version of the app.

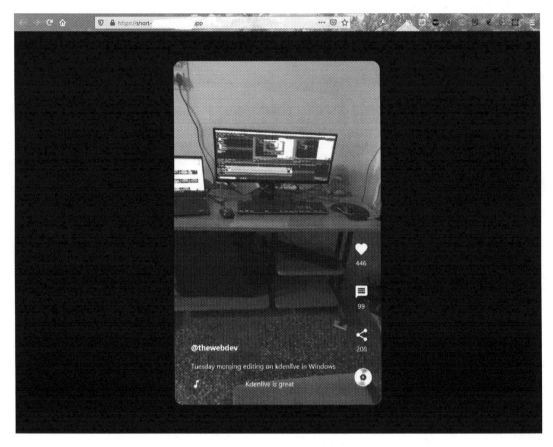

Figure 3-1. *Deployed version*

Work with React first and then move to the back end. Open your terminal and create a `short-video-mern` folder. Inside it, use `create-react-app` to create a new app called **short-video-frontend**. The following are the commands.

```
mkdir short-video-mern
cd short-video-mern
npx create-react-app short-video-frontend
```

Firebase Hosting Initial Setup

Since the front-end site is hosted through Firebase, you can create the basic setting while create-react-app creates the React app. Following the setup instructions in Chapter 1, I created short-video-mern in the Firebase console.

React Basic Setup

Go back to the React project and cd to the short-video-frontend directory. Start the
React app with npm start.

```
cd short-video-frontend
npm start
```

The deleting of the files and basic setup in index.js, App.js, and App.css is like
what was done in Chapter 2. Follow those instructions.

Figure 3-2 shows how the app looks on localhost.

Figure 3-2. *Initial app*

Creating a Video Component

Next, create a components folder inside the src folder. Create two files—Video.js and
Video.css—inside the components folder. In the Video.js file, add a video tag and a
vertical video link. I used the link to my YouTube short video on my channel.

The following is the Video.js content.

```
import React from 'react'
import './Video.css'
const Video = () => {
    return (
        <div className="video">
            <video
                src="https://res.cloudinary.com/dxkxvfo2o/video/upload/
                v1608169738/video1_cvrjfm.mp4"
                className="video__player"
                loop
```

```
            >
            </video>
        </div>
    )
}
export default Video
```

Include the Video component in the App.js file and on localhost. The updated code is marked in bold.

```
import './App.css';
import Video from './components/Video';

function App() {
  return (
    <div className="app">
            <div className="app__videos">
                <Video />
                <Video />
            </div>
    </div>
  );
}
```

export default App;

Next, put the basic styles in the App.css file, including the styles for scroll-snap-type, which are for scrolling. You also need to center everything. Next, put some more styles for the app__videos class and hide the scrollbar.

```
html{
    scroll-snap-type: y mandatory;
}

.app{
    height: 100vh;
    background-color: black;
```

```css
    display: grid;
    place-items: center;
}

.app__videos{
    position:relative;
    height: 800px;
    border-radius: 20px;
    overflow: scroll;
    width: 80%;
    max-width: 500px;
    scroll-snap-type: y mandatory;
}

.app__videos::-webkit-scrollbar{
    display: none;
}

.app__videos{
    -ms-overflow-style: none;
    scrollbar-width: none;
}
```

Figure 3-3 shows how the app looks on localhost.

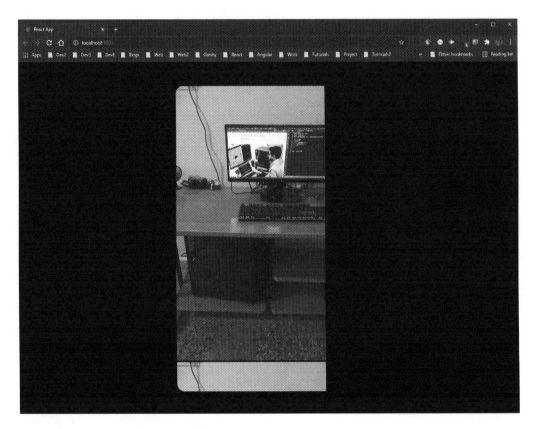

Figure 3-3. *Video shown*

You need to style the video and video__player classes in the Video.css file also. You are again using scroll-snap-type here.

```
.video{
    position: relative;
    background-color: white;
    width: 100%;
    height:100%;
    scroll-snap-align: start;
}

.video__player{
    object-fit: fill;
    width: 100%;
    height: 100%;
}
```

The snap feature is done. It smoothly takes you to the next video as you scroll, as seen in Figure 3-4. Also, the edges have been made perfect on all sides through CSS.

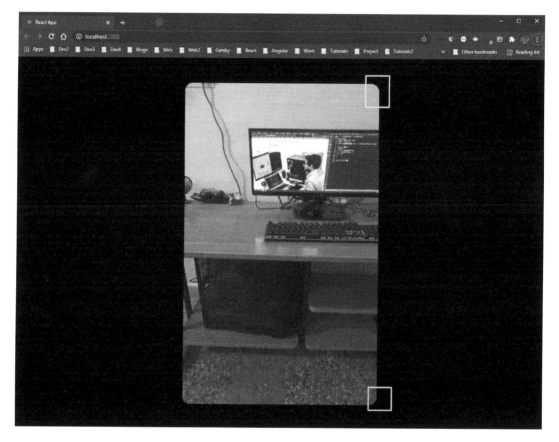

Figure 3-4. *Snap feature*

Right now, the videos won't play. To make them play, you must use a reference (or ref). React works on a virtual DOM. Generally, you only need to access the DOM (Document Object Model) in special cases, and you use refs to access DOM elements. In this case, you need to access the `<video>` HTML element so that you can access the `play()` and `pause()` properties, which are only available through refs.

First, import the `useRef` and `useState` hooks to get the `videoRef` variable, which is used inside the video element, where you create an `onClick` handler to fire a `handleVideoPress` function.

Inside the `handleVideoPress` function, use the `playing` state variable to check if the video plays, and then set it to pause with `videoRef.current.pause()` and change the playing state to false. You do the reverse in the `else` block.

The updated Video.js content is marked in bold.

```
import React , { useRef, useState } from 'react'
import './Video.css'

const Video = () => {
    const [playing, setPlaying] = useState(false)
    const videoRef = useRef(null)
    const handleVideoPress = () => {
        if(playing){
            videoRef.current.pause()
            setPlaying(false)
        } else {
            videoRef.current.play()
            setPlaying(true)
        }
    }
    return (
        <div className="video">
            <video
                src="https://res.cloudinary.com/dxkxvfo2o/video/upload/
                v1608169738/video1_cvrjfm.mp4"
                className="video__player"
                loop
                ref={videoRef}
                onClick={handleVideoPress}
            >
            </video>
        </div>
    )
}

export default Video
```

Click the video to play it on localhost. Click it again to pause.

Creating a Video Footer Component

Let's work on the second component, which shows the username, video title, and a rolling ticker in the video's footer.

Create two files—VideoFooter.js and VideoFooter.css—inside the components folder. Then include the VideoFooter component in the Video.js file. The updated code is marked in bold.

```
import React , { useRef, useState } from 'react'
import './Video.css'
import VideoFooter from './VideoFooter'

const Video = () => {
    ...
    return (
        <div className="video">
            <video
                src="https://res.cloudinary.com/dxkxvfo2o/video/upload/
                v1608169738/video1_cvrjfm.mp4"
                className="video__player"
                loop
                ref={videoRef}
                onClick={handleVideoPress}
            >
            </video>
            <VideoFooter />
        </div>
    )
}

export default Video
```

Next, add an h3 tag containing the username and a p tag containing the description in the VideoFooter.js file.

```
import React from 'react'
import './VideoFooter.css'

const VideoFooter = () => {
    return (
        <div className="videoFooter">
            <div className="videoFooter__text">
                <h3>@nabendu82</h3>
                <p>Macbook Air to new Windows editing beast</p>
            </div>
        </div>
    )
}

export default VideoFooter
```

Next, style them in the VideoFooter.css file.

```
.videoFooter{
    position: relative;
    color: white;
    bottom: 150px;
    margin-left: 40px;
    display: flex;
}

.videoFooter__text{
    flex: 1;
}

.videoFooter__text > h3{
    padding-bottom: 20px;
}

.videoFooter__text > p{
    padding-bottom: 20px;
}
```

Figure 3-5 shows the text on localhost.

Figure 3-5. *Initial footer*

Let's first install Material-UI, which provides the icons. Do two npm installs as per the Material-UI documentation. Install the core through the integrated terminal in the short-video-frontend folder.

```
npm i @material-ui/core @material-ui/icons
```

It's time to use it in the VideoFooter.js file. Include the music note icon, MusicNoteIcon, inside the videoFooter__ticker div, which you imported from Material-UI.

The updated content is marked in bold.

```
import React from 'react'
import './VideoFooter.css'
import MusicNoteIcon from '@material-ui/icons/MusicNote'
```

```
const VideoFooter = () => {
    return (
        <div className="videoFooter">
            <div className="videoFooter__text">
                <h3>@nabendu82</h3>
                <p>Macbook Air to new Windows editing beast</p>
                <div className="videoFooter__ticker">
                    <MusicNoteIcon className="videoFooter__icon" />
                </div>
            </div>
        </div>
    )
}
```

```
export default VideoFooter
```

The project features a nice ticker. For this, you install a package called `react-ticker` in the `short-video-frontend` folder.

```
npm i react-ticker
```

Next, include the ticker as per the documentation and a record (or rotating disc) image in the `VideoFooter.js` file. As you can see at the bottom of the news channels, the ticker is moving text across the screen. A record/rotating disc image is also shown, to which you add nice animations very shortly.

The updated content is marked in bold.

```
import React from 'react'
import './VideoFooter.css'
import MusicNoteIcon from '@material-ui/icons/MusicNote'
import Ticker from 'react-ticker'

const VideoFooter = () => {
    return (
        <div className="videoFooter">
            <div className="videoFooter__text">
                <h3>@nabendu82</h3>
                <p>Macbook Air to new Windows editing beast</p>
```

```
            <div className="videoFooter__ticker">
                <MusicNoteIcon className="videoFooter__icon" />
                <Ticker mode="smooth">
                    {(({ index }) => (
                      <>
                        <p>I am a Windows PC</p>
                      </>
                    )}
                </Ticker>
            </div>
        </div>
        <img className="videoFooter__record" src="https://static.
        thenounproject.com/png/934821-200.png" alt="video footer" />
      </div>
  )
}

export default VideoFooter
```

Next, add styles for both the ticker and the recorded image in the VideoFooter.
css file. Here, you align the ticker with the music icon and add animation to move the
recorded image.

Add the following content to the VideoFooter.css file.

```
.videoFooter__icon{
    position: absolute;
}

.videoFooter__ticker > .ticker{
    height: fit-content;
    margin-left: 30px;
    width: 60%;
}

.videoFooter__record{
    animation: spinTheRecord infinite 5s linear;
    height: 50px;
    filter: invert(1);
```

```
    position: absolute;
    bottom: 0;
    right: 20px;
}

@keyframes spinTheRecord {
    from {
        transform: rotate(0deg)
    }
    to {
        transform: rotate(360deg)
    }
}
```

Figure 3-6 shows the footer component, including a scrolling ticker and rotating disc, on localhost.

Figure 3-6. *Footer complete*

Creating a Video Sidebar Component

Let's now create a sidebar component, which shows icons on the right side of the video.

Create two files—VideoSidebar.js and VideoSidebar.css—inside the components folder. You also need to include the Video.js file.

The updated code is marked in bold.

```
import React , { useRef, useState } from 'react'
import './Video.css'
import VideoFooter from './VideoFooter'
import VideoSidebar from './VideoSidebar'

const Video = () => {
    ...
    return (
        <div className="video">
            <video
                src="https://res.cloudinary.com/dxkxvfo2o/video/upload/
                v1608169738/video1_cvrjfm.mp4"
                className="video__player"
                loop
                ref={videoRef}
                onClick={handleVideoPress}
            >
            </video>
            <VideoFooter />
            <VideoSidebar />
        </div>
    )
}

export default Video
```

Next, update the VideoSidebar.js file. Here, you are using different Material-UI icons. You also use a state variable that saves whether the like icon has been pressed; if so, it changes from a hollow icon to a filled icon, and the count also changes.

```
import React, { useState } from 'react'
import './VideoSidebar.css'
import FavoriteIcon from '@material-ui/icons/Favorite'
import FavoriteBorderIcon from '@material-ui/icons/FavoriteBorder'
import MessageIcon from '@material-ui/icons/Message'
import ShareIcon from '@material-ui/icons/Share'

const VideoSidebar = () => {
    const [liked, setLiked] = useState(false)
    return (
        <div className="videoSidebar">
            <div className="videoSidebar__button">
                { liked ? <FavoriteIcon fontSize="large" onClick={e =>
                setLiked(false)} /> : <FavoriteBorderIcon fontSize="large"
                onClick={e => setLiked(true)} /> }
                <p>{liked ? 101 : 100}</p>
            </div>
            <div className="videoSidebar__button">
                <MessageIcon fontSize="large" />
                <p>345</p>
            </div>
            <div className="videoSidebar__button">
                <ShareIcon fontSize="large" />
                <p>109</p>
            </div>
        </div>
    )
}

export default VideoSidebar
```

Next, update the VideoSidebar.css file.

```
.videoSidebar{
    position: absolute;
    top: 50%;
```

```
    right: 10px;
    color: white;
}

.videoSidebar__button{
    padding: 20px;
    text-align: center;
}
```

Figure 3-7 shows these lovely icons, and the video sidebar is done.

Figure 3-7. *Sidebar completed*

Making Components Dynamic

All the data from the App.js file is passed to child components. You make the components dynamic so that you can pass props to them. Like in React, you pass data from a parent component to a child component with props. The video sidebar is the first component to work on. In VideoSidebar.js, pass the numbers as props.

The updated content is marked in bold.

```
...
const VideoSidebar = ({ likes, shares, messages }) => {
    const [liked, setLiked] = useState(false)
    return (
        <div className="videoSidebar">
            <div className="videoSidebar__button">
                { liked ? <FavoriteIcon fontSize="large" onClick={e =>
                setLiked(false)} /> : <FavoriteBorderIcon fontSize="large"
                onClick={e => setLiked(true)} /> }
                <p>{liked ? likes + 1 : likes }</p>
            </div>
            <div className="videoSidebar__button">
                <MessageIcon fontSize="large" />
                <p>{messages}</p>
            </div>
            <div className="videoSidebar__button">
                <ShareIcon fontSize="large" />
                <p>{shares}</p>
            </div>
        </div>
    )
}

export default VideoSidebar
```

Similarly, pass the strings as props in the VideoFooter.js file.

The updated content is marked in bold.

```
...
const VideoFooter = ({ channel, description, song }) => {
    return (
        <div className="videoFooter">
            <div className="videoFooter__text">
                <h3>@{channel} </h3>
                <p>{description}</p>
                <div className="videoFooter__ticker">
                    <MusicNoteIcon className="videoFooter__icon" />
                    <Ticker mode="smooth">
                        {(({ index }) => (
                          <>
                            <p>{song}</p>
                          </>
                        )}
                    </Ticker>
                </div>
            </div>
            <img className="videoFooter__record" src="https://static.
            thenounproject.com/png/934821-200.png" alt="video footer" />
        </div>
    )
}

export default VideoFooter
```

You want to further drill the props from the app component to have different video files. Let's add these props to the Video.js file and use them.

The updated content is marked in bold.

```
...
const Video = ({ url, channel, description, song, likes, shares, messages
}) => {
    ...
    return (
```

79

```
        <div className="video">
            <video
                src={url}
                className="video__player"
                loop
                ref={videoRef}
                onClick={handleVideoPress}
            >
            </video>
            <VideoFooter channel={channel} description={description}
            song={song}  />
            <VideoSidebar likes={likes} shares={shares}
            messages={messages}   />
        </div>
    )
}

export default Video
```

In App.js, you pass all the props and can pass two different videos.
The updated content is marked in bold.

```
...
function App() {
  return (
    <div className="app">
      <div className="app__videos">
        <Video
            url="https://res.cloudinary.com/dxkxvfo2o/video/upload/
            v1608169738/video1_cvrjfm.mp4"
            channel="nabendu82"
            description="Macbook Air to new Windows editing beast"
            song="I am a Windows PC"
            likes={345}
            shares={200}
            messages={90}
        />
```

```
      <Video
        url="https://res.cloudinary.com/dxkxvfo2o/video/upload/
        v1608169739/video2_mecbdo.mp4"
        channel="thewebdev"
        description="Tuesday morning editing on kdenlive in Windows"
        song="Kdenlive is great"
        likes={445}
        shares={290}
        messages={109}
      />
    </div>
  </div>
  );
}
export default App;
```

The front end is complete, and it's time to start the back end.

Initial Back-End Setup

Let's move to the back end, starting with the Node.js code. Open a new terminal window and create a new short-video-backend folder in the root directory. After moving to the short-video-backend directory, enter the git init command, which is required for Heroku later.

```
mkdir short-video-backend
cd short-video-backend
git init
```

Next, create the package.json file by entering the npm init command in the terminal. You are asked a bunch of questions; for most of them, simply press the Enter key. You can provide the **description** and the **author**, but they are not mandatory. You generally make the entry point at server.js, which is standard (see Figure 3-8).

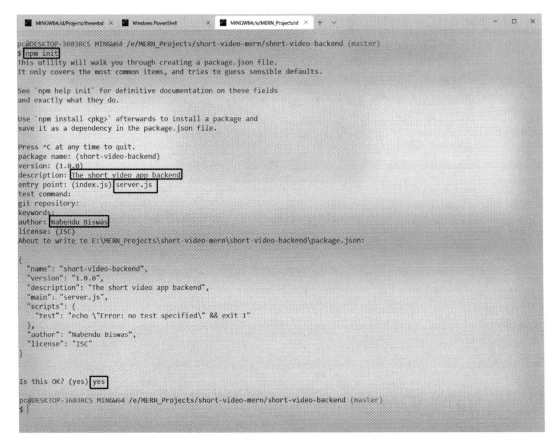

Figure 3-8. *Initial server setup*

Once package.json is created, you need to create the .gitignore file with node_
modules in it since you don't want to push node_modules to Heroku later. The following is
the content of the .gitignore file.

```
node_modules
```

Next, open package.json. The line "type" : "module" is required to have React-like
imports enabled in Node.js. Include a start script to run the server.js file.

The updated content is marked in bold.

```
{
  "name": "short-video-backend",
  "version": "1.0.0",
  "description": " The short video app backend",
  "main": "server.js",
```

```
  "type": "module",
  "scripts": {
    "test": "echo \"Error: no test specified\" && exit 1",
    "start": "node server.js"
  },
  "author": "Nabendu Biswas",
  "license": "ISC"
}
```

You need to install two packages before starting. Open the terminal and install Express and Mongoose in the short-video-backend folder. As discussed in Chapter 2, Express is the Node.js framework through which you can easily build back-end code. Mongoose is the library required to bind Node.js and MongoDB, so it is the bridge responsible for creating schemas in Node.js code.

```
npm i express mongoose
```

MongoDB Setup

The MongoDB setup is the same as described in Chapter 1. Follow those instructions and create a new project named **short-video-mern**.

Before moving forward, install nodemon in the short-video-backend folder. It helps the changes in server.js to restart the Node server instantaneously.

```
npm i nodemon
```

Initial Route Setup

Next, create a server.js file in the short-video-backend folder. Here, you import the Express and Mongoose packages. Then use Express to create a port variable to run on port 9000.

The first API endpoint is a simple GET request created by app.get(), which shows the text **Hello TheWebDev** if successful.

Then, listen on port with `app.listen()`.

```
import express from 'express'
import mongoose from 'mongoose'

//App Config
const app = express()
const port = process.env.PORT || 9000

//Middleware

//DB Config

//API Endpoints
app.get("/", (req, res) => res.status(200).send("Hello TheWebDev"))

//Listener
app.listen(port, () => console.log(`Listening on localhost: ${port}`))
```

In the terminal, type **nodemon server.js** to see the **Listening on localhost: 9000** console log. To check that the route is working correctly, go to `http://localhost:9000/` to see the endpoint text, as shown in Figure 3-9.

Figure 3-9. *localhost*

Database User and Network Access

In MongoDB, you need to create a database user and give network access. The process is the same as explained in Chapter 1. Follow those instructions, and then get the user credentials and connection URL.

In `server.js`, create a `connection_url` variable and paste the URL within the string from MongoDB. You need to provide the password that you saved earlier and a database name.

The updated code is marked in bold.

...

```
//App Config
const app = express()
const port = process.env.PORT || 9000
const connection_url = ' mongodb+srv://admin:yourpassword@cluster0.ryj4g.
mongodb.net/shortVideoDB?retryWrites=true&w=majority'

//Middleware

//DB Config
mongoose.connect(connection_url, {
    useNewUrlParser: true,
    useCreateIndex: true,
    useUnifiedTopology: true
})

//API Endpoints
app.get("/", (req, res) => res.status(200).send("Hello TheWebDev"))

...
```

MongoDB Schema and Routes

Next, let's create the schema file required by MongoDB. It tells you about the way fields are stored in MongoDB. Create a dbModel.js file inside the short-video-backend folder.

Here, shortVideos is considered a collection name, and you store a value like shortVideoSchema in the database. It consists of an object with a URL, channel, description, song, likes, shares, and message keys.

```
import mongoose from 'mongoose'
const shortVideoSchema = mongoose.Schema({
    url: String,
    channel: String,
    description: String,
    song: String,
    likes: String,
```

```
    shares: String,
    messages: String
})
```

```
export default mongoose.model('shortVideos', shortVideoSchema)
```

You can now use the schema to create the endpoint that adds data to the database.

In server.js, create a POST request to the /v2/posts endpoint. The load is in req. body to MongoDB. Then use create() to send dbVideos. If it's a success, you receive status 201; otherwise, you receive status 500.

Next, create the GET endpoint to /v2/posts to get the data from the database. You are using find() here. You receive status 200 if successful (otherwise, status 500).

The updated code is marked in bold.

```
import express from 'express'
import mongoose from 'mongoose'
import Videos from './dbModel.js'
...

//API Endpoints
app.get("/", (req, res) => res.status(200).send("Hello TheWebDev"))

app.post('/v2/posts', (req, res) => {
    const dbVideos = req.body
    Videos.create(dbVideos, (err, data) => {
        if(err)
            res.status(500).send(err)
        else
            res.status(201).send(data)
    })
})

app.get('/v2/posts', (req, res) => {
    Videos.find((err, data) => {
        if(err) {
            res.status(500).send(err)
        } else {
```

```
            res.status(200).send(data)
        }
    })
})

//Listener
app.listen(port, () => console.log(`Listening on localhost: ${port}`))
```

To check the routes, let's use the awesome Postman app. Send a GET request to `http://localhost:9000` to check if it's working in Postman (see Figure 3-10).

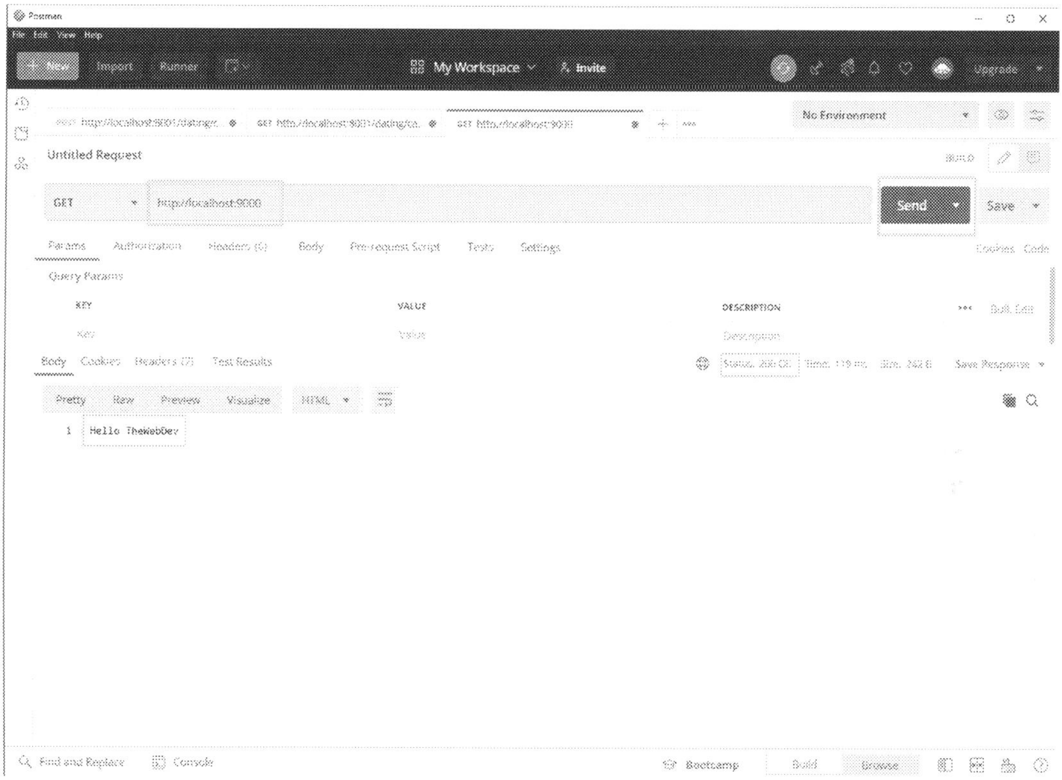

Figure 3-10. *Get request*

Before moving forward with the POST request, you need to complete two things. First, implement CORS. Open the terminal and install CORS in the `short-video-backend` folder.

```
npm i cors
```

In server.js, import CORS and then use it with app.use(). You also need to use the express.json() middleware.

The updated code is marked in bold.

```
import express from 'express'
import mongoose from 'mongoose'
import Cors from 'cors'
import Videos from './dbModel.js'

...

//Middleware
app.use(express.json())
app.use(Cors())

...
```

In Postman, change the request to POST and then add the http://localhost:9000/v2/posts endpoint.

Next, click **Body** and select **raw**. Select **JSON(application/json)** from the drop-down menu. In the text editor, copy the data from the App.js file. Make the data JSON by adding double quotes to the keys.

Then, click the **Send** button. If everything is correct, you get **Status: 201 Created**, as seen in Figure 3-11.

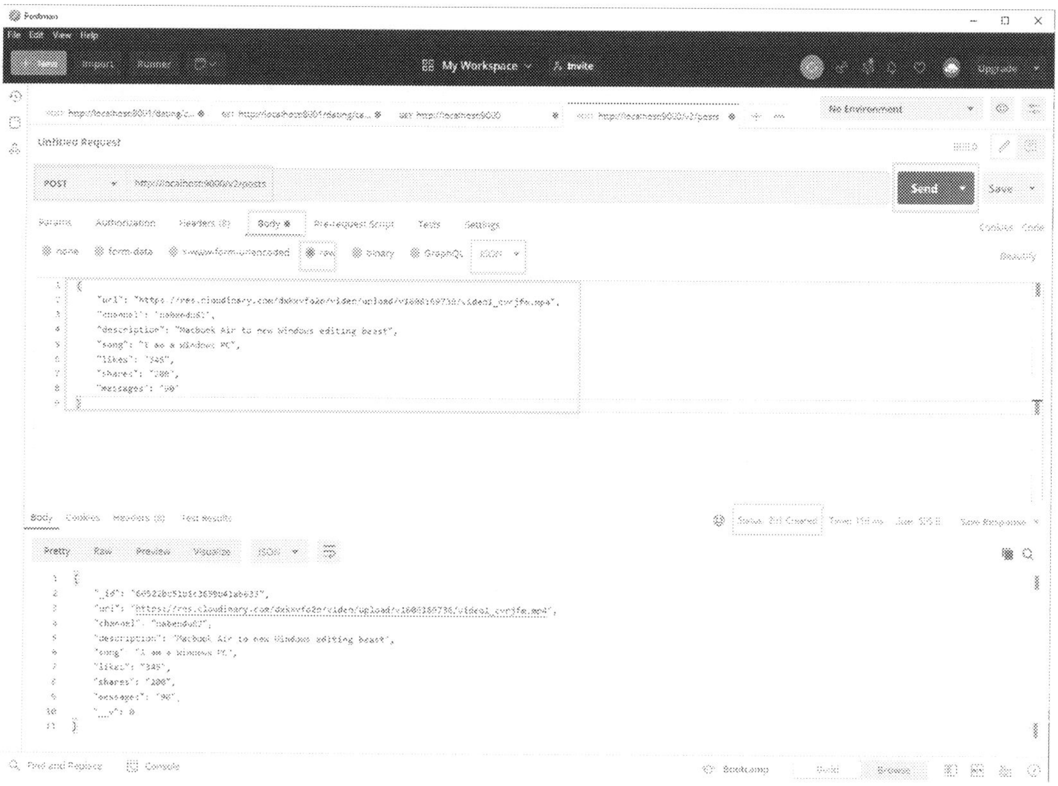

Figure 3-11. *Success Message POST*

I inserted other data similarly. You need to test the GET endpoint. Change the request to GET and click the **Send** button. If everything is correct, you get **Status: 200 OK**, as seen in Figure 3-12.

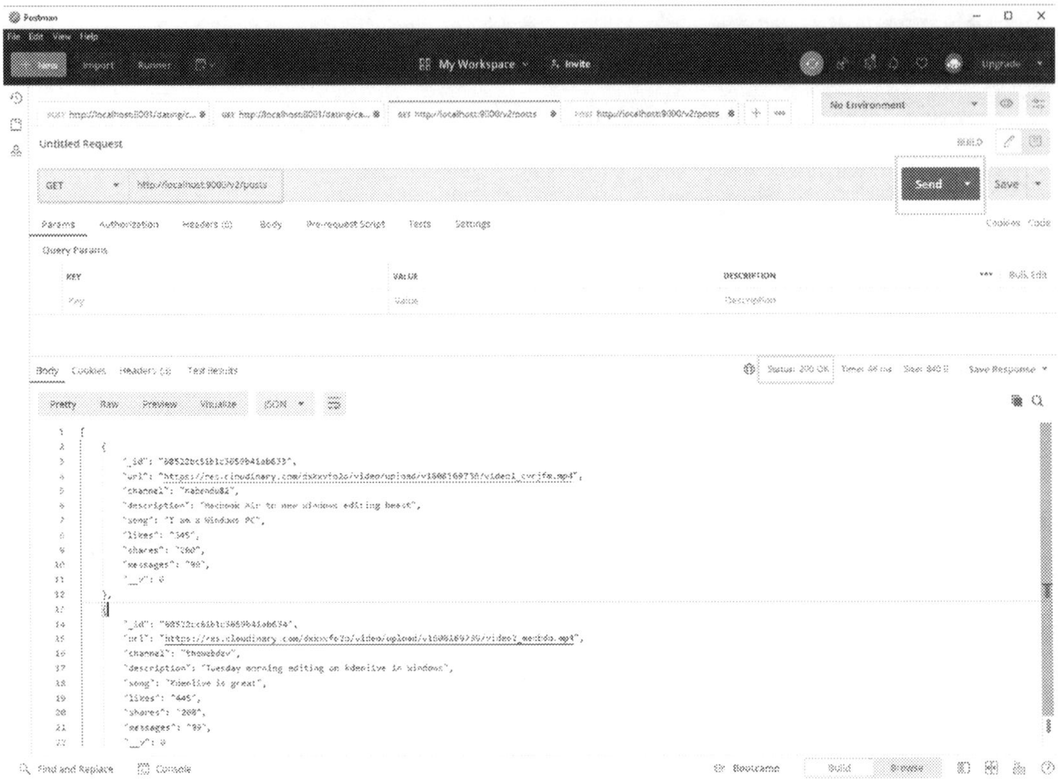

Figure 3-12. *Success Message GET*

Integrating the Back End with the Front End

Let's hook the back end to the front end with the axios package. Open the short-video-frontend folder and install it.

```
npm i axios
```

Next, create a new axios.js file inside the components folder and create an instance of axios. The base URL is http://localhost:9000.

```
import axios from 'axios'

const instance = axios.create({
    baseURL: "http://localhost:9000"
})

export default instance
```

In App.js, import the local axios. Then use the useEffect hook to do the API call to /v2/posts endpoint. Once you receive the data, store it in the videos state variable using setVideos().

In the return statement, get rid of the hard-coded stuff. After that, map through the videos array and pass the props to the video component.

The updated content is marked in bold.

```
import React, { useState, useEffect } from 'react';
import './App.css';
import Video from './components/Video';
import axios from './components/axios';

function App() {
  const [videos, setVideos] = useState([])
  useEffect(() => {
    async function fetchData() {
        const res = await axios.get("/v2/posts")
        setVideos(res.data)
        return res
    }
    fetchData()
  }, [])

  return (
    <div className="app">
      <div className="app__videos">
        {videos.map(({ url, channel, description, song, likes, shares,
        messages }) => (
            <Video
              key={url}
              url={url}
              channel={channel}
              description={description}
              song={song}
              likes={likes}
              shares={shares}
              messages={messages}
```

```
                />
            )}
        </div>
    </div>
  );
}

export default App;
```

You can see the data at `http://localhost:3000/`. The app is now complete. But there is a small issue with the number of likes; it shows 3451 instead of 346 (see Figure 3-13).

Figure 3-13.

This issue occurs because string numbers are being passed from the database. In `VideoSidebar.js`, add a + in front of the likes to change the string to a number.

...

```
        <div className="videoSidebar__button">
            { liked ? <FavoriteIcon fontSize="large" onClick={e =>
            setLiked(false)} /> : <FavoriteBorderIcon fontSize="large"
            onClick={e => setLiked(true)} /> }
            <p>{liked ? +likes + 1 : likes}</p>
        </div>
```

...

Deploying the Back End to Heroku

Go to www.heroku.com to deploy the back end. Follow the same procedure that you did in Chapter 1 and create an app named **short-video-backend**.

After successfully deploying, go to the link. Figure 3-14 shows the correct text.

Figure 3-14.

In axios.js, change the endpoint to https://short-video-backend.herokuapp.com. If everything is working fine, your app should run.

```
import axios from 'axios'
const instance = axios.create({
    baseURL: " https://short-video-backend.herokuapp.com"
})
export default instance
```

Deploying the Front End to Firebase

It's time to deploy the front end in Firebase. Follow the same procedure that you did in Chapter 1. After this process, the site should be live and working properly, as seen in Figure 3-15).

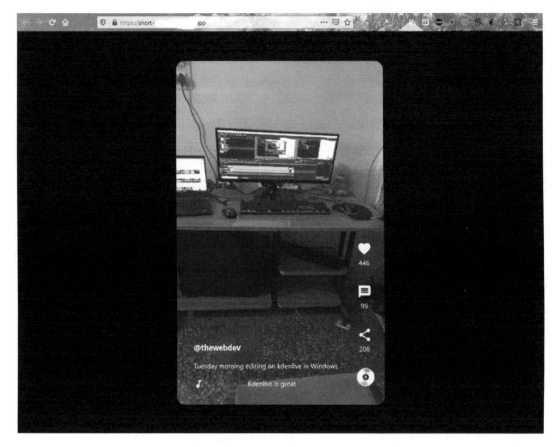

Figure 3-15.

Summary

In this chapter, we have created a short video sharing app. We build the frontend in ReactJS and hosted it in Firebase. The backend was build in NodeJS and hosted in Heroku. The database was build in MongoDB.

CHAPTER 4

Building a Messaging App with MERN

Welcome to your third MERN project, where you build an awesome messaging app using the MERN framework. The back end is hosted in Heroku, and the front-end site is hosted in Firebase.

Material-UI provides the icons in the project. Pusher is used since MongoDB is not a real-time database like Firebase and a chat application requires real-time data. It is a functional chat application with Google authentication so that different users can log in with their Google accounts to chat. Figure 4-1 shows a fully functional hosted and finished app.

© Nabendu Biswas 2021
N. Biswas, *MERN Projects for Beginners*, https://doi.org/10.1007/978-1-4842-7138-4_4

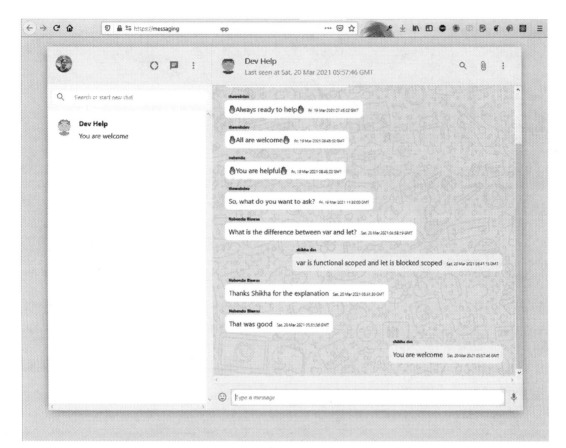

Figure 4-1. *Final hosted app*

Go to your terminal and create a `messaging-app-mern` folder. Inside it, use the
create-react-app to create a new app called **messaging-app-frontend**.

```
mkdir messaging-app-mern
cd messaging-app-mern
npx create-react-app messaging-app-frontend
```

Firebase Hosting Initial Setup

Since the front-end site is hosted through Firebase, you can create the basic setting while
create-react-app creates the React app. Following the setup instructions from Chapter 1,
I created **messaging-app-mern** in the Firebase console.

React Basic Setup

Let's return to the React project and cd to the messaging-app-frontend directory. Start the React app with npm start.

```
cd messaging-app-frontend
npm start
```

The deleting of the files and basic setup in index.js, App.js, and App.css is like what was done in Chapter 2. Follow those instructions.

Figure 4-2 shows how the app looks on localhost.

Messaging App MERN

Figure 4-2. *Initial app*

Creating a Sidebar Component

Let's create a sidebar component that shows the avatar of the logged-in user and other icons, including a search bar. Before creating the sidebar component, add the basic styles in the App.js file. In App.js, create an app__body class that contains all the code. The updated content is marked in bold.

```
import './App.css';

function App() {
  return (
    <div className="app">
      <div className="app__body">

      </div>
    </div>
  );
}

export default App;
```

Next, style the container in App.css to get a centered container with a box-shadow.

```
.app{
    display: grid;
    place-items: center;
    height: 100vh;
    background-color: #dadbd3;
}

.app__body{
    display: flex;
    background-color: #ededed;
    margin-top: -50px;
    height: 90vh;
    width: 90vw;
    box-shadow: -1px 4px 20px -6px rgba(0, 0, 0, 0.75);
}
```

Go to localhost. You should see the big shadow box shown in Figure 4-3.

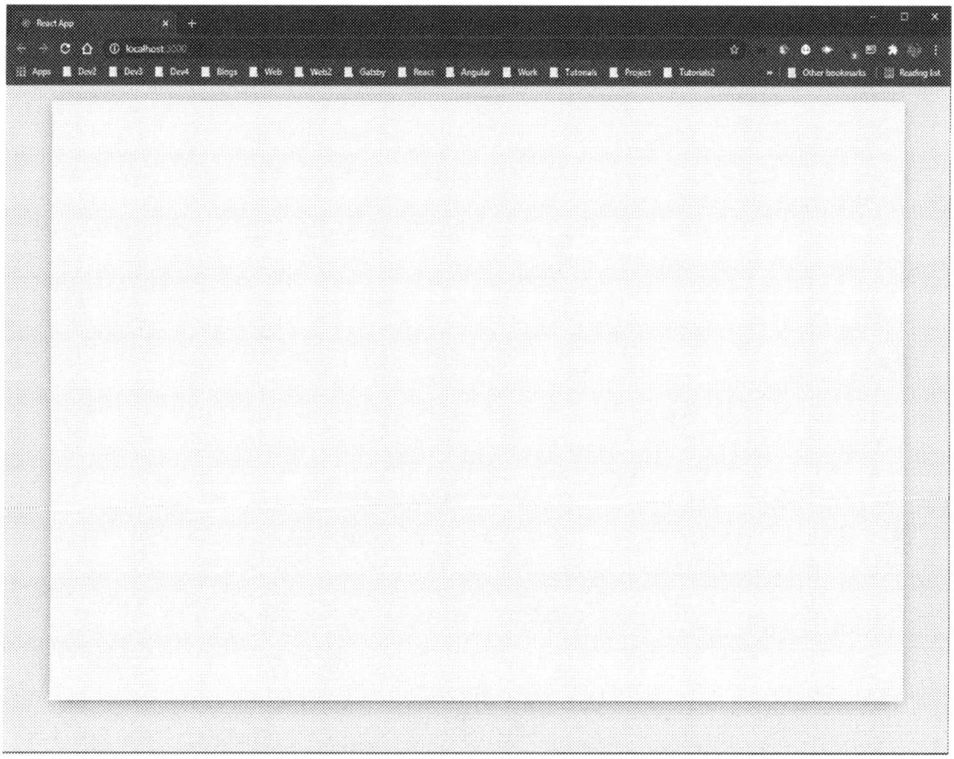

Figure 4-3. *Initial background*

Next, create a components folder inside the src folder. Then create two files—Sidebar.js and Sidebar.css—inside the components folder. Put the content in the Sidebar.js file. The following is the content for the Sidebar.js file.

```
import React from 'react'
import './Sidebar.css'

const Sidebar = () => {
    return (
        <div className="sidebar">
            <div className="sidebar__header"></div>
            <div className="sidebar__search"></div>
            <div className="sidebar__chats"></div>
        </div>
    )
}

export default Sidebar
```

Next, install Material-UI (https://material-ui.com) to get the icons. Do two npm installs according to the Material-UI documentation. Install the core through the integrated terminal in the messaging-app-frontend folder.

```
npm i @material-ui/core @material-ui/icons
```

Next, let's use these icons in the Sidebar.js file. Import them and then use them inside the sidebar__header class. The updated content is marked in bold.

```
import React from 'react'
import './Sidebar.css'
import DonutLargeIcon from '@material-ui/icons/DonutLarge'
import ChatIcon from '@material-ui/icons/Chat'
import MoreVertIcon from '@material-ui/icons/MoreVert'
import { Avatar, IconButton } from '@material-ui/core'

const Sidebar = () => {
    return (
        <div className="sidebar">
            <div className="sidebar__header">
                <Avatar />
                <div className="sidebar__headerRight">
                    <IconButton>
                        <DonutLargeIcon />
                    </IconButton>
                    <IconButton>
                        <ChatIcon />
                    </IconButton>
                    <IconButton>
                        <MoreVertIcon />
                    </IconButton>
                </div>
            </div>
            <div className="sidebar__search"></div>
            <div className="sidebar__chats"></div>
        </div>
    )
}
export default Sidebar
```

Let's add the sidebar header styles in the `Sidebar.css` file. A flexbox is used to achieve this.

```css
.sidebar {
    display: flex;
    flex-direction: column;
    flex: 0.35;
}

.sidebar__header {
    display: flex;
    justify-content: space-between;
    padding: 20px;
    border-right: 1px solid lightgray;
}

.sidebar__headerRight {
    display: flex;
    align-items: center;
    justify-content: space-between;
    min-width: 10vw;
}

.sidebar__headerRight > .MuiSvgIcon-root{
    margin-right: 2vw;
    font-size: 24px !important;
}
```

Next, let's import the sidebar component in `App.js` for it to show on localhost. The updated content is marked in bold.

```jsx
import './App.css';
import Sidebar from './components/Sidebar';

function App() {
  return (
    <div className="app">
      <div className="app__body">
          <Sidebar />
      </div>
```

101

```
    </div>
  );
}
```

```
export default App;
```

Figure 4-4 shows the aligned icons on localhost.

Next, create the search bar in `Sidebar.js`. Import `SearchOutlined` from Material-UI and use it with the `sidebar__searchContainer` class. Place an input box beside it.

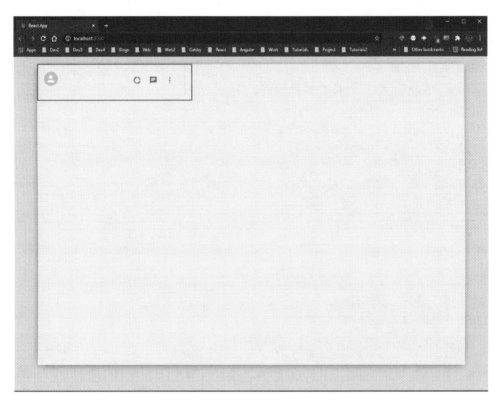

Figure 4-4. *Icons aligned*

```
import { SearchOutlined } from '@material-ui/icons'
```

```
const Sidebar = () => {
    return (
        <div className="sidebar">
            <div className="sidebar__header">
```

```
            <Avatar src="https://pbs.twimg.com/profile_
            images/1020939891457241088/fcbu814K_400x400.jpg"/>
            <div className="sidebar__headerRight">
                ...
            </div>
        </div>
        <div className="sidebar__search">
            <div className="sidebar__searchContainer">
                <SearchOutlined />
                <input placeholder="Search or start new chat"
                type="text" />
            </div>
        </div>
            <div className="sidebar__chats"></div>
        </div>
    )
}

export default Sidebar
```

I used an image from my Twitter account as the avatar. The updated content is marked in bold.

The search bar is styled in the Searchbar.css file. A lot of flexboxes are used to style it. Add this new content to the existing content.

```
.sidebar__search {
    display: flex;
    align-items: center;
    background-color: #f6f6f6;
    height: 39px;
    padding: 10px;
}

.sidebar__searchContainer{
    display: flex;
    align-items: center;
    background-color: white;
    width: 100%;
```

```
    height: 35px;
    border-radius: 20px;
}

.sidebar__searchContainer > .MuiSvgIcon-root{
    color: gray;
    padding: 10px;
}
.sidebar__searchContainer > input {
    border: none;
    outline-width: 0;
    margin-left: 10px;
}
```

Figure 4-5 shows everything on localhost.

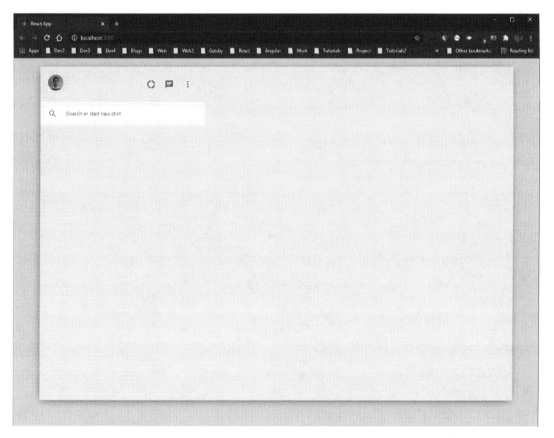

Figure 4-5. *Search bar*

Creating a Sidebar Chat Component

Let's build the sidebar chat component now. Inside the components folder, create two files—SidebarChat.js and SidebarChat.css. Use them in the Sidebar.js file. The updated content is marked in bold.

```
...
import SidebarChat from './SidebarChat'

const Sidebar = () => {
    return (
        <div className="sidebar">
            <div className="sidebar__header">
                ...
            </div>
            <div className="sidebar__search">
                ...
            </div>
            <div className="sidebar__chats">
                <SidebarChat />
                <SidebarChat />
                <SidebarChat />
        </div>
        </div>
    )
}
export default Sidebar
```

Before coding the sidebar chat component, let's style the sidebar__chats div, which contains the SidebarChat component in the Sidebar.css file. Add this new content to the existing content.

```
.sidebar__chats{
    flex: 1;
    background-color: white;
    overflow: scroll;
}
```

In the SidebarChat.js file, there is a simple, functional component. An API endpoint provides random avatars if you pass random stings to it. The seed state variable is used; it changes each time with a random string from within useEffect.

```
import React, { useEffect, useState } from 'react'
import { Avatar } from '@material-ui/core'
import './SidebarChat.css'

const SidebarChat = () => {
    const [seed, setSeed] = useState("")

    useEffect(() => {
        setSeed(Math.floor(Math.random() * 5000))
    }, [])

    return (
        <div className="sidebarChat">
            <Avatar src={`https://avatars.dicebear.com/api/human/
            b${seed}.svg`} />
            <div className="sidebarChat__info">
                <h2>Room name</h2>
                <p>Last message...</p>
            </div>
        </div>
    )
}

export default SidebarChat
```

Next, let's style the rooms a bit in the SidebarChat.css file. Here, you are again using a flexbox and a bit of padding.

```
.sidebarChat{
    display: flex;
    padding: 20px;
    cursor: pointer;
    border-bottom: 1px solid #f6f6f6;
}
```

```
.sidebarChat:hover{
    background-color: #ebebeb;
}
.sidebarChat__info > h2 {
    font-size: 16px;
    margin-bottom: 8px;
}
.sidebarChat__info {
    margin-left: 15px;
}
```

Figure 4-6 shows the sidebar chat component on localhost.

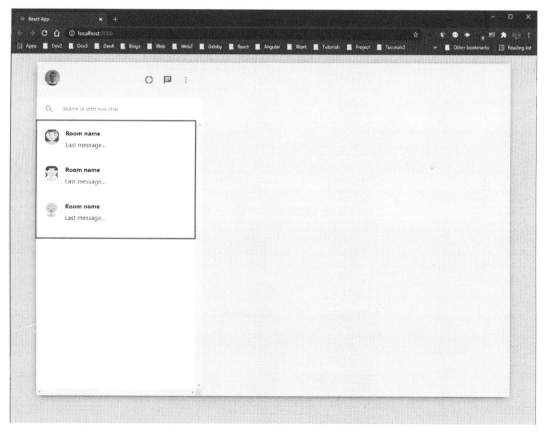

Figure 4-6. *Sidebar chat*

Creating a Chat Component

Let's start working on the chat component. Create two files—Chat.js and Chat.css—inside the components folder. Put this basic structure in the Chat.js file. Random strings are used to show a random avatar icon.

```
import React, { useEffect, useState } from 'react'
import { Avatar, IconButton } from '@material-ui/core'
import { AttachFile, MoreVert, SearchOutlined } from '@material-ui/icons'
import './Chat.css'

const Chat = () => {
    const [seed, setSeed] = useState("")
    useEffect(() => {
        setSeed(Math.floor(Math.random() * 5000))
    }, [])

    return (
        <div className="chat">
            <div className="chat__header">
                <Avatar src={`https://avatars.dicebear.com/api/human/
                b${seed}.svg`} />
                <div className="chat__headerInfo">
                    <h3>Room Name</h3>
                    <p>Last seen at...</p>
                </div>
                <div className="chat__headerRight">
                    <IconButton>
                        <SearchOutlined />
                    </IconButton>
                    <IconButton>
                        <AttachFile />
                    </IconButton>
                    <IconButton>
                        <MoreVert />
                    </IconButton>
                </div>
            </div>
```

```
            <div className="chat__body"></div>
            <div className="chat__footer"></div>
        </div>
    )
}

export default Chat
```

Next, style the chat header in the Chat.css file, and add a nice background image to the chat__body class.

```css
.chat{
    display: flex;
    flex-direction: column;
    flex: 0.65;
}
.chat__header{
    padding: 20px;
    display: flex;
    align-items: center;
    border-bottom: 1px solid lightgray;
}
.chat__headerInfo {
    flex: 1;
    padding-left: 20px;
}
.chat__headerInfo > h3 {
    margin-bottom: 3px;
    font-weight: 500;
}
.chat__headerInfo > p {
    color: gray;
}
.chat__body{
    flex: 1;
```

```
  background-image: url("https://user-images.githubusercontent.com/
  15075759/28719144-86dc0f70-73b1-11e7-911d-60d70fcded21.png");
  background-repeat: repeat;
  background-position: center;
  padding: 30px;
  overflow: scroll;
}
```

Render the chat component from the App.js file. The updated content is marked in bold.

```
import './App.css';
import Sidebar from './components/Sidebar';
import Chat from './components/Chat';

function App() {
  return (
    <div className="app">
      <div className="app__body">
          <Sidebar />
          <Chat />
      </div>
    </div>
  );
}

export default App;
```

Head over to localhost. Figure 4-7 shows the header for the chat is done, and a nice background image is displayed.

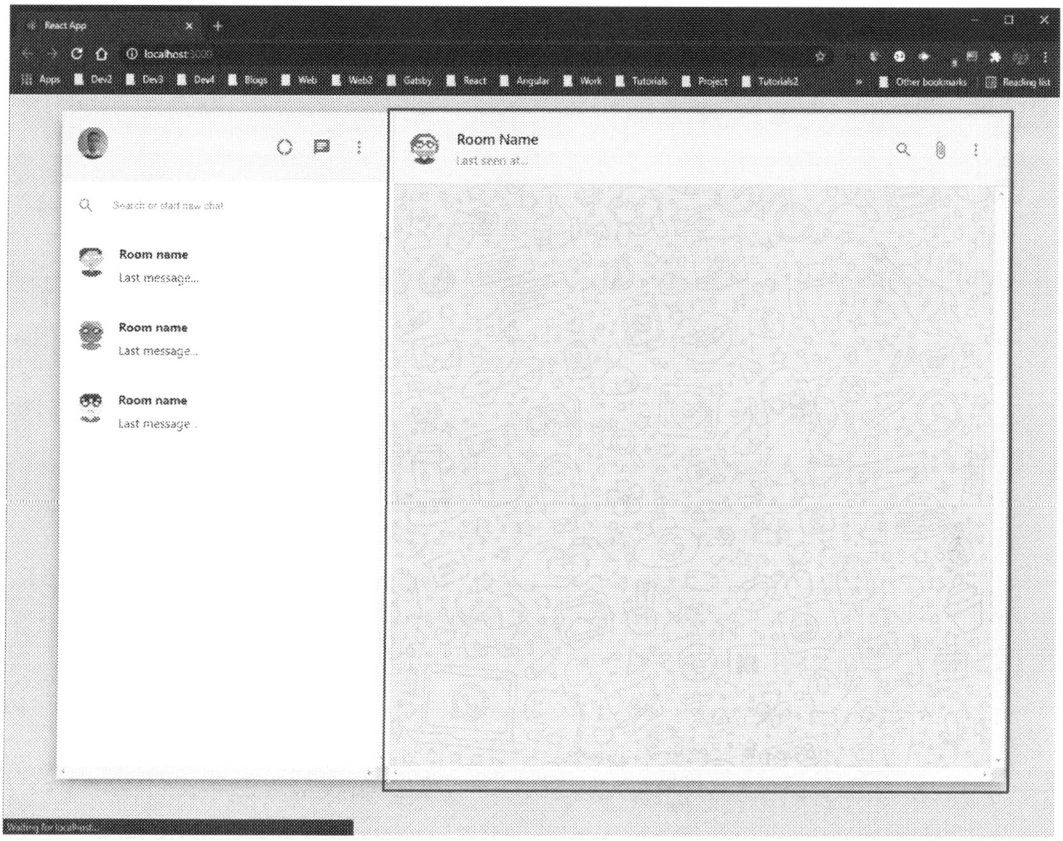

Figure 4-7. *Chat component*

Next, go back to the Chat.js file and put the hard-coded message in a p tag in the chat__message class. Two span tags are used for the name and timestamp.

Note the chat__receiver class for the chat user. The updated content is marked in bold.

```
...
const Chat = () => {
    const [seed, setSeed] = useState("")
    useEffect(() => {
        setSeed(Math.floor(Math.random() * 5000))
    }, [])

    return (
        <div className="chat">
            <div className="chat__header">
```

111

```
            ...
        </div>
        <div className="chat__body">
            <p className="chat__message">
                <span className="chat__name">Nabendu</span>
                This is a message
                <span className="chat__timestamp">
                    {new Date().toUTCString()}
                </span>
            </p>
            <p className="chat__message chat__receiver">
                <span className="chat__name">Parag</span>
                This is a message back
                <span className="chat__timestamp">
                    {new Date().toUTCString()}
                </span>
            </p>
            <p className="chat__message">
                <span className="chat__name">Nabendu</span>
                This is a message again again
                <span className="chat__timestamp">
                    {new Date().toUTCString()}
                </span>
            </p>
        </div>
        <div className="chat__footer"></div>
    </div>
    )
}

export default Chat
```

Add the styles in the Chat.css file.

```
.chat__message{
    position: relative;
    font-size: 16px;
```

```
    padding: 10px;
    width: fit-content;
    border-radius: 10px;
    background-color: #ffffff;
    margin-bottom: 30px;
}

.chat__receiver{
    margin-left: auto;
    background-color: #dcf8c6;
}
.chat__timestamp{
    margin-lefl: 10px;
    font-size: xx-small;
}
.chat__name{
    position: absolute;
    top: -15px;
    font-weight: 800;
    font-size: xx-small;
}
```

Figure 4-8 shows the three messages on localhost.

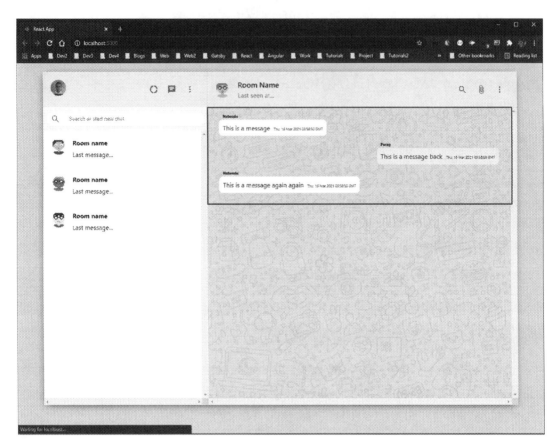

Figure 4-8. *Chat messages*

Creating a Chat Footer Component

Let's complete the chat__footer div. There are two more icons and an input box inside a form. The updated code for Chat.js is marked in bold.

```
...
import { AttachFile, MoreVert, SearchOutlined, InsertEmoticon } from
'@material-ui/icons'
import MicIcon from '@material-ui/icons/Mic'
import './Chat.css'
...
const Chat = () => {
...
    return (
```

```
        <div className="chat">
            <div className="chat__header">
              ...
            </div>
            <div className="chat__body">
              ...
            </div>
            <div className="chat__footer">
                <InsertEmoticon />
                <form>
                    <input
                        placeholder="Type a message"
                        type="text"
                    />
                    <button type="submit">Send a message</button>
                </form>
                <MicIcon />
            </div>
        </div>
    )
}

export default Chat
```

It's time to style the chat__footer div. Note display: none for the button. Since it is wrapped in a form, you can use enter in it. Add the following content in the Chat.css file.

```
.chat__footer{
    display: flex;
    justify-content: space-between;
    align-items:center;
    height: 62px;
    border-top: 1px solid lightgray;
}
```

```css
.chat__footer > form {
    flex: 1;
    display: flex;
}

.chat__footer > form > input {
    flex: 1;
    outline-width: 0;
    border-radius: 30px;
    padding: 10px;
    border: none;
}

.chat__footer > form > button {
    display: none;
}

.chat__footer > .MuiSvgIcon-root {
    padding: 10px;
    color: gray;
}
```

Figure 4-9 shows the footer on localhost.

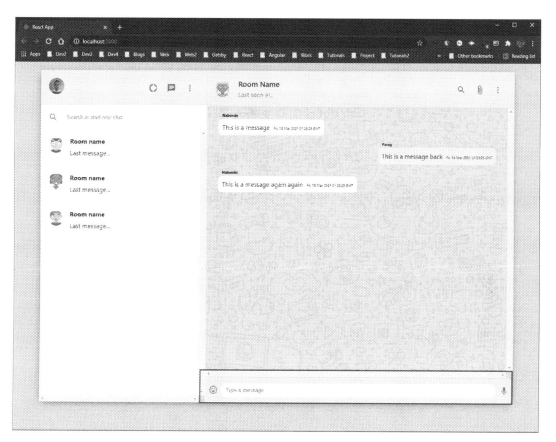

Figure 4-9. *Footer complete*

Initial Back-End Setup

Let's move to the back end, starting with the Node.js code. Open a new terminal window and create a new messaging-app-backend folder in the root directory. After moving to the messaging-app-backend directory, enter the git init command, which is required for Heroku later.

```
mkdir messaging-app-backend
cd messaging-app-backend
git init
```

Next, create the package.json file by entering the npm init command in the terminal. You are asked a bunch of questions; for most of them, simply press the Enter key. You can provide the **description** and the **author**, but they are not mandatory. You generally make the entry point at server.js, which is standard (see Figure 4-10).

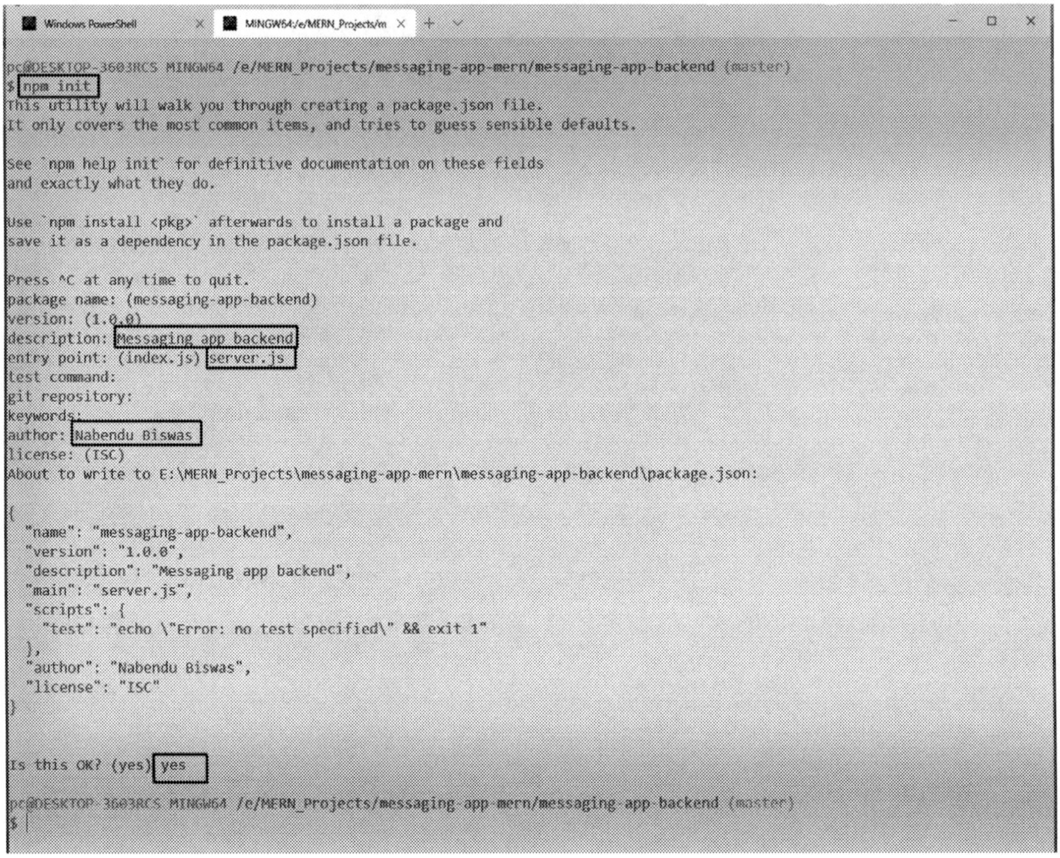

Figure 4-10. *Initial back-end setup*

Once package.json is created, you need to create the .gitignore file with node_modules in it since you don't want to push node_modules to Heroku later. The following is the .gitignore file content.

```
node_modules
```

Next, open package.json. The line "type": "module is required to have React-like imports enabled in Node.js. Include a start script to run the server.js file. The updated content is marked in bold.

```
{
  "name": "messaging-app-backend",
  "version": "1.0.0",
  "description": "Messaging app backend",
  "main": "server.js",
```

```
"type": "module",
"scripts": {
  "test": "echo \"Error: no test specified\" && exit 1",
  "start": "node server.js"
},
"author": "Nabendu Biswas",
"license": "ISC"
}
```

Finally, you need to install two packages before starting. Open the terminal and install Express and Mongoose in the messaging-app-backend folder.

```
npm i express mongoose
```

MongoDB Setup

The MongoDB setup is the same as described in Chapter 1. Follow those instructions and create a new project named **messaging-app-mern**.

Before moving forward, install nodemon in the messaging-app-backend folder. It helps the changes in server.js to restart the Node server instantaneously.

```
npm i nodemon
```

Initial Route Setup

Create a server.js file in the messaging-app-backend folder, where you import the Express and Mongoose packages. Then use Express to create a port variable to run on port 9000.

The first API endpoint is a simple GET request created by app.get(), which shows the text **Hello TheWebDev** if successful.

Then, listen on port with app.listen().

```
import express from 'express'
import mongoose from 'mongoose'

//App Config
const app = express()
const port = process.env.PORT || 9000
```

```
//Middleware

//DB Config

//API Endpoints
app.get("/", (req, res) => res.status(200).send("Hello TheWebDev"))

//Listener
app.listen(port, () => console.log(`Listening on localhost: ${port}`))
```

In the terminal, type **nodemon server.js** to see the **Listening on localhost: 9000** console log. To check that the route is working correctly, go to `http://localhost:9000/` to see the endpoint text, as shown in Figure 4-11.

Hello TheWebDev

Figure 4-11. *Initial route*

Database User and Network Access

In MongoDB, you need to create a database user and give network access. The process is the same as explained in Chapter 1. Follow those instructions, and then get the user credentials and connection URL.

In the `server.js` file, create a `connection_url` variable and paste the URL within the string from MongoDB. You need to provide the password that you saved earlier and a database name.

The updated code is marked in bold.

```
...

//App Config
const app = express()
const port = process.env.PORT || 9000
const connection_url = ' mongodb+srv://admin:<password>@cluster0.ew283.
mongodb.net/messagingDB?retryWrites=true&w=majority'

//Middleware

//DB Config
```

```
mongoose.connect(connection_url, {
    useNewUrlParser: true,
    useCreateIndex: true,
    useUnifiedTopology: true
})

//API Endpoints
app.get("/", (req, res) => res.status(200).send("Hello TheWebDev"))

...
```

MongoDB Schema and Routes

Let's now create the schema file required by MongoDB. It tells you about the way fields are stored in MongoDB. Create a dbMessages.js file inside the messaging-app-backend folder.

Here, messagingmessages is considered a collection name, and you store a value like messagingSchema in the database. It consists of an object with a message, name, timestamp, and received keys.

```
import mongoose from 'mongoose'
const messagingSchema = mongoose.Schema({
    message: String,
    name: String,
    timestamp: String,
    received: Boolean
})

export default mongoose.model('messagingmessages', messagingSchema)
```

You can now use the schema to create the endpoint that adds data to the database.

In server.js, create a POST request to the /messages/new endpoint. The load is in req.body to MongoDB. Then use create() to send dbMessage. If it's a success, you receive status 201; otherwise, you receive status 500.

Next, create the GET endpoint to /messages/sync to get the data from the database. You are using find() here. You receive status 200 if successful (otherwise, status 500).

The updated code is marked in bold.

```
import express from 'express'
import mongoose from 'mongoose'
import Messages from './dbMessages.js'

...
//API Endpoints
app.get("/", (req, res) => res.status(200).send("Hello TheWebDev"))

app.post('/messages/new', (req, res) => {
    const dbMessage = req.body
    Messages.create(dbMessage, (err, data) => {
        if(err)
            res.status(500).send(err)
        else
            res.status(201).send(data)
    })
})

app.get('/messages/sync', (req, res) => {
    Messages.find((err, data) => {
        if(err) {
            res.status(500).send(err)
        } else {
            res.status(200).send(data)
        }
    })
})

//Listener
app.listen(port, () => console.log(`Listening on localhost: ${port}`))
```

To check the routes, use the Postman app. Download it and install it.

Send a GET request to http://localhost:9000 to check if it's working from Postman, as seen in Figure 4-12.

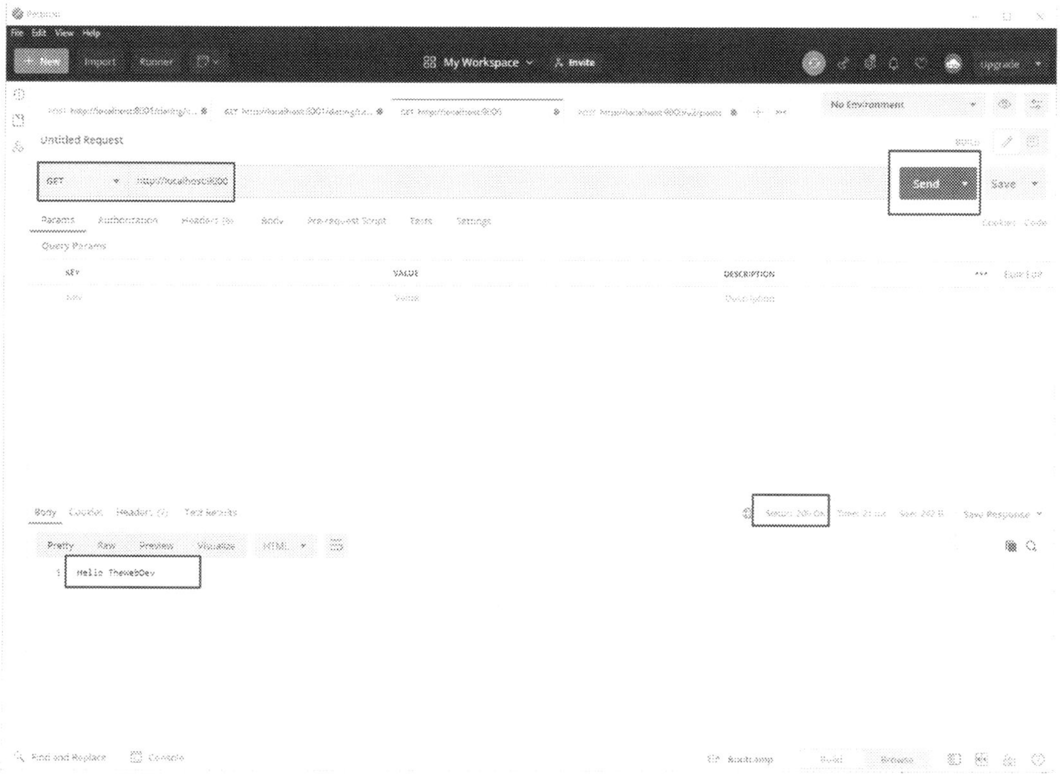

Figure 4-12. *Initial GET request*

Before moving forward with the POST request, you need to complete two things. First, implement CORS; otherwise, you get cross-origin errors when you deploy the app. Open the terminal and install CORS in the messaging-app-backend folder.

```
npm i cors
```

In server.js, import CORS and then use it with app.use(). You also need to use the express.json() middleware. The updated code is marked in bold.

```
import express from 'express'
import mongoose from 'mongoose'
import Cors from 'cors'
import Messages from './dbMessages.js'

...
```

```
//Middleware
app.use(express.json())
app.use(Cors())
```

...

In Postman, you need to change the request to POST and then add the `http://localhost:9000/messages/new` endpoint.

Next, click **Body** and select **raw**. Select **JSON(application/json)** from the drop-down menu. In the text editor, enter the data as shown in Figure 4-13. Make the data JSON by adding double quotes to the keys.

Next, click the **Send** button. If everything is correct, you get **Status: 201 Created**, as seen in Figure 4-13.

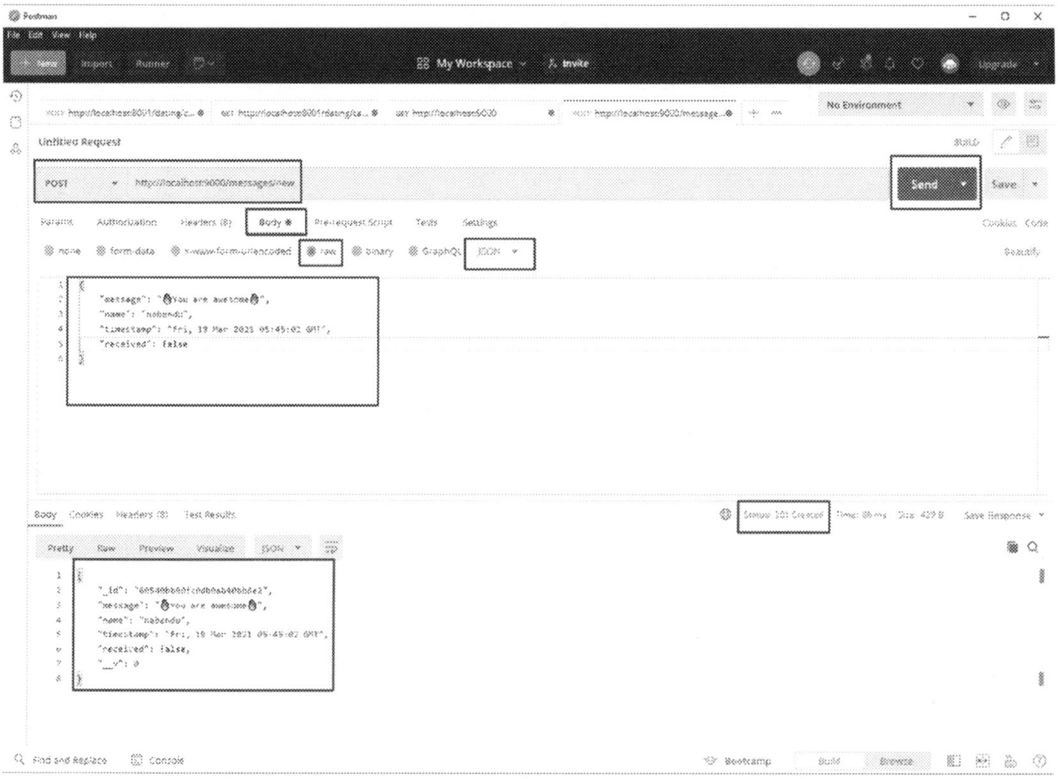

Figure 4-13. *POST request*

I similarly inserted other data, but with **received** as **true**. You need to test the GET /messages/sync endpoint. Change the request to GET and click the **Send** button. If everything is correct, you get **Status: 200 OK**, as seen in Figure 4-14.

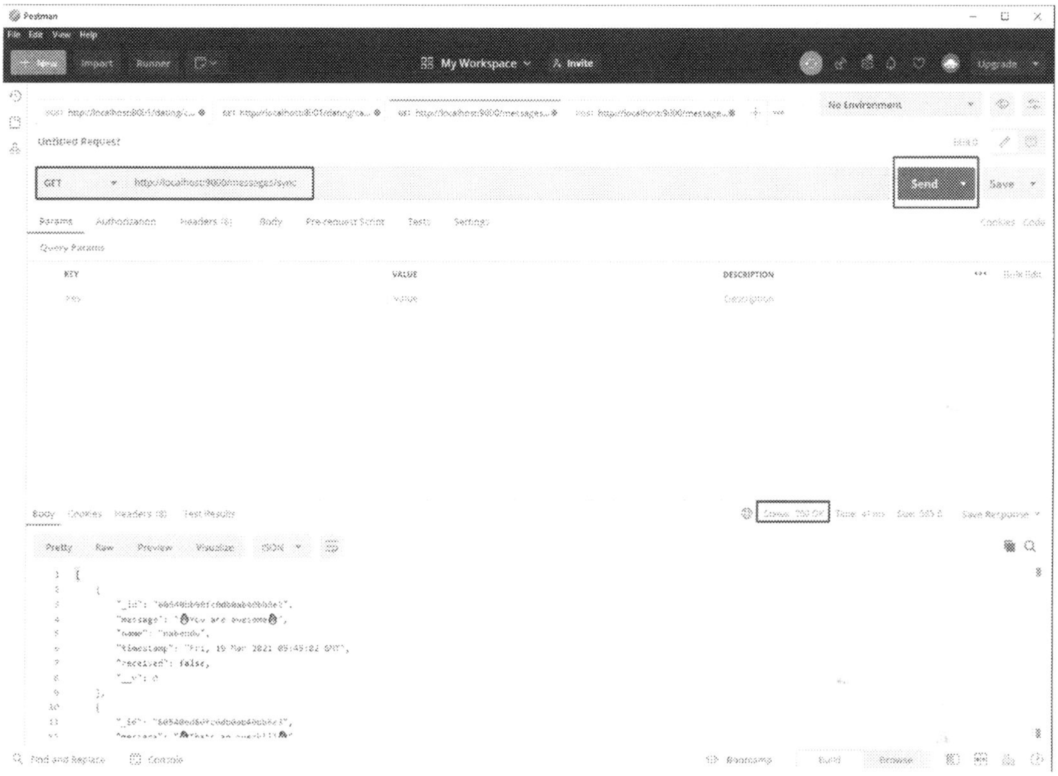

Figure 4-14. *GET request*

Sometimes you get a server error with POST requests. The error is **UnhandledPromiseRejectionWarning: MongooseServerSelectionError: connection**. If you get this error, go to your **Network Access** tab, and click the **ADD IP ADDRESS** button. After that, click the **ADD CURRENT IP ADDRESS** button, and then click **Confirm**, as seen in Figure 4-15.

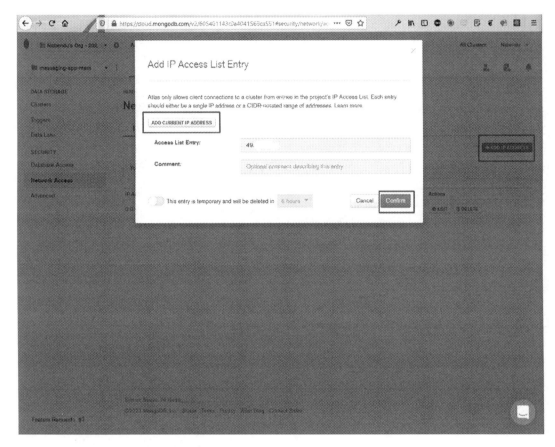

Figure 4-15. *Network error fix*

Configuring Pusher

Since MongoDB is not a real-time database, it's time to add a pusher to the app to get real-time data. Go to `https://pusher.com` and sign up. The Pusher app dashboard is shown in Figure 4-16. Click the **Manage** button.

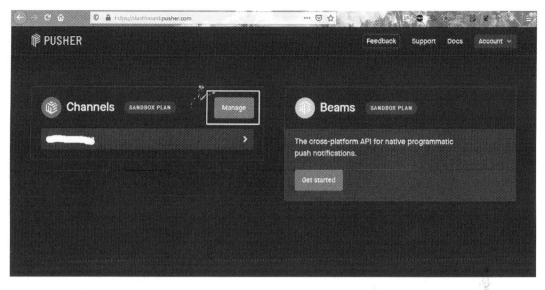

Figure 4-16. *Pusher dashboard*

On the next screen, click the **Create app** button, as seen in Figure 4-17.

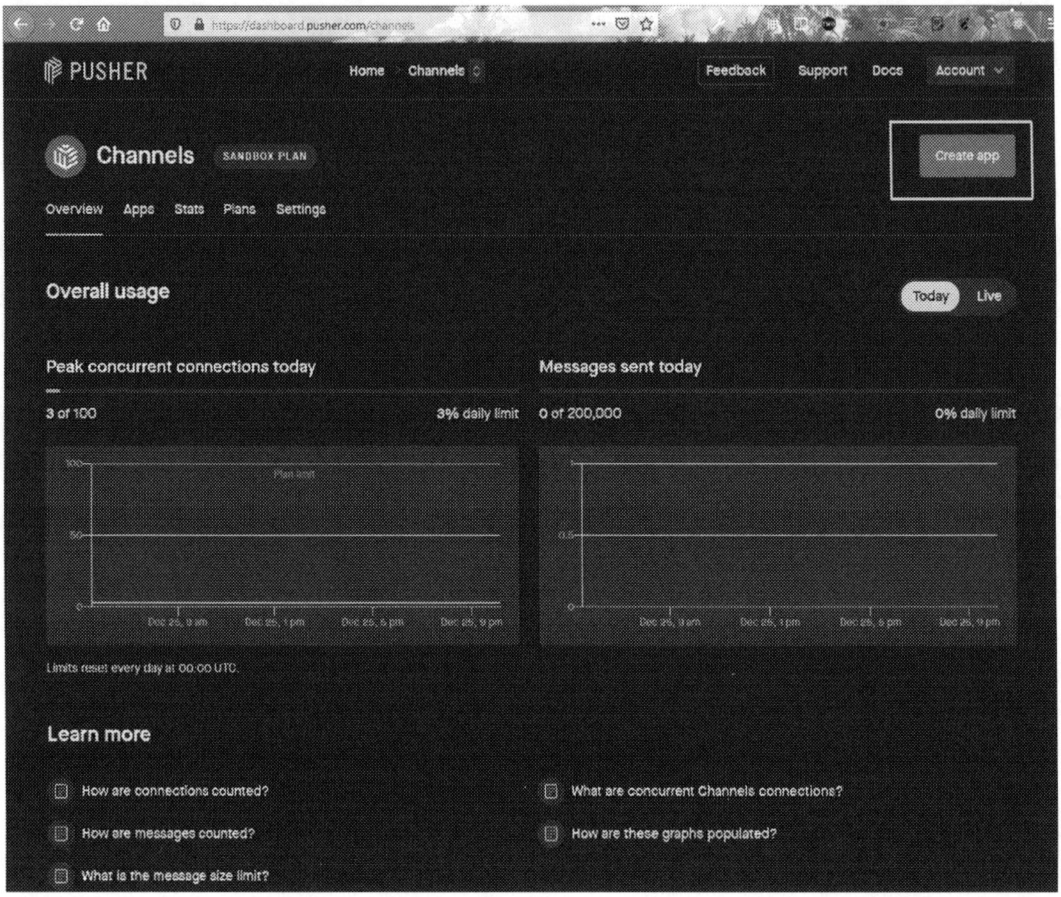

Figure 4-17. *Create app in Pusher*

In the popup window, name the app **messaging-app-mern**. The front end is React, and the back end is Node.js, as seen in Figure 4-18.

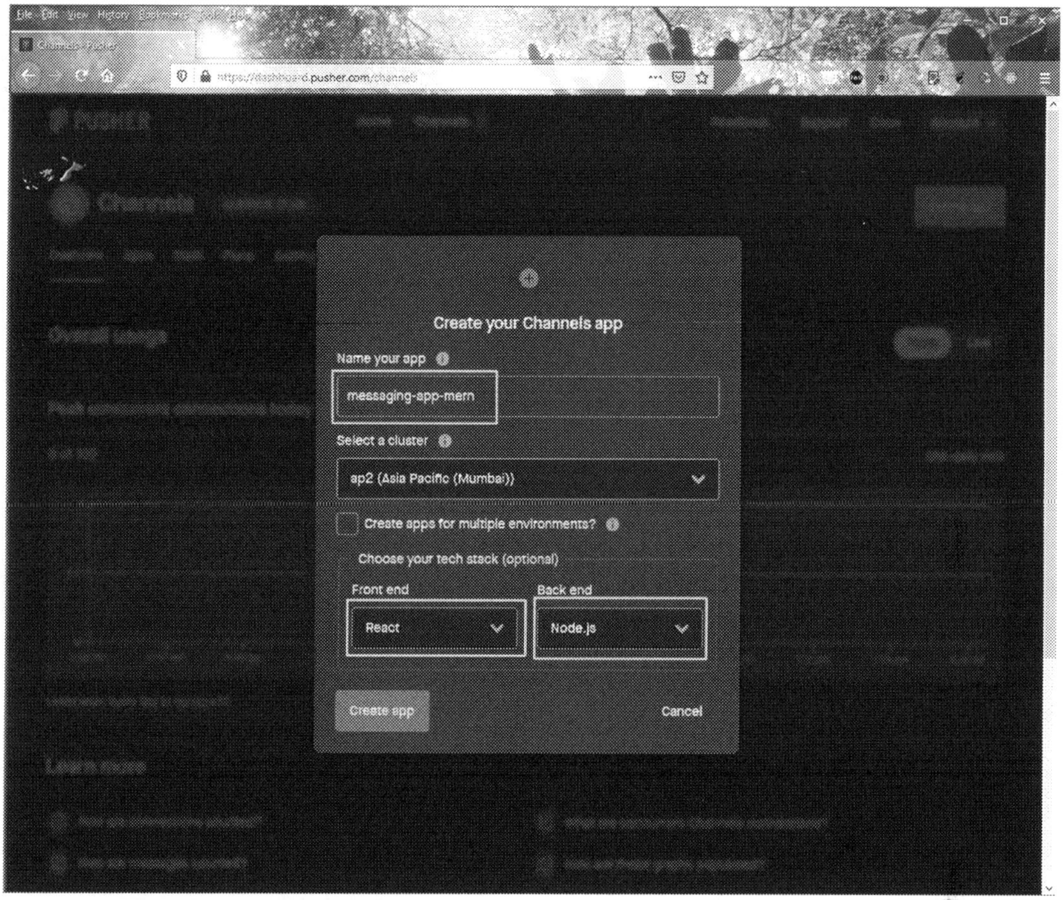

Figure 4-18. *Front end and back end*

In the next screen, you get the code for both the front end and the back end of Pusher, as seen in Figure 4-19.

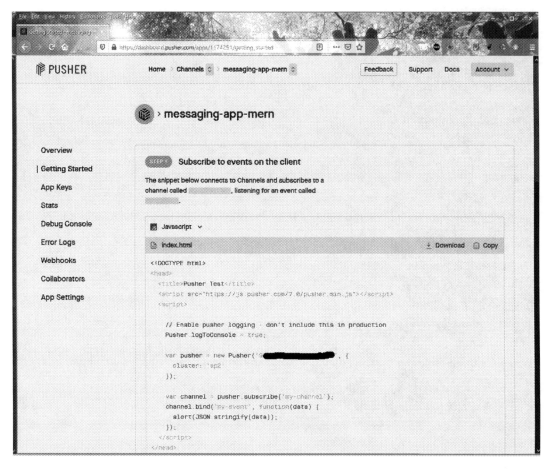

Figure 4-19. *Back-end code*

Adding Pusher to the Back End

As explained in the previous section, you need to stop the server and install Pusher. In the messaging-app-backend folder, install it with the following command.

```
npm i pusher
```

In the server.js file, import it and then use the Pusher initialization code. Get the initialization code from the Pusher website (https://pusher.com). To add the code, open a database connection with db.once. Then watch the message collection from MongoDB with watch().

Inside changeStream, if operationType is inserted, you insert the data in the pusher. The updated code is marked in bold.

```
...
import Pusher from 'pusher'
...
//App Config
const app = express()
const port = process.env.PORT || 9000
const connection_url = ' mongodb+srv://admin:<password>@cluster0.ew283.
mongodb.net/messagingDB?retryWrites=true&w=majority'
const pusher = new Pusher({
    appId: "11xxxx",
    key: "9exxxxxxxxxxxxxx",
    secret: "b7xxxxxxxxxxxxxxx",
    cluster: "ap2",
    useTLS: true
});

//API Endpoints
const db = mongoose.connection
db.once("open", () => {
    console.log("DB Connected")
    const msgCollection = db.collection("messagingmessages")
    const changeStream = msgCollection.watch()
    changeStream.on('change', change => {
        console.log(change)
        if(change.operationType === "insert") {
            const messageDetails = change.fullDocument
            pusher.trigger("messages", "inserted", {
                name: messageDetails.name,
                message: messageDetails.message,
                timestamp: messageDetails.timestamp,
                received: messageDetails.received
            })
```

```
        } else {
            console.log('Error trigerring Pusher')
        }
    })
})
app.get("/", (req, res) => res.status(200).send("Hello TheWebDev"))

...

//Listener
app.listen(port, () => console.log(`Listening on localhost: ${port}`))
```

To test this, you need to send a POST request from Postman. At the same time, you need to be in the **Debug console** in Pusher.

Figure 4-20 shows the message displayed in the Debug console log.

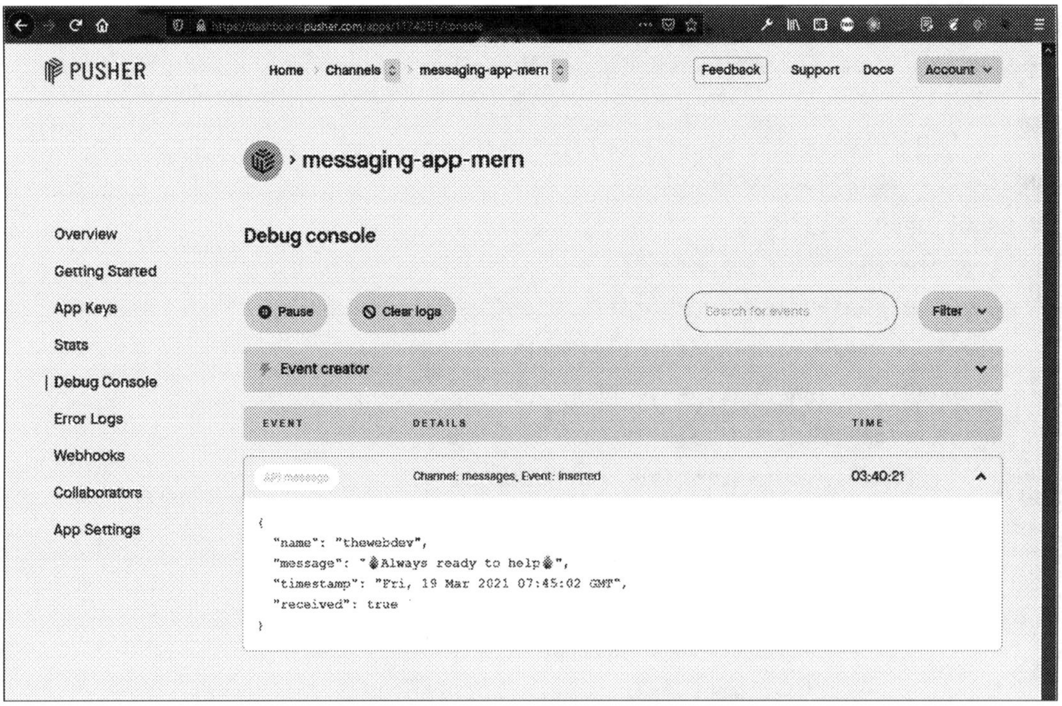

Figure 4-20. *Message in Pusher*

In the server, the console logs show the same, as seen in Figure 4-21.

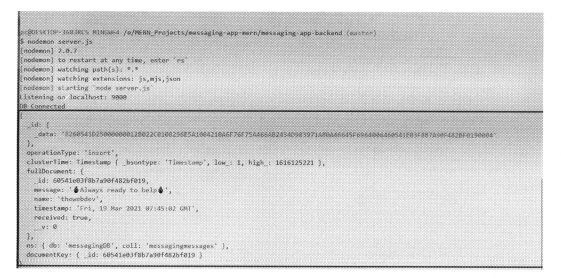

Figure 4-21. *Server logs*

Adding Pusher to the Front End

It's time to move back to the front end and use Pusher. First, you need to install the
pusher-js package in the messaging-app-frontend folder.

```
npm i pusher-js
```

Use the following code and insert the new data in the front end in the App.js file.
The updated content is marked in bold.

```
...
import React, { useEffect, useState } from 'react'
import Pusher from 'pusher-js'
function App() {
  const [messages, setMessages] = useState([])

  useEffect(() => {
    const pusher = new Pusher('9exxxxxxxxxxxx', {
      cluster: 'ap2'
    });

    const channel = pusher.subscribe('messages');
    channel.bind('inserted', (data) => {
```

```
      setMessages([...messages, data])
    });

    return () => {
      channel.unbind_all()
      channel.unsubscribe()
    }
  }, [messages])

  console.log(messages)

  return (
    <div className="app">
      ...
    </div>
  );
}

export default App;
```

Go to Postman and send another POST request. Figure 4-22 shows the data from the console log on localhost.

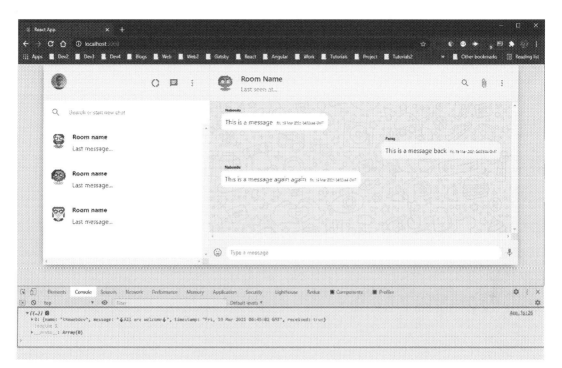

Figure 4-22. *Console log*

Integrating the Back End with the Front End

You want to get all the messages when the app initially loads, and then push the messages. You must hit the GET endpoint, and you need Axios for that. Open the `messaging-app-frontend` folder and install it.

```
npm i axios
```

Next, create a new `axios.js` file inside the `components` folder and create an instance of `axios`. The base URL is `http://localhost:9000`.

```
import axios from 'axios'

const instance = axios.create({
    baseURL: "http://localhost:9000"
})

export default instance
```

Next, return to App.js and include the local axios first. Then use axios in the useEffect hook to get all the data from the /messages/sync endpoint. After receiving the messages, you set it through setMessages(). Finally, pass the messages as props to the chat component.

The updated content is marked in bold.

```
...
import axios from './components/axios'

function App() {
  const [messages, setMessages] = useState([])

  useEffect(() => {
    axios.get("/messages/sync").then(res => {
      setMessages(res.data)
    })
  }, [])

  useEffect(() => {
    ...
  }, [messages])

  return (
    <div className="app">
      <div className="app__body">
        <Sidebar />
        <Chat messages={messages} />
      </div>
    </div>
  );
}

export default App;
```

In the Chat.js file, use this message's props and map through it to display on the screen.

Add the chat__receiver class if the message contains the received key. The updated content is marked in bold.

```
...
const Chat = ({ messages }) => {
    const [seed, setSeed] = useState("")
    useEffect(() => {
        setSeed(Math.floor(Math.random() * 5000))
    }, [])

    return (
        <div className="chat">
            <div className="chat__header">
                ...
            </div>
            <div className="chat__body">
                {messages.map(message => (
                    <p className={`chat__message ${message.received &&
                    'chat__receiver'}`}>
                        <span className="chat__name">{message.name}</span>
                            {message.message}
                        <span className="chat__timestamp">
                            {message.timestamp}
                        </span>
                    </p>
                ))}
            </div>
            <div className="chat__footer">
                ...
            </div>
        </div>
    )
}

export default Chat
```

You can see all the messages on localhost. If you post a new message through Postman, you get it in the chat, as seen in Figure 4-23.

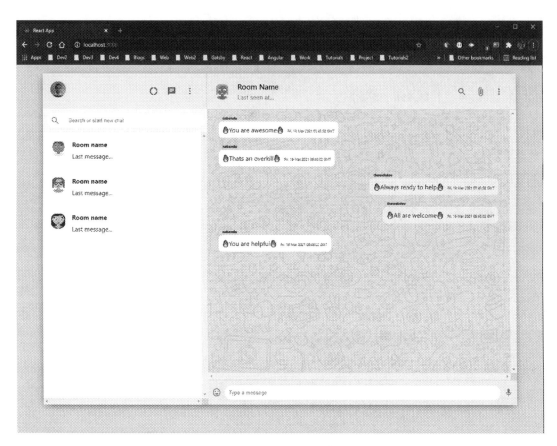

Figure 4-23. *New messages*

Add the logic to POST directly from the message box. First, import the local `axios` and then create an input state variable.

Then do the **value** and **onChange** React thing on input and attach a `sendMessage` function to the `onClick` event handler of the button.

Inside the `sendMessage` function, do a POST call to the `/messages/new` endpoint with the required data. The updated content in `Chat.js` is marked in bold.

```
import axios from './axios'
...
const Chat = ({ messages }) => {
    const [seed, setSeed] = useState("")
    const [input, setInput] = useState("")

    const sendMessage = async (e) => {
```

```
    e.preventDefault()
    await axios.post('/messages/new', {
        message: input,
        name: "thewebdev",
        timestamp: new Date().toUTCString(),
        received: true
    })
    setInput("")
}
useEffect(() => {
    setSeed(Math.floor(Math.random() * 5000))
}, [])

return (
    <div className="chat">
        <div className="chat__header">
          ...
        </div>
        <div className="chat__body">
          ...
        </div>
        <div className="chat__footer">
            <InsertEmoticon />
            <form>
                <input
                    value={input}
                    onChange={e => setInput(e.target.value)}
                    placeholder="Type a message"
                    type="text"
                />
                <button onClick={sendMessage} type="submit">Send a
                message</button>
            </form>
            <MicIcon />
        </div>
```

```
        </div>
    )
}
export default Chat
```

You can type text in the input box, and when you press the Enter key, the message is instantly shown in the chat, as seen in Figure 4-24.

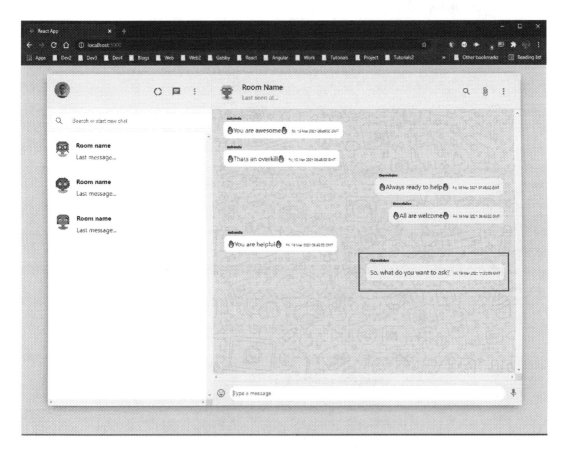

Figure 4-24. *Message from input*

Additional Setup

Next, let's add Google authentication to the project so that the user can log in with their Google account.

For Google authentication, you need an additional setting in the Firebase console. Click the **Settings** icon in the top-right corner of the screen. After that, click the **Project settings** button, as seen in Figure 4-25.

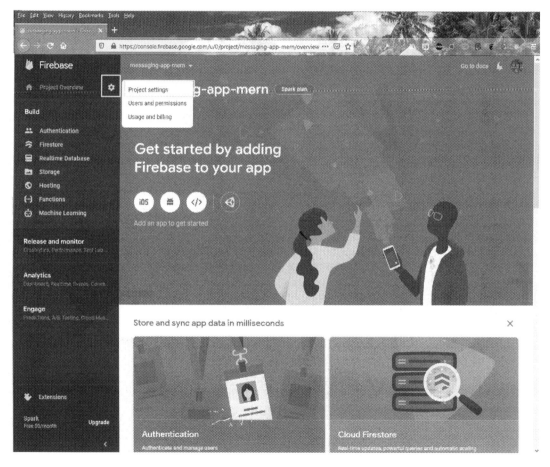

Figure 4-25. *Additional settings*

On the next page, click the web icon on the bottom of the page, as seen in Figure 4-26.

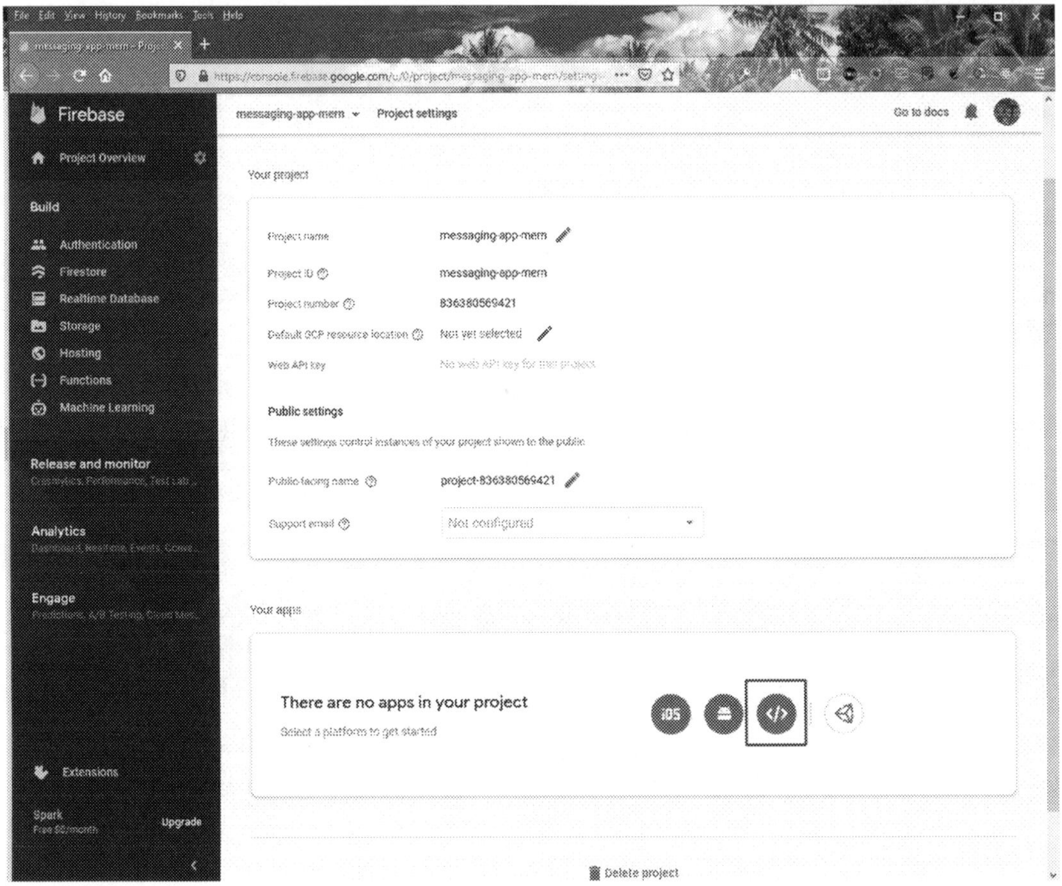

Figure 4-26. *Web icon*

On the next page, enter the name of the app (**messaging-app-mern** in my case).
Select the **Firebase hosting** check box. Click the **Register app** button (see Figure 4-27).

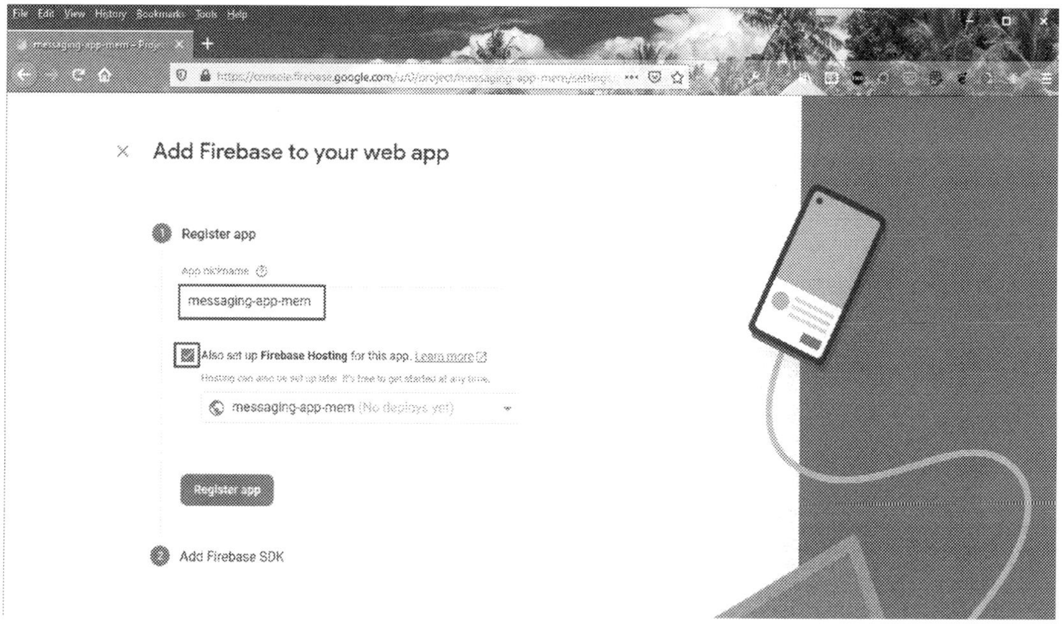

Figure 4-27. *Firebase hosting*

On the next page, click the **Next** button (see Figure 4-28).

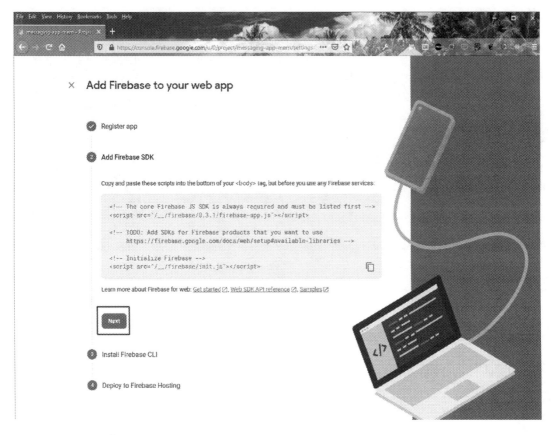

Figure 4-28. *The next screen*

On the next page, run the `firebase-tools` globally install Firebase from the terminal. Note that this is a one-time setup on your machine since it is used with the `-g` option (see Figure 4-29).

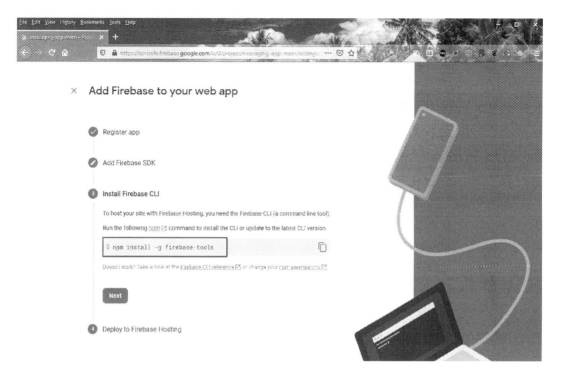

Figure 4-29. *Global install*

Ignore the next set of commands, and click the **Continue to the console** button (see Figure 4-30).

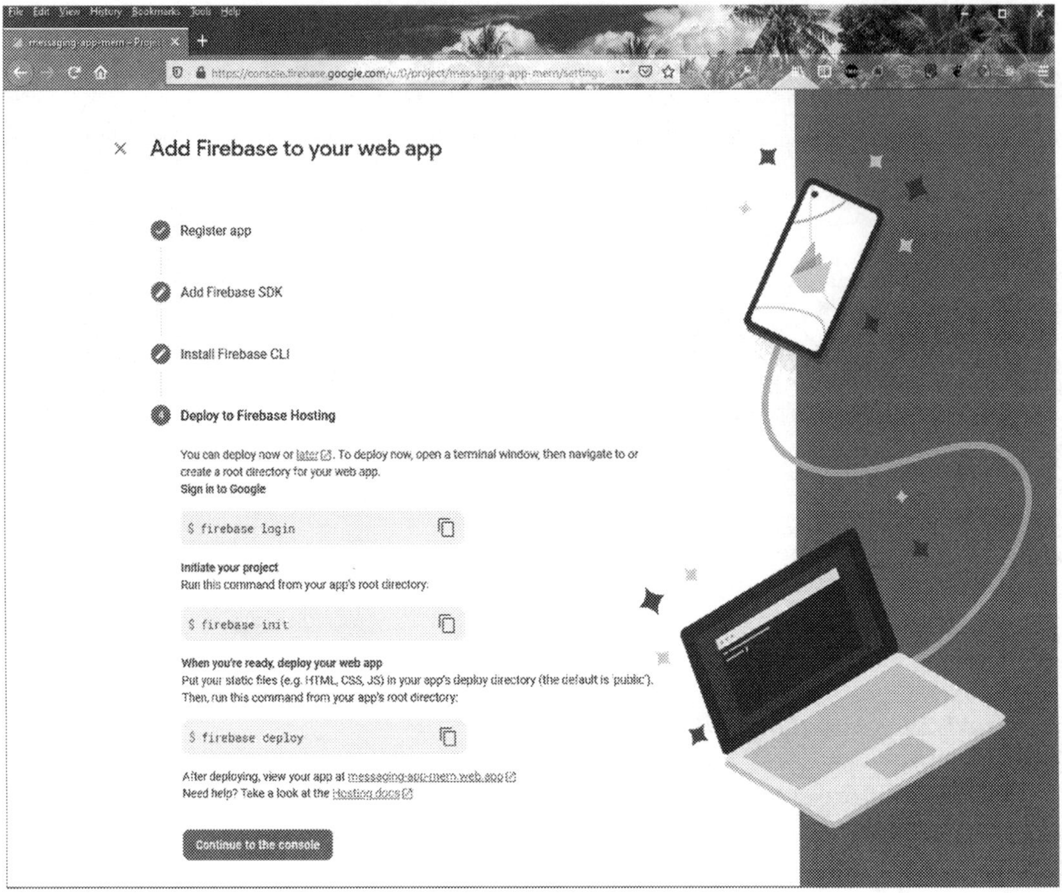

Figure 4-30. *Continue*

Next, scroll down the page and select the **Config** radio button. Then copy the
firebaseConfig data, as seen in Figure 4-31.

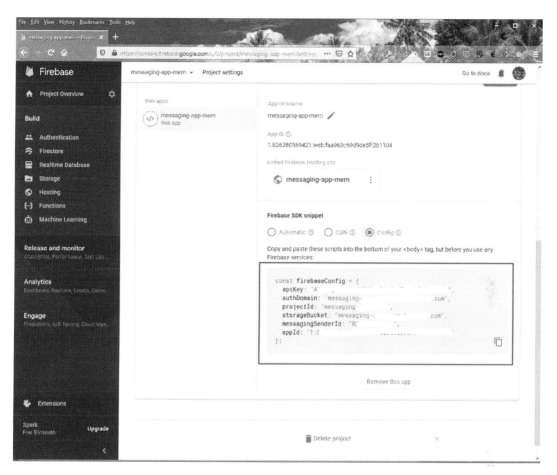

Figure 4-31. *Config details*

Open the code in Visual Studio Code and create a `firebase.js` file inside the `src` folder. Paste the content from VSCode.

Initialize the Firebase app and use the database. Use `auth, provider` from Firebase. The following is the `firebase.js` content.

```
import firebase from 'firebase/app';
import 'firebase/auth';          // for authentication
import 'firebase/storage';       // for storage
import 'firebase/database';      // for realtime database
import 'firebase/firestore';     // for cloud firestore

const firebaseConfig = {
    apiKey: "Axxxxxxxxxxxxxxxxxxxxxxxxxxxxxxxxx",
    authDomain: "messaging-xxxxxxxxxxxxxxxx.com",
```

```
    projectId: "messaging-xxxxx",
    storageBucket: "messaging-app-xxxxxxxxxxxxxxxxx",
    messagingSenderId: "83xxxxxxxxxxxx",
    appId: "1:836xxxxxxxxxxxxxxxxxxxxxxxxxxxxxx"
};

const firebaseApp = firebase.initializeApp(firebaseConfig)
const db = firebaseApp.firestore()
const auth = firebase.auth()
const provider = new firebase.auth.GoogleAuthProvider()

export { auth, provider }
export default db
```

In the terminal, you need to install all the Firebase dependencies in the messaging-app-frontend folder.

```
npm i firebase
```

Creating a Login Component

Create two files—Login.js and Login.css—inside the components folder. In the Login.js file, there is a simple functional component showing a logo and a **Sign in with Google** button. The following is the Login.js content.

```
import React from 'react'
import { Button } from '@material-ui/core'
import './Login.css'

const Login = () => {
    const signIn = () => {

    }

    return (
        <div className="login">
            <div className="login__container">
                <img src="logo512.png" alt="whatsapp" />
                <div className="login__text">
```

```
                <h1>Sign in to Messaging App</h1>
            </div>
            <Button onClick={signIn}>Sign In with Google</Button>
        </div>
    </div>
  )
}

export default Login
```

Let's create the styles in the Login.css file. The following is the Login.css content.

```
.login{
    background-color: #f8f8f8;
    height: 100vh;
    width: 100vw;
    display: grid;
    place-items: center;
}

.login__container{
    padding: 100px;
    text-align: center;
    background-color: white;
    border-radius: 10px;
    box-shadow: -1px 4px 20px -6px rgba(0, 0, 0, 0.75);
}

.login__container > img {
    object-fit: contain;
    height: 100px;
    margin-bottom: 40px;
}

.login__container > button {
    margin-top: 50px;
    text-transform: inherit !important;
```

```
    background-color: #0a8d48 !important;
    color: white;
}
```

Next, let's show a login component if you receive no user. A temporary state variable is created to show it in the App.js file. The updated content is marked in bold.

```
...
import Login from './components/Login';

function App() {
  const [messages, setMessages] = useState([])
  const [user, setUser] = useState(null)
  ...
  return (
    <div className="app">
      { !user ? <Login /> : (
        <div className="app__body">
          <Sidebar />
          <Chat messages={messages} />
        </div>
      )}
    </div>
  );
}

export default App;
```

Figure 4-32 shows the login screen on localhost.

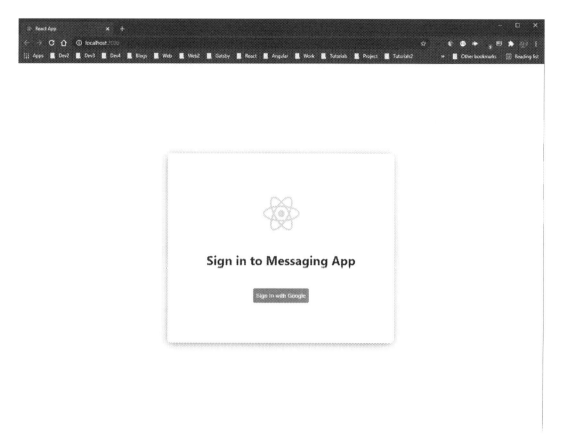

Figure 4-32. *Login screen*

Adding Google Authentication

Before using the sign-in method, return to Firebase and click the **Authentication** tab and then the **Get started** button, as seen in Figure 4-33.

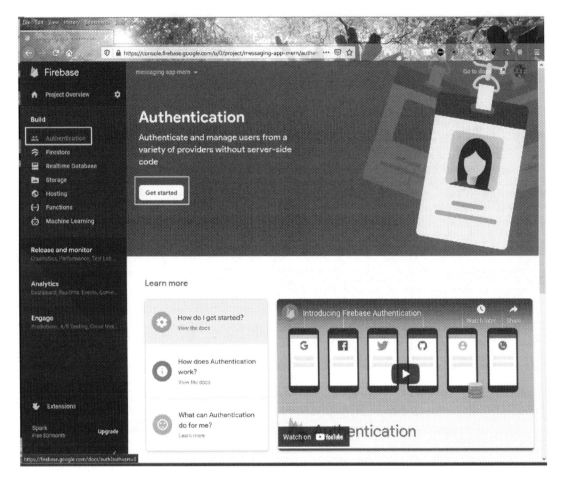

Figure 4-33. *Get started*

On the next screen, click the **Edit configuration** icon for Google authentication, as seen in Figure 4-34.

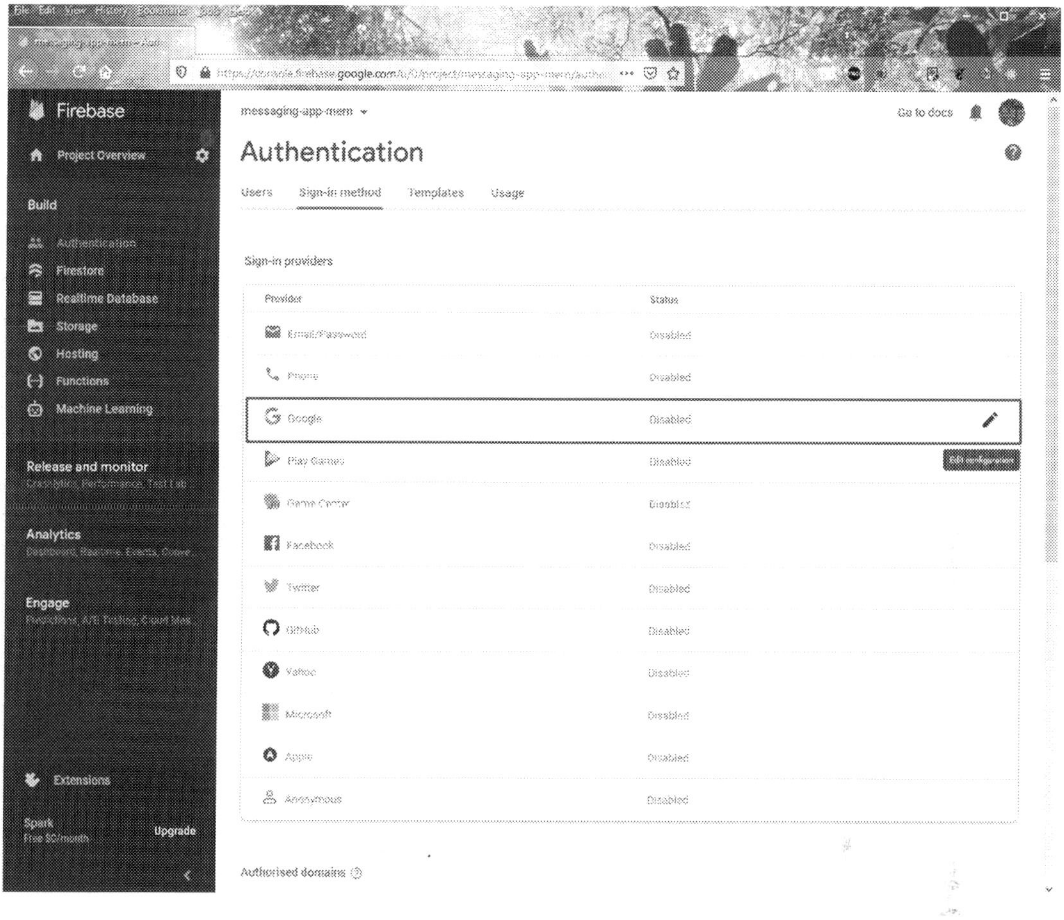

Figure 4-34. *Google login*

In the popup window, click the **Enable** button. Next, enter your Gmail id and click the **Save** button (see Figure 4-35).

```
...
import { auth, provider } from '../firebase'
const Login = () => {
    const signIn = () => {
        auth.signInWithPopup(provider)
            .then(result => console.log(result))
            .catch(error => alert(error.message))
    }

    return (
        <div className="login">
```

153

```
        ...
    </div>
  )
}
export default Login
```

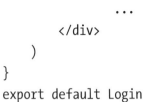

Figure 4-35. *Enable Google login*

Next, in the Login.js file, you need to import auth, provider from the local Firebase file. After that, use the signInWithPopup() method to get the results. The updated content is marked in bold.

Click the **Sign in with Google** button on localhost. A Gmail authentication popup window opens. After clicking the username, you see all the information about the logged-in user in the console, as seen in Figure 4-36.

Using Redux and Context API

Let's dispatch the user data into the data layer, and here the Redux/Context API comes into play.

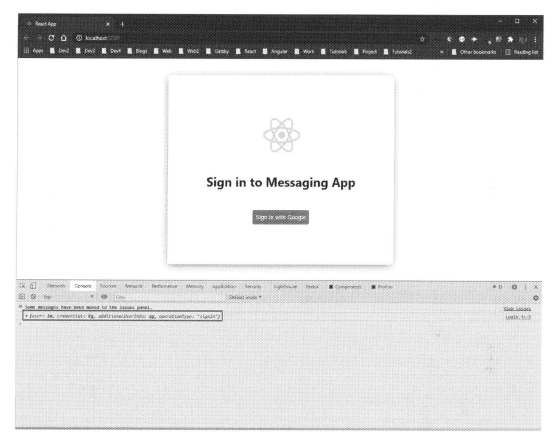

Figure 4-36. *Google authentication success*

You want the user information to be stored in a global state. First, create a new `StateProvider.js` file. Use the useContext API to create a `StateProvider` function. The following is the content. You can learn more about the `useContext` hook in my React hooks YouTube video at `www.youtube.com/watch?v=oSqqs16RejM`.

```
import React, { createContext, useContext, useReducer } from "react"

export const StateContext = createContext()

export const StateProvider = ({ reducer, initialState, children }) => (
```

```
    <StateContext.Provider value={useReducer(reducer, initialState)}>
        {children}
    </StateContext.Provider>
)

export const useStateValue = () => useContext(StateContext)
```

Next, create a `reducer.js` file inside the `components` folder. This is a concept similar to the reducer in a Redux component. You can learn more about it at `www.youtube.com/watch?v=mOGOROTchDY`. The following is the content.

```
export const initialState = { user: null }

export const actionTypes = {
    SET_USER: "SET_USER"
}

const reducer = (state, action) => {
    console.log(action)
    switch(action.type) {
        case actionTypes.SET_USER:
            return {
                ...state,
                user: action.user
            }
        default:
            return state
    }
}

export default reducer
```

In the `index.js` file, wrap the app component with the `StateProvider` component after importing the required files. The updated content is marked in bold.

```
...
import { StateProvider } from './components/StateProvider';
import reducer, { initialState } from './components/reducer';

ReactDOM.render(
  <React.StrictMode>
```

```
  <StateProvider initialState={initialState} reducer={reducer}>
    <App />
  </StateProvider>
</React.StrictMode>,
document.getElementById('root')
);
```

When you get the user data back from Google, you dispatch it to the reducer in the Login.js file, and it is stored in the data layer.

Here, useStateValue is a hook. In fact, it is an example of a custom hook. The updated content is marked in bold.

```
...
import { actionTypes } from './reducer'
import { useStateValue } from './StateProvider'

const Login = () => {
    const [{}, dispatch] = useStateValue()

    const signIn = () => {
        auth.signInWithPopup(provider)
            .then(result => {
                dispatch({
                    type: actionTypes.SET_USER,
                    user: result.user
                })
            })
            .catch(error => alert(error.message))
    }

    return (
        <div className="login">
            ...
        </div>
    )
}
export default Login
```

In the App.js file, use the useStateValue hook, and extract the global user from it. Then, you log in based on it. The updated content is marked in bold.

```
...
import { useStateValue } from './components/StateProvider';

function App() {
  const [messages, setMessages] = useState([])
  const [{ user }, dispatch] = useStateValue()
  ...
  return (
    <div className="app">
      ...
    </div>
  );
}

export default App;
```

If you sign in on localhost, you are taken to the app, as seen in Figure 4-37.

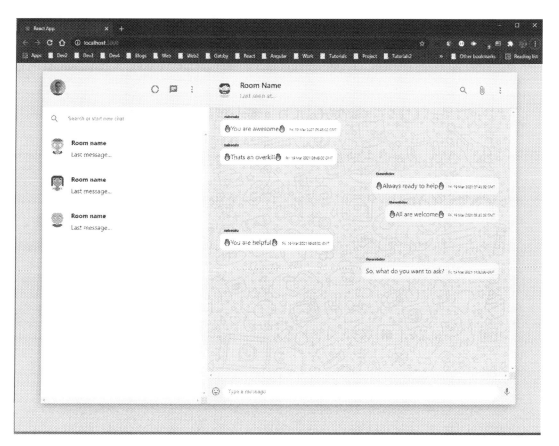

Figure 4-37. *Logged in*

Using Redux Data in Other Components

You have access to the user's data, so you can use it anywhere. Let's use the user's Google image as the avatar in the Sidebar.js file. Let's remove the extra rooms because this project has only one room where everyone can chat.

The updated content is marked in bold.

```
...
import { useStateValue } from './StateProvider';

const Sidebar = () => {
    const [{ user }, dispatch] = useStateValue()

    return (
        <div className="sidebar">
```

```
        <div className="sidebar__header">
            <Avatar src={user?.photoURL} />
            <div className="sidebar__headerRight">
                ...
            </div>
        </div>
        <div className="sidebar__search">
            ...
        </div>
        <div className="sidebar__chats">
            <SidebarChat />
        </div>
    </div>
  )
}

export default Sidebar
```

Figure 4-38 shows the logged-in user's Google image in the top-left corner of the page on localhost.

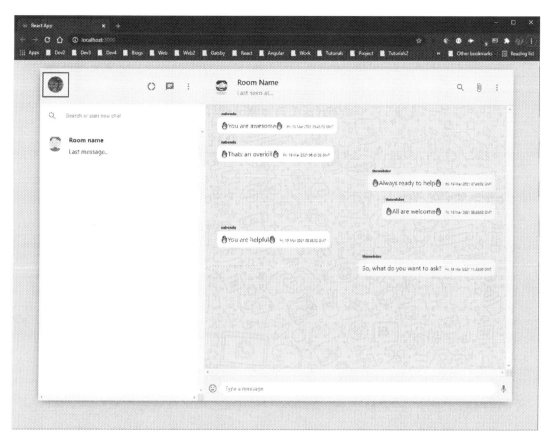

Figure 4-38. *Login image*

In Chat.js, use the useStateValue hook to get the user's display name. Then check whether message.name is equal to user.displayName to display the chat__receiver class. Fix the hard-coded **Last seen at...** message in the chat__header in the Chat.js file; update so that it shows the time that the last person messaged. Also change the room name to **Dev Help**.

The updated content is marked in bold.

```
...
import { useStateValue } from './StateProvider';

const Chat = ({ messages }) => {
  ...
  const [{ user }, dispatch] = useStateValue()

  const sendMessage = async (e) => {          e.preventDefault()
      await axios.post('/messages/new', {
```

```
            message: input,
            name: user.displayName,
            timestamp: new Date().toUTCString(),
            received: true
        })
        setInput("")
    }
    ...
    return (
        <div className="chat">
            <div className="chat__header">
                <Avatar src={`https://avatars.dicebear.com/api/human/
                b${seed}.svg`} />
                <div className="chat__headerInfo">
                    <h3>Dev Help</h3>
                    <p>Last seen at {" "}
                        {messages[messages.length -1]?.timestamp}
                    </p>
                </div>
            </div>
            <div className="chat__body">
                {messages.map(message => (
                    <p className={`chat__message ${message.name === user.
                    displayName && 'chat__receiver'}`}>
                        ...
                    </p>
                ))}
            </div>
            <div className="chat__footer">
                ...
            </div>
        </div>
    )
}

export default Chat
```

Type something and click Enter. You can see that the message was received.
Figure 4-39 shows the scene has been updated.

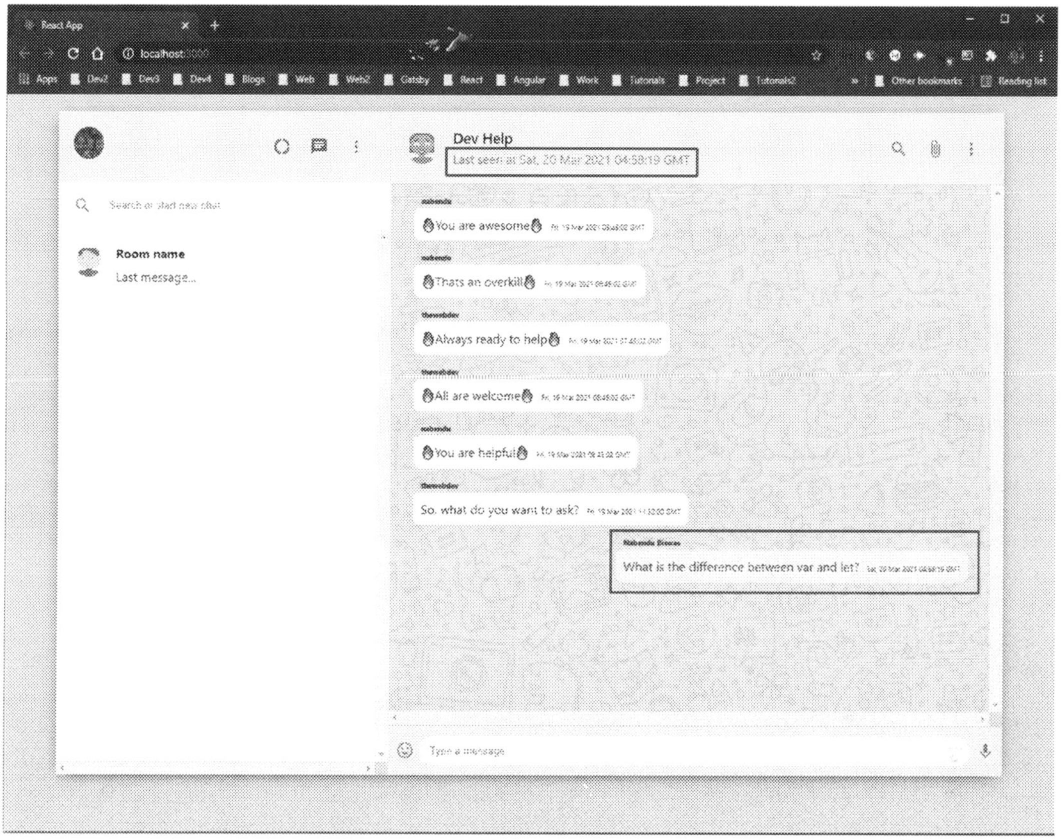

Figure 4-39. *Time updates*

The last thing to change is the hard-coded message in the sidebar. You need to
show the last message here. First, send the messages from the App.js file to the sidebar
component.

The updated content is marked in bold.

```
...
function App() {
  ...
  return (
    <div className="app">
```

```
      { !user ? <Login /> : (
        <div className="app__body">
          <Sidebar messages={messages} />
          <Chat messages={messages} />
        </div>
      )}
    </div>
  );
}
export default App;
```

After that from the `Sidebar.js` file to the `SidebarChat` component. The updated content is marked in bold.

```
...
const Sidebar = ({ messages }) => {
    const [{ user }, dispatch] = useStateValue()
    return (
        <div className="sidebar">
            <div className="sidebar__header">
                    ...
            </div>
            <div className="sidebar__search">
                    ...
            </div>
            <div className="sidebar__chats">
                <SidebarChat messages={messages} />
            </div>
        </div>

    )
}
```

`export default Sidebar`

Finally, in the `SidebarChat.js` file, show the last message instead of the hard-coded message, and change the room name to **Dev Help**.

The updated content is marked in bold.

```
...
const SidebarChat = ({ messages }) => {
    ...
    return (
        <div className="sidebarChat">
            <Avatar src={`https://avatars.dicebear.com/api/human/b${seed}.
            svg`} />
            <div className="sidebarChat__info">
                <h2>Dev Help</h2>
                <p>{messages[messages.length -1]?.message}</p>
            </div>
        </div>
    )
}

export default SidebarChat
```

The app is complete. Figure 4-40 shows the latest message in the sidebar. I also tested my login in a different Google account.

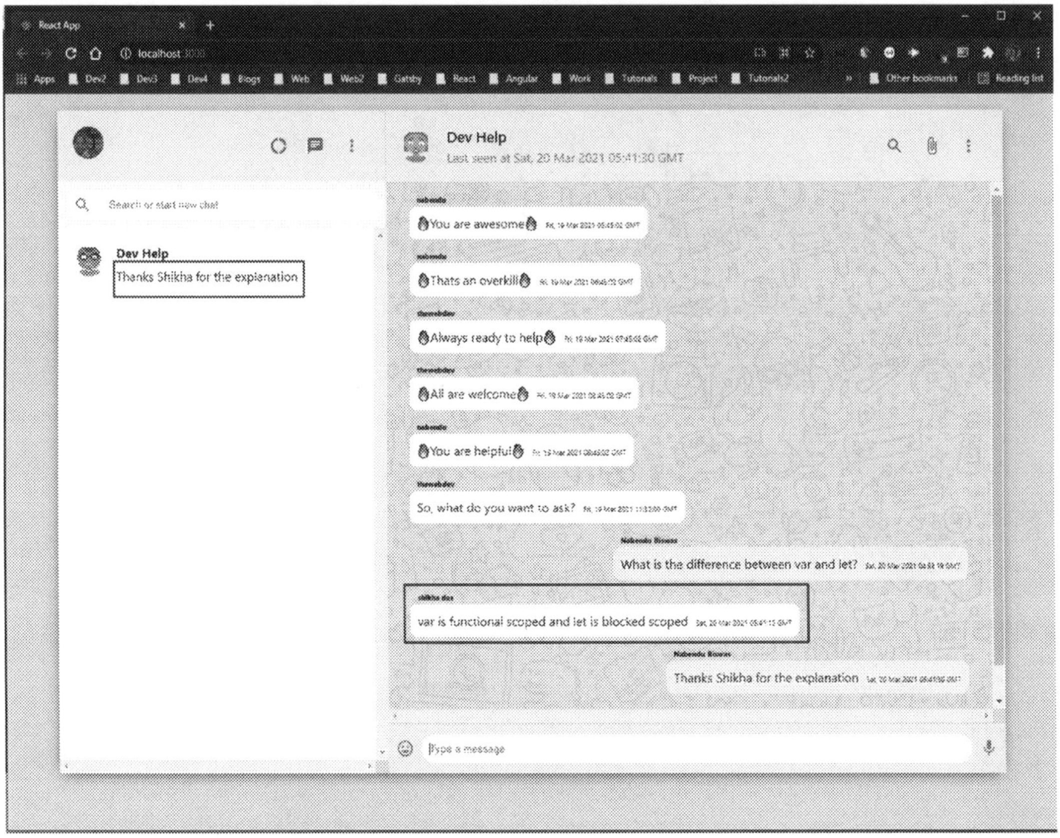

Figure 4-40. *App complete*

Deploying the Back End to Heroku

Go to www.heroku.com to deploy the back end. Follow the same procedure that you did in Chapter 1 and create an app named **messaging-app-backend**.

After successfully deploying, go to https://messaging-app-backend.herokuapp.com. Figure 4-41 shows the correct text.

Figure 4-41. *Initial route check*

In axios.js, change the endpoint to https://messaging-app-backend.herokuapp.com. If everything is working fine, your app should run.

```
import axios from 'axios'
const instance = axios.create({
    baseURL: " https://messaging-app-backend.herokuapp.com "
})

export default instance
```

Deploying the Front End to Firebase

It's time to deploy the front end in Firebase. Follow the same procedure that you did in Chapter 1. After this process, the site should be live and working properly, as seen in Figure 4-42.

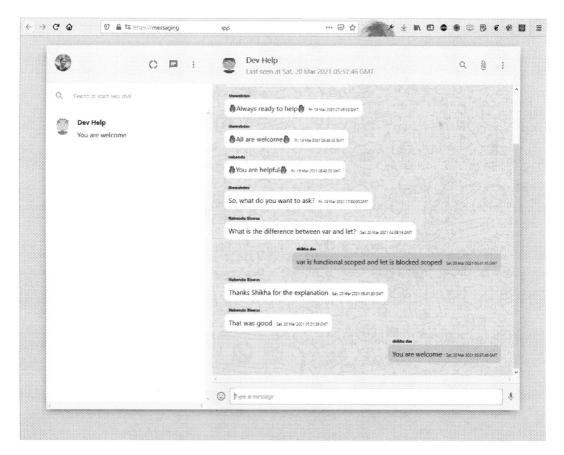

Figure 4-42. *Final app*

Summary

In this chapter, you created a simple but functional chat app. Firebase hosted it on the Internet. You learned to add Google authentication, by which you can log in with a Google account. You also learned to store the chats in a MongoDB database with API routes created using Node.js.

CHAPTER 5

Building a Photo-Based Social Network with MERN

In this chapter, you are going to build an awesome photo-based social network using the MERN framework. The back end is hosted in Heroku, and the front-end site is hosted using Firebase. The authentication functionality is also handled by Firebase.

Material-UI provides the icons in the project. Pusher is used since MongoDB is not a real-time database like Firebase. You want the posts to reflect the moment someone hits the Submit button.

With this functional photo-based social network, you can upload pictures from your computer and write a description. The user login is through email. The final hosted app is shown in Figure 5-1.

© Nabendu Biswas 2021
N. Biswas, *MERN Projects for Beginners*, https://doi.org/10.1007/978-1-4842-7138-4_5

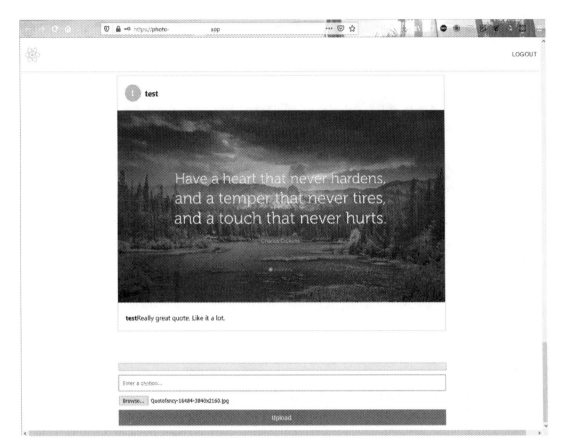

Figure 5-1. *Final app*

First, go to your terminal and create a photo-social-mern folder. Inside, it uses the **create-react-app** to create a new app called **photo-social-frontend**. The following are the commands.

```
mkdir photo-social-mern
cd photo-social-mern
npx create-react-app photo-social-frontend
```

Firebase Hosting Initial Setup

Since the front-end site is hosted through Firebase, you can create the basic setting while create-react-app creates the React app. Following the setup instructions from Chapter 1, I created **photo-social-mern** in the Firebase console.

Since authentication functionality is used, you need to do the additional configuration mentioned in Chapter 4 and use `firebaseConfig`, which you need to copy (see Figure 5-2).

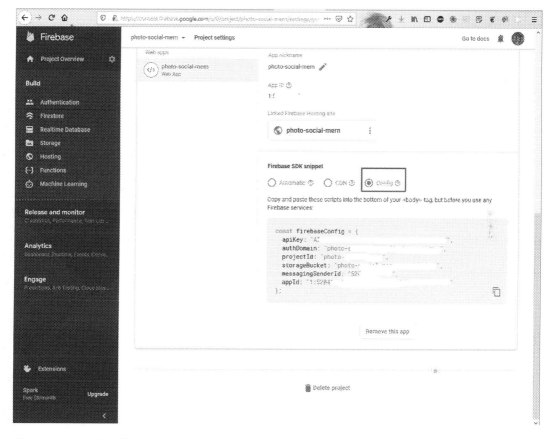

Figure 5-2. *Config*

Open the code in Visual Studio Code (VSCode) and create a `firebase.js` file inside the `src` folder and paste the config content there.

```
const firebaseConfig = {
    apiKey: "AIxxxxxxxxxxxxxxxxxxxxxxxxxxxxxxxxxY",
    authDomain: "photo-xxxxxxxxxxxxxxxxxxxxxxxx.com",
    projectId: "photo-xxxxxxxxxx",
    storageBucket: "photo-xxxxxxxxxx",
    messagingSenderId: "52xxxxxxx",
    appId: "1:52xxxxxxxxxxxxxxxxxxxxxxxxxxxxxxxxxx"
};
```

React Basic Setup

Return to the React project and cd to the photo-social-frontend directory. Start the React app with npm start.

```
cd photo-social-frontend
npm start
```

The deleting of the files and basic setup in index.js, App.js, and App.css is like what was done in Chapter 2. Follow those instructions. Figure 5-3 shows how the app looks on localhost.

Photo Social Network MERN

Figure 5-3. *Initial app*

Creating a Header Component

Let's create the app header, which is a nice logo. In the App.js file, create a div with the app__header class name and use the React logo from the public folder, which comes with every React project. The updated content is marked in bold.

```
import './App.css';

function App() {
  return (
    <div className="app">
      <div className="app__header">
        <img className="app__headerImage" src="logo192.png" alt="Header" />
      </div>
    </div>
  );
}

export default App;
```

Next, start writing styles in the App.css file. Here, you are writing styles for the app, app__header, and the app__headerImage class.

```css
.app {
  background-color: #fafafa;
}

.app__header{
  background-color: white;
  padding: 20px;
  border-bottom: 1px solid lightgray;
  object-fit: contain;
}

.app__headerImage {
  object-fit: contain;
  margin-left: 10px;
  height: 40px;
}
```

Figure 5-4 shows the logo on localhost.

Figure 5-4. *Perfect logo*

Creating a Post Component

Let's now create the post component, which contains the logged-in user's avatar, including a photo and a brief description. Create a components folder inside the src folder. Then, create two files—Post.js and Post.css—inside the components folder.

The Post.js file is a simple functional component that contains the username, image, and post.

```
import React from 'react'
import './Post.css'
const Post = () => {
    return (
        <div className="post">
            <h3>TWD</h3>
            <img className="post__image" src="https://www.techlifediary.
            com/wp-content/uploads/2020/06/react-js.png" alt="React" />
            <h4 className="post__text"><strong>thewebdev</strong>🔥Build a
            Messaging app with MERN (MongoDB, Express, React JS, Node JS)
            🔥</h4>
        </div>
    )
}

export default Post
```

In the App.js file, include the Post component three times. The updated content is marked in bold.

```
import './App.css';
import Post from './components/Post';

function App() {
  return (
    <div className="app">
      <div className="app__header">
        <img className="app__headerImage" src="logo192.png" alt="Header" />
      </div>
        <Post />
        <Post />
        <Post />
    </div>
  );
}

export default App;
```

The icons come from Material-UI (`https://material-ui.com`). First, do two npm installs as per the documentation. Install the core through the integrated terminal in the `photo-social-frontend` folder.

```
npm i @material-ui/core @material-ui/icons
```

In `Post.js`, add an avatar icon from Material-UI. You are using it along with the h3 tag inside a `post__header` div. The updated content is marked in bold.

```
...
import { Avatar } from '@material-ui/core'

const Post = () => {
    return (
        <div className="post">
            <div className="post__header">
                <Avatar
                    className="post__avatar"
                    alt="TWD"
                    src="/static/images/avatar/1.jpg"
                />
                <h3>TWD</h3>
            </div>
            <img className="post__image" src="https://www.techlifediary.
            com/wp-content/uploads/2020/06/react-js.png" alt="React" />
            ...
        </div>
    )
}

export default Post
```

Next, add the styles in the Post.css file.

```css
.post {
    background-color: white;
    max-width: 800px;
    border: 1px solid lightgray;
    margin-bottom: 45px;
}
.post__image {
    width: 100%;
    object-fit: contain;
    border-top: 1px solid lightgray;
    border-bottom: 1px solid lightgray;
}
.post__text {
    font-weight: normal;
    padding: 20px;
}

.post__header {
    display: flex;
    align-items: center;
    padding: 20px;
}
.post__avatar {
    margin-right: 10px;
}
```

Figure 5-5 shows how the app now looks on localhost.

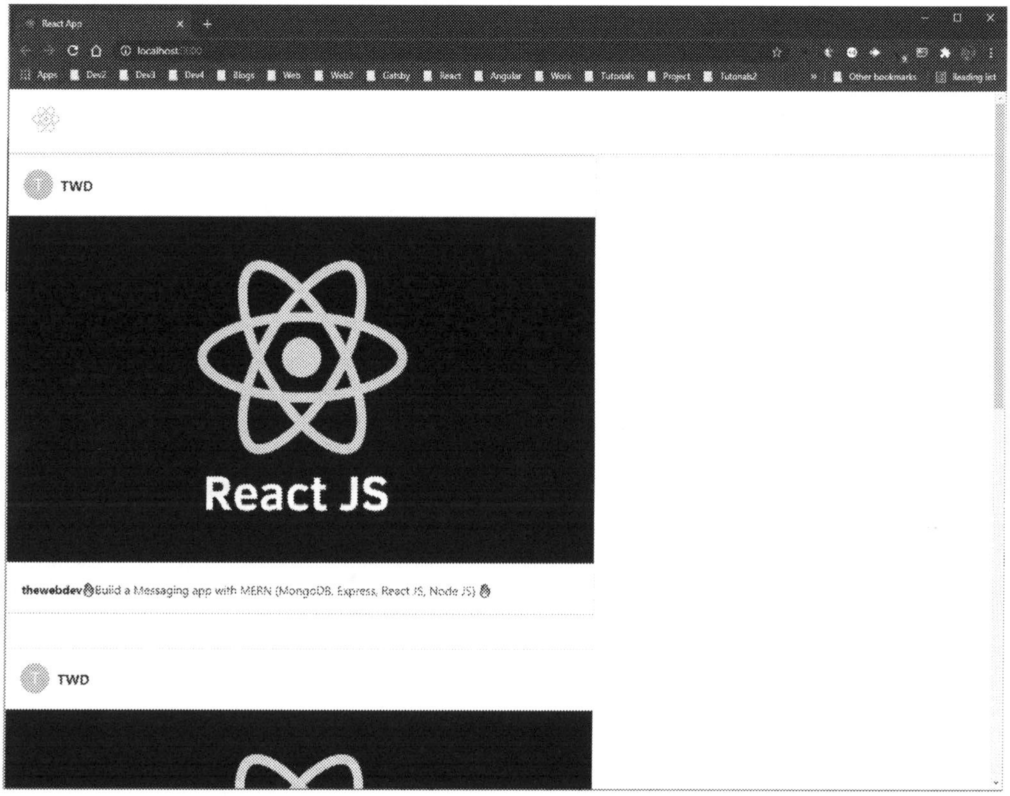

Figure 5-5. *Styled post*

Making Components Dynamic

Let's make everything dynamic and pass the username, caption, and image URL as props. In Post.js, make the following changes. The updated content is marked in bold.

```
...
import { Avatar } from '@material-ui/core'

const Post = ({ username, caption, imageUrl }) => {
    return (
        <div className="post">
            <div className="post__header">
                <Avatar
                    className="post__avatar"
                    alt= {username}
```

```
                  src="/static/images/avatar/1.jpg"
            />
            <h3> {username}</h3>
        </div>
        <img className="post__image" src={imageUrl} alt="React" />
        <h4 className="post__text"><strong>{username}</strong>
        {caption}</h4>
      </div>
    )
}
```

```
export default Post
```

Next, let's optimize the code in App.js. Here, you use the useState hook to create new state posts. The posts here are objects inside an array.

Inside the return statement, map through the posts array and show each post. The updated content is marked in bold.

```
...
import React, { useEffect, useState } from 'react';

function App() {
  const [posts, setPosts] = useState([
    {
      username: "TWD",
      caption: "🔥Build a Messaging app with MERN Stack🔥",
      imageUrl: "https://www.techlifediary.com/wp-content/uploads/2020/06/
      react-js.png"
    },
    {
      username: "nabendu82",
      caption: "Such a beautiful world",
      imageUrl: "https://quotefancy.com/media/wallpaper/3840x2160/126631-
      Charles-Dickens-Quote-And-a-beautiful-world-you-live-in-when-it-is.jpg"
    }
  ])
  return (
```

```
    <div className="app">
      <div className="app__header">
        <img className="app__headerImage" src="logo192.png" alt="Header" />
      </div>
        {posts.map(post => (
            <Post username={post.username} caption={post.caption}
            imageUrl={post.imageUrl} />
        ))}
    </div>
  );
}

export default App;
```

Figure 5-6 shows it on localhost.

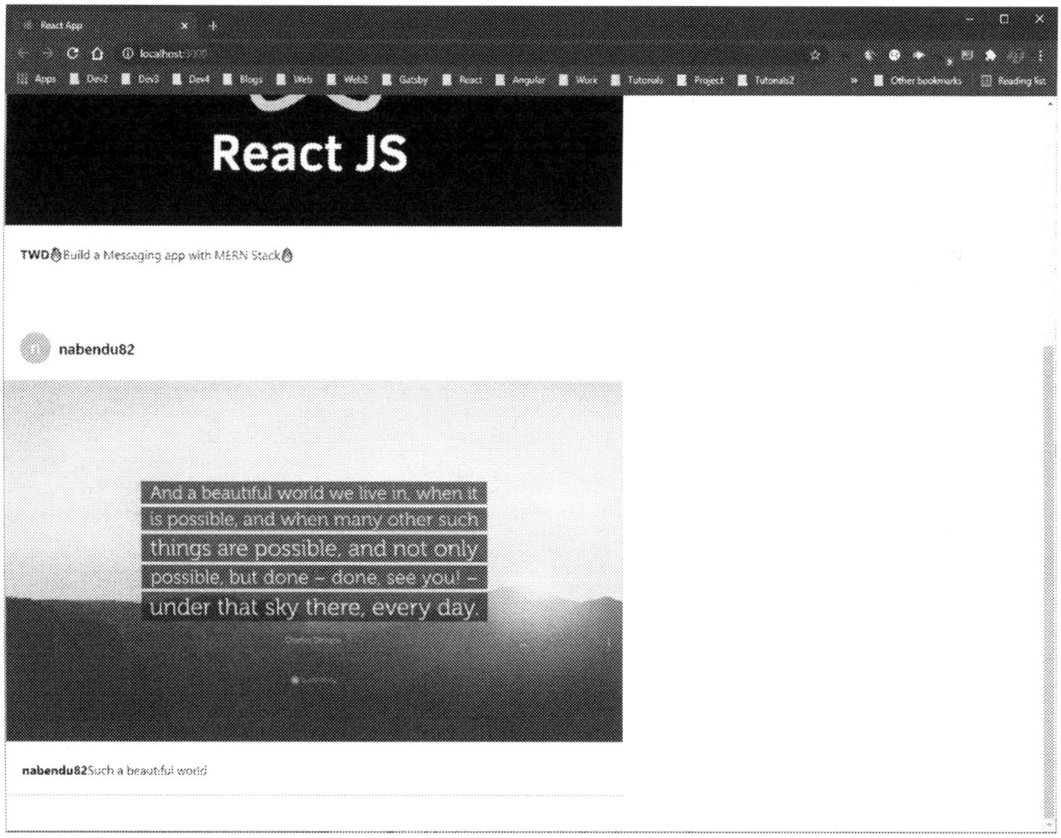

Figure 5-6. *Everything dynamic*

Firebase Authentication Setup

Let's work on the Firebase authentication, which allows you to log in to the app and post. This project uses email-based authentication, which is different from the Google authentication in the previous chapter.

You need to return to Firebase. Click the **Authentication** tab and then the **Get started** button, as seen in Figure 5-7.

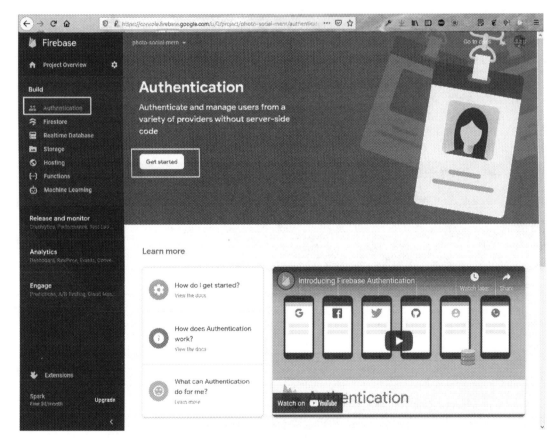

Figure 5-7. *Get started*

On the next screen, click the Edit icon for **Email/Password**, as seen in Figure 5-8.

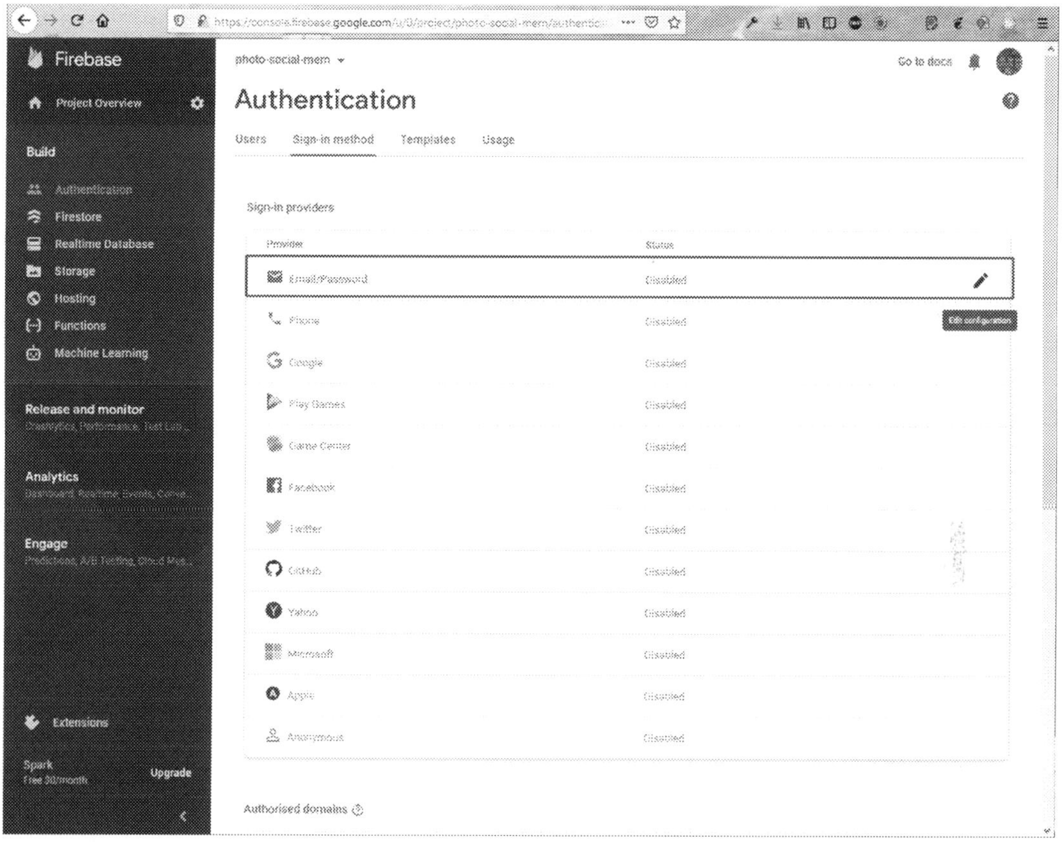

Figure 5-8. *Email and password*

In the popup window, click the **Enable** button, and then click the **Save** button, as seen in Figure 5-9.

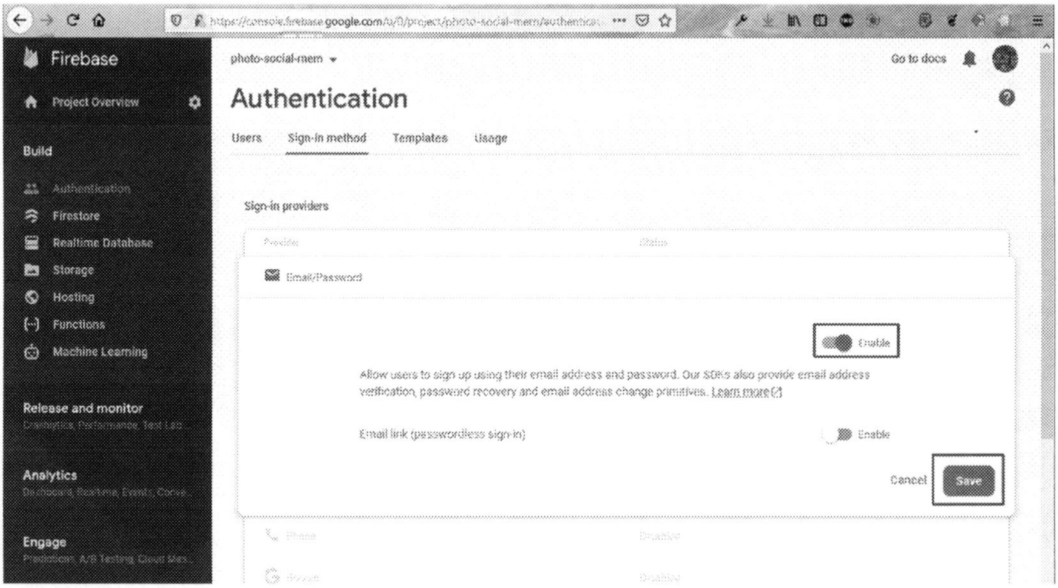

Figure 5-9. *Enable email and password*

Creating a Modal for Signup

Now, let's show a sign-up modal from Material-UI . The code for this is from `https://material-ui.com/components/modal/#modal`.

First, import several dependencies and two styles in the `App.js` file. After that you have the constant of **classes** and **modalStyle**. The **open** state is initially set to **false**.

Inside return, set the **open** state to **true** for the modal and sign-up button .

The updated content is marked in bold.

```
...
import { makeStyles } from '@material-ui/core/styles';
import Modal from '@material-ui/core/Modal';
import { Button, Input } from '@material-ui/core';
function getModalStyle() {
  const top = 50;
  const left = 50;
  return {
    top: `${top}%`,
    left: `${left}%`,
```

```
      transform: `translate(-${top}%, -${left}%)`,
   };
}
const useStyles = makeStyles((theme) => ({
  paper: {
    position: 'absolute',
    width: 400,
    backgroundColor: theme.palette.background.paper,
    border: '2px solid #000',
    boxShadow: theme.shadows[5],
    padding: theme.spacing(2, 4, 3),
  },
}));

function App() {
  const classes = useStyles();
  const [modalStyle] = React.useState(getModalStyle);
  const [open, setOpen] = useState(false)
  ...
  return (
    <div className="app">
      <Modal open={open} onClose={() => setOpen(false)}>
        <div style={modalStyle} className={classes.paper}>
          <h2>Modal Code</h2>
        </div>
      </Modal>
      <div className="app__header">...</div>
      <Button onClick={() => setOpen(true)}>Sign Up</Button>
        {posts.map(post => (
            <Post ={post.username} caption={post.caption} imageUrl={post.
            imageUrl} />
        ))}
    </div>
  );
}

export default App;
```

On localhost, click the **SIGN UP** button to get the modal with text (see Figure 5-10).

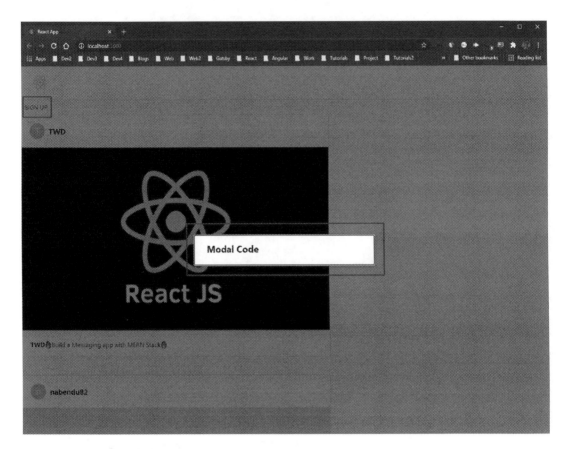

Figure 5-10. *Modal popup*

Before creating the form, you need to create three state variables—username, email, and password—in the App.js file.

Fields for the username, email, and password are inside the modal in the App.js file. There is also a button that includes an onClick handler calling a signUp function.

The updated content is marked in bold.

```
...

function App() {
  ...
  const [username, setUsername] = useState('')
  const [email, setEmail] = useState('')
  const [password, setPassword] = useState('')
```

```
...
const signUp = e => {
  e.preventDefault()
}

return (
  <div className="app">
    <Modal open={open} onClose={() => setOpen(false)}>
      <div style={modalStyle} className={classes.paper}>
        <form className="app__signup">
          <center>
            <img className="app__headerImage" src="logo192.png"
            alt="Header" />
          </center>
            <Input placeholder="username"
              type="text"
              value={username}
              onChange={e => setUsername(e.target.value)}
            />
            <Input placeholder="email"
              type="text"
              value={email}
              onChange={e => setEmail(e.target.value)}
            />
            <Input placeholder="password"
              type="password"
              value={password}
              onChange={e => setPassword(e.target.value)}
            />
            <Button type="submit" onClick={signUp}>Sign Up</Button>
        </form>
      </div>
    </Modal>
```

```
      <div className="app__header">...</div>
      ...
   </div>
  );
}

export default App;
```

In the App.css file, add styles for the app__signup class.

```
.app__signup {
  display: flex;
  flex-direction: column;
}
```

Figure 5-11 shows that clicking the **SIGN UP** button on localhost opens a form.

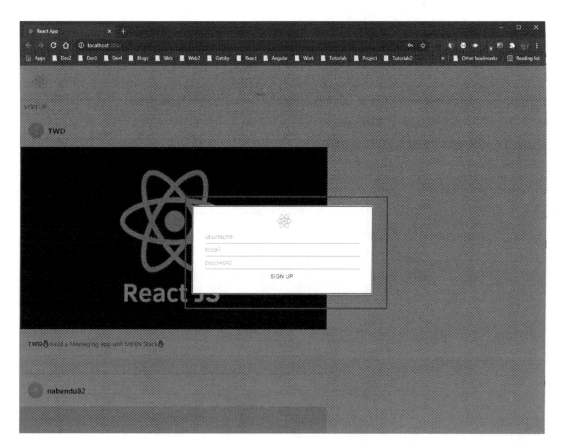

Figure 5-11. *Sign-up form*

Sign up with Firebase

Let's start with the Firebase setup for authentication. First, install all dependencies for Firebase in the photo-social-frontend folder.

```
npm i firebase
```

Next, update the firebase.js file to use the config to initialize the app. The updated content is marked in bold.

```
import firebase from 'firebase';

const firebaseConfig = {
    ...
};

const firebaseApp = firebase.initializeApp(firebaseConfig)
const db = firebaseApp.firestore()
const auth = firebase.auth()
const storage = firebase.storage()

export { db, auth, storage }
```

Let's add authentication to the app. First, import auth from the local Firebase, and then add a new user state variable in the App.js file.

Add code to the signUp function that uses createUserWithEmailAndPassword from Firebase and passes the email and password. After that, update the user and set the displayName as the **username**. Use the useEffect hook to monitor any user changes, and use setUser() to update the user variable.

Inside the return, check if the user is logged in and then show either the **Log out** button or the **Sign up** button.

The updated content is marked in bold.

```
import { auth } from './firebase'
...

function App() {
  ...
  const [user, setUser] = useState(null)
  ...
```

```
  useEffect(() => {
    const unsubscribe = auth.onAuthStateChanged(authUser => {
      if(authUser) {
        console.log(authUser)
        setUser(authUser)
      } else {
        setUser(null)
      }
    })
    return () => {
      unsubscribe()
    }
  }, [user, username])
  const signUp = (e) => {
    e.preventDefault()
    auth.createUserWithEmailAndPassword(email, password)
      .then(authUser => authUser.user.updateProfile({ displayName: username }))
      .catch(error => alert(error.message))

    setOpen(false)
  }
  return (
    <div className="app">
      <Modal open={open} onClose={() => setOpen(false)}>...</Modal>
      <div className="app__header">...</div>
      {user ? <Button onClick={() => auth.signOut()}>Logout</Button> :
      <Button onClick={() => setOpen(true)}>Sign Up</Button>}
      ...
    </div>
  );
}

export default App;
```

The authentication is working properly on localhost. You can sign up a new user, as seen in Figure 5-12.

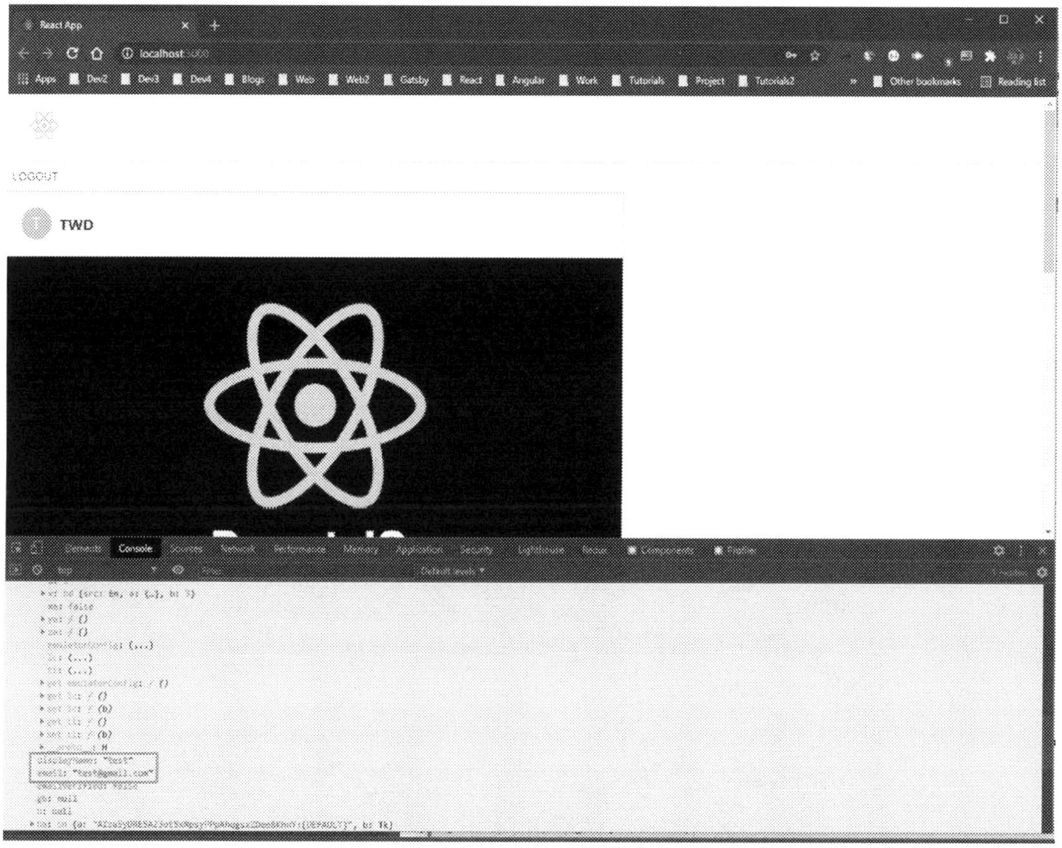

Figure 5-12. *User sign-up*

Sign in with Firebase

Now let's work on the sign-in functionality by creating a new sign-in button and a new modal component in the App.js file.

First, create the openSignIn state variable and function in the App.js file. The function contains signInWithEmailAndPassword from Firebase.

Note that only email and a password are used, but there is a new openSignIn state variable and its setOpenSignIn setter. The updated content is marked in bold.

```
...
function App() {
  ...
  const [openSignIn, setOpenSignIn] = useState(false)
```

```
...
  const signIn = e => {
    e.preventDefault()
    auth.signInWithEmailAndPassword(email, password)
      .catch(error => alert(error.message))
    setOpenSignIn(false)
  }

  return (
    <div className="app">
      <Modal open={open} onClose={() => setOpen(false)}>...</Modal>
      <Modal open={openSignIn} onClose={() => setOpenSignIn(false)}>
        <div style={modalStyle} className={classes.paper}>
          <form className="app__signup">
            <center>
              <img className="app__headerImage" src="logo192.png"
              alt="Header" />
            </center>
              <Input placeholder="email" type="text" value={email}
                onChange={e => setEmail(e.target.value)}  />
              <Input placeholder="password" type="password"
              value={password}
                onChange={e => setPassword(e.target.value)}  />
              <Button type="submit" onClick={signIn}>Sign In</Button>
          </form>
        </div>
      </Modal>
      <div className="app__header">...</div>
      {user ? <Button onClick={() => auth.signOut()}>Logout</Button> : (
          <div className="app__loginContainer">
            <Button onClick={() => setOpenSignIn(true)}>Sign In</Button>
            <Button onClick={() => setOpen(true)}>Sign Up</Button>
          </div>
        )}}
      ...
    </div>
```

```
  );
}
```

```
export default App;
```

There is a new **SIGN IN** button on localhost. It opens a popup window to enter credentials (see Figure 5-13). Use the same credentials that you entered for the SIGN IN button, and you can log in successfully.

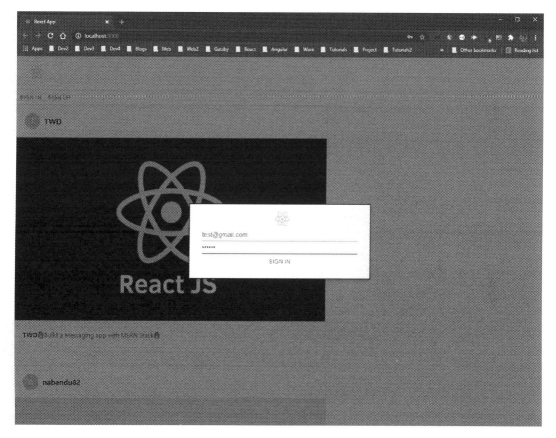

Figure 5-13. *Sign-in popup*

Adding Posts and Images

The Firebase user authentication is complete. Add the code for the posts and upload the images. You return to this part once you start the back end.

Create new files—ImageUpload.js and ImageUpload.css—inside the components folder and import them into the App.js file. Next, pass the prop username from ImageUpload in the App.js file.

In App.js, create a new div with an app__posts class name, and contain the posts in it. The updated content of the App.js file is marked in bold.

```
...
import ImageUpload from './components/ImageUpload';
...
function App() {
...
  return (
    <div className="app">
        ...
        {user ? <Button onClick={() => auth.signOut()}>Logout</Button> :(
            ...
        )}
        <div className="app__posts">
          {posts.map(post => (
              <Post username={post.username} caption={post.caption}
              imageUrl={post.imageUrl} />
          ))}
        </div>
        {user?.displayName ? <ImageUpload username={user.displayName} /> :
        <h3 className="app__notLogin">Need to login to upload</h3>}
    </div>
  );
}

export default App;
```

In the ImageUpload.js file, start with the basic content. There is an input box for the caption and another for the image. There is also a button and a progress bar.

The following is the content of the ImageUpload.js file.

```
import React, { useState } from 'react'
import './ImageUpload.css'
const ImageUpload = ({ username }) => {
    const [image, setImage] = useState(null)
    const [progress, setProgress] = useState(0)
    const [caption, setCaption] = useState('')
const handleChange = e => {
        if(e.target.files[0]) {
            setImage(e.target.files[0])
        }
    }

const handleUpload = () => {}
    return (
        <div className="imageUpload">
            <progress className="imageUpload__progress" value={progress}
            max="100" />
            <input
                type="text"
                placeholder="Enter a caption..."
                className="imageUpload__input"
                value={caption}
                onChange={e => setCaption(e.target.value)}
            />
            <input className="imageUpload__file" type="file"
            onChange={handleChange} />
            <button className="imageUpload__button"
            onClick={handleUpload}>Upload</button>
        </div>
    )
}

export default ImageUpload
```

The front end is almost complete, but you need to complete the styling. First, add styles in the ImageUpload.css file. The following is the content for this file.

```css
.imageUpload {
    display: flex;
    flex-direction: column;
    max-width: 800px;
    width: 100%;
    margin: 10px auto;
}

.imageUpload__progress{
    width: 100%;
    margin-bottom: 10px;
}

.imageUpload__input{
    padding: 10px;
    margin-bottom: 10px;
}

.imageUpload__file {
    margin-bottom: 10px;
}

.imageUpload__button {
    border: none;
    color: lightgray;
    background-color: #6082a3;
    cursor: pointer;
    padding: 10px;
    font-weight: bolder;
    font-size: 0.9rem;
}

.imageUpload__button:hover {
    color: #6082a3;
    background-color: lightgray;
}
```

Figure 5-14 shows the image upload on localhost.

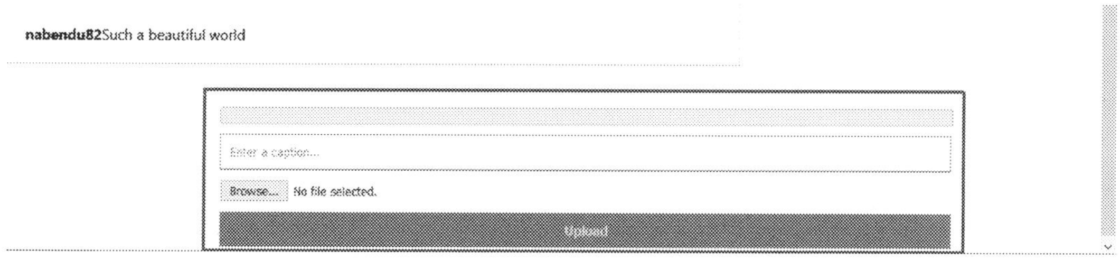

Figure 5-14. *Image upload*

Add the styles in the App.css file. The updated code is marked in bold. It keeps the existing code for app__signup and app__headerImage.

```
.app {
  display:grid;
  place-items: center;
  background-color: #fafafa;
}

.app__header{
  display: flex;
  justify-content: space-between;
  position: sticky;
  top: 0;
  z-index: 1;
  width: 100%;
  background-color: white;
  padding: 20px;
  border-bottom: 1px solid lightgray;
  object-fit: contain;
}

.app__notLogin{
  margin-bottom: 20px;
}
```

```css
.app__loginContainer{
  margin-right: 10px;
}

.app__posts {
  padding: 20px;
}
```

There is a small fix in App.js to move the user code inside the app__header div. The updated code is marked in bold.

```jsx
...
function App() {
...
  return (
    <div className="app">
      ...
      <div className="app__header">
        <img className="app__headerImage" src="logo192.png" alt="Header" />
        {user ? <Button onClick={() => auth.signOut()}>Logout</Button> :(
          <div className="app__loginContainer">
            <Button onClick={() => setOpenSignIn(true)}>Sign In</Button>
            <Button onClick={() => setOpen(true)}>Sign Up</Button>
          </div>
        )}
      </div>
      ...
    </div>
  );
}

export default App;
```

Figure 5-15 shows the app in desktop view on localhost.

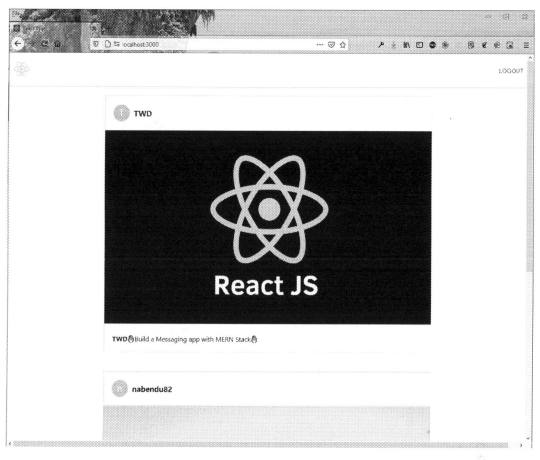

Figure 5-15. *Front-end complete*

Initial Back-End Setup

Let's move to the back end, starting with the Node.js code. Open a new terminal window and create a new photo-social-backend folder in the root directory. After moving to the photo-social-backend directory, enter the git init command, which is required for Heroku later.

```
mkdir photo-social-backend
cd photo-social-backend
git init
```

Next, create the `package.json` file by entering the `npm init` command in the terminal. You are asked a bunch of questions; for most of them, simply press the Enter key. You can provide the **description** and the **author**, but they are not mandatory. You generally make the entry point at `server.js,` which is standard (see Figure 5-16).

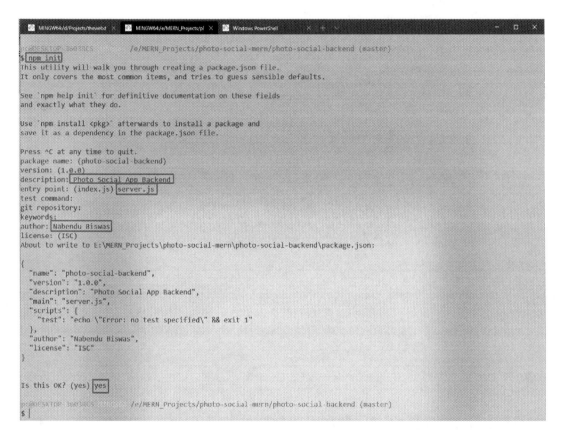

Figure 5-16. *Initial back end*

Once `package.json` is created, you need to create the `.gitignore` file with `node_modules` in it since you don't want to push node_modules to Heroku later. The following is the `.gitignore` file content.

node_modules

Next, open `package.json`. The line "`type`": "`module` is required to have React-like imports enabled in Node.js. Include a start script to run the `server.js` file. The updated content is marked in bold.

```
{
  "name": "messaging-app-backend",
  "version": "1.0.0",
  "description": "Messaging app backend",
  "main": "server.js",
  "type": "module",
  "scripts": {
    "test": "echo \"Error: no test specified\" && exit 1",
    "start": "node server.js"
  },
  "author": "Nabendu Biswas",
  "license": "ISC"
}
```

Finally, you need to install two packages before starting. Open the terminal, and install Express and Mongoose in the photo-social-backend folder.

```
npm i express mongoose
```

MongoDB Setup

The MongoDB setup is the same as described in Chapter 1. Follow those instructions and create a new project named **photo-social-mern**.

Before moving forward, install nodemon in the photo-social-backend folder. It helps the changes in server.js to restart the Node server instantaneously.

```
npm i nodemon
```

Initial Route Setup

Create a server.js file in the photo-social-backend folder. Here, you import the Express and Mongoose packages. Then use Express to create a port variable to run on port 9000.

The first API endpoint is a simple GET request created by app.get(), which shows the text **Hello TheWebDev** if successful.

Then listen on port with app.listen().

```
import express from 'express'
import mongoose from 'mongoose'

//App Config
const app = express()
const port = process.env.PORT || 9000

//Middleware

//DB Config

//API Endpoints
app.get("/", (req, res) => res.status(200).send("Hello TheWebDev"))

//Listener
app.listen(port, () => console.log(`Listening on localhost: ${port}`))
```

In the terminal, type **nodemon server.js** to see the **Listening on localhost: 9000** console log. To check that the route is working correctly, go to http://localhost:9000/ to see the endpoint text, as shown in Figure 5-17.

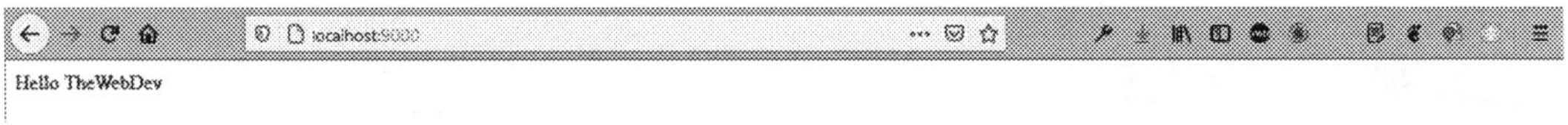

Hello TheWebDev

Figure 5-17. *Initial route*

Database User and Network Access

In MongoDB, you need to create a database user and give network access. The process is the same as explained in Chapter 1. Follow those instructions, and then get the user credentials and connection URL.

In the server.js file, create a connection_url variable and paste the URL within the string from MongoDB. You need to provide the password that you saved earlier and a database name.

The updated code is marked in bold.

```
...

//App Config
const app = express()
const port = process.env.PORT || 9000
const connection_url = ' mongodb+srv://admin:<password>@cluster0.giruc.
mongodb.net/photoDB?retryWrites=true&w=majority'

//Middleware

//DB Config
mongoose.connect(connection_url, {
    useNewUrlParser: true,
    useCreateIndex: true,
    useUnifiedTopology: true
})

//API Endpoints
app.get("/", (req, res) => res.status(200).send("Hello TheWebDev"))

...
```

MongoDB Schema and Routes

Let's create the model for the post. Create a postModel.js file inside the
photo-social-backend folder.

First, create a schema with the required parameters to be passed, and then export it.

```
import mongoose from 'mongoose'

const postsModel = mongoose.Schema({
    caption: String,
    user: String,
    image: String
})

export default mongoose.model('posts', postsModel)
```

You now use the schema to create the endpoint that adds data to the database.

In server.js, create a POST request to the /upload endpoint. The load is in req.body to MongoDB. Then use create() to send dbPost. If it's a success, you receive status 201; otherwise, you receive status 500.

Next, create the GET endpoint to /sync to get the data from the database. You are using find() here. You receive status 200 if successful (otherwise, status 500).

The updated code is marked in bold.

```
import express from 'express'
import mongoose from 'mongoose'
import Posts from './postModel.js'
...

//API Endpoints
app.get("/", (req, res) => res.status(200).send("Hello TheWebDev"))

app.post('/upload', (req, res) => {
    const dbPost = req.body
    Posts.create(dbPost, (err, data) => {
        if(err)
            res.status(500).send(err)
        else
            res.status(201).send(data)
    })
})

app.get('/sync', (req, res) => {
    Posts.find((err, data) => {
        if(err) {
            res.status(500).send(err)
        } else {
            res.status(200).send(data)
        }
    })
})

//Listener
app.listen(port, () => console.log(`Listening on localhost: ${port}`))
```

Before moving forward with the POST request, you need to complete two things. First, implement CORS; otherwise, you get cross-origin errors later when you deploy the app. Open the terminal and install CORS in the `photo-social-backend` folder.

```
npm i cors
```

In `server.js`, import CORS and then use it with `app.use()`. You also need to use the `express.json()` middleware. The updated code is marked in bold.

```
import express from 'express'
import mongoose from 'mongoose'
import Cors from 'cors'
import Posts from './postModel.js'

...

//Middleware
app.use(express.json())
app.use(Cors())

...
```

In Postman, you need to change the request to POST and then add the `http://localhost:9000/upload` endpoint.

After that, click **Body** and then select **raw**. Change to **JSON (application/json)** from drop-down menu. In the text editor, enter the data as shown in Figure 5-18. One thing to change is to make the data JSON by adding double quotes to keys also.

Next, click the **Send** button. If everything is correct, you get **Status: 201 Created**, as seen in Figure 5-18.

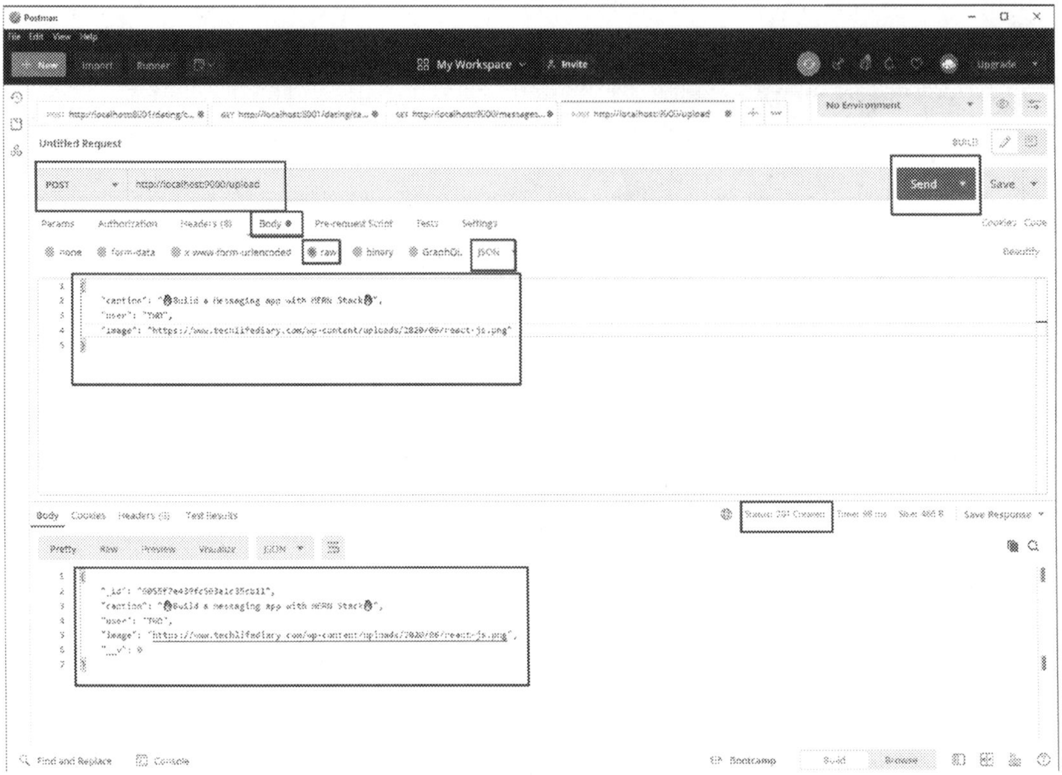

Figure 5-18. *Postman POST*

I inserted other data in a similar way. You need to test the GET /sync endpoint. Change the request to GET and click the **Send** button. If everything is correct, you get **Status: 200 OK**, as seen in Figure 5-19.

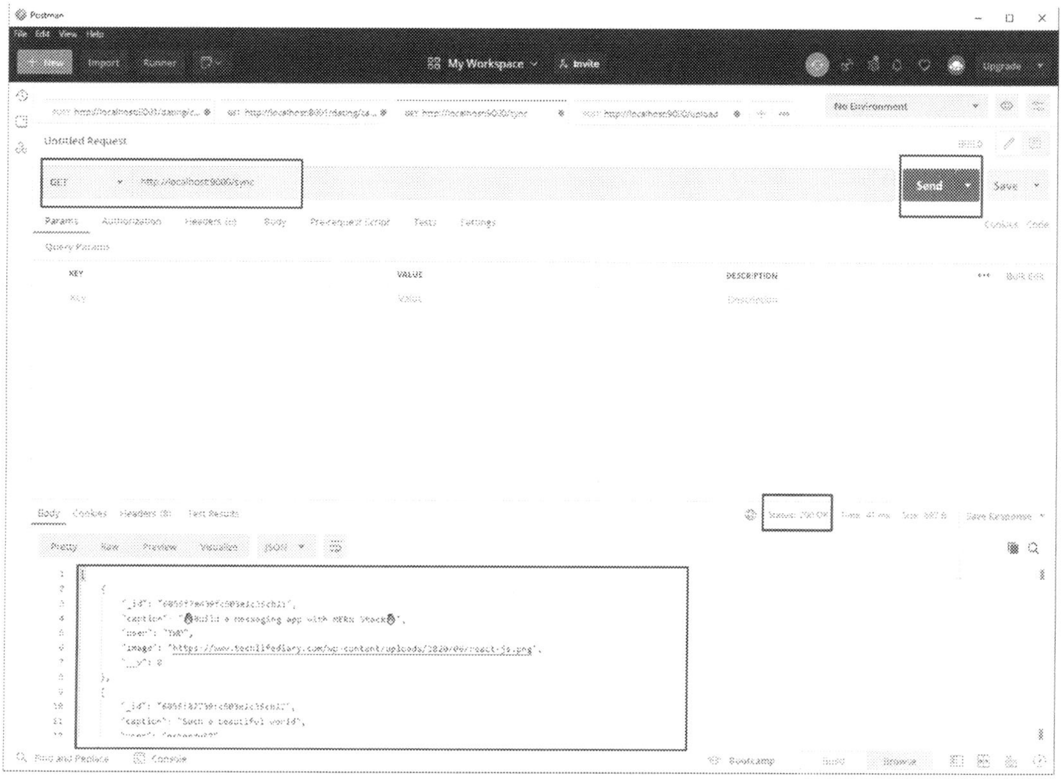

Figure 5-19. *Postman GET*

Sometimes you get an error in the server while POST requests. The error is
UnhandledPromiseRejectionWarning: MongooseServerSelectionError: connection.

If you get this error, go to your **Network Access** tab, and click the **ADD IP ADDRESS**
button. After that, click **ADD CURRENT IP ADDRESS** button, and click **Confirm**, as seen
in Figure 5-20.

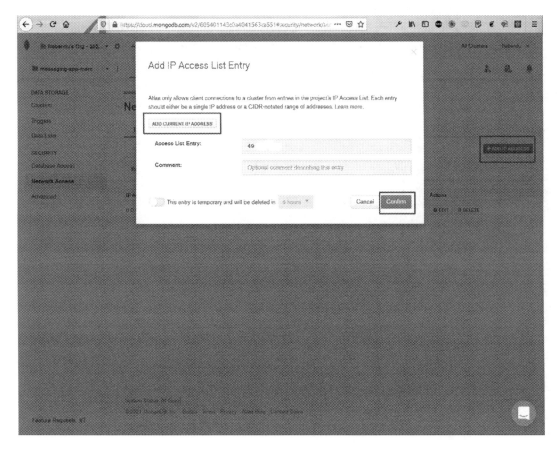

Figure 5-20. *Add current IP*

Integrating the Back End with the Front End

You want to get all the messages when the app initially loads, and then push the messages. You need to hit the GET endpoint, and for that you need Axios. Open the photo-social-frontend folder and install it.

```
npm i axios
```

Next, create a new axios.js file inside the src folder and then create an instance of axios. The base URL is http://localhost:9000.

```
import axios from 'axios'

const instance = axios.create({
    baseURL: "http://localhost:9000"
})

export default instance
```

In the ImageUpload.js file, import storage from Firebase and Axios. Update handleUpload(), which fires after you click the Upload button.

First, take the uploaded image path in the uploadTask variable and put it in the database. Check state_changed because the snapshot changes. Depending on how much hass uploaded, update the progress bar in setProgress.

After that, you need to do error management. Get the image URL from Firebase.

Next, take the caption, username, and URL and do an axios.post to /upload to push it in MongoDB.

The updated code is marked in bold.

```
...
import { storage } from "../firebase";
import axios from '../axios'
const ImageUpload = ({ username }) => {
    ...
    const [url, setUrl] = useState("");
    const handleChange = e => {...}
    const handleUpload = () => {
        const uploadTask = storage.ref(`images/${image.name}`).put(image);
        uploadTask.on(
            "state_changed",
            (snapshot) => {
                const progress = Math.round(
                    (snapshot.bytesTransferred / snapshot.totalBytes) * 100
                );
                setProgress(progress);
            },
```

```
            (error) => {
                console.log(error);
            },
            () => {
                storage
                    .ref("images")
                    .child(image.name)
                    .getDownloadURL()
                    .then((url) => {
                        setUrl(url);
                        axios.post('/upload', {
                            caption: caption,
                            user: username,
                            image: url
                        })
                        setProgress(0);
                        setCaption("");
                        setImage(null);
                    });
            }
        );
    };
    return (...)
}
```

```
export default ImageUpload
```

You need to set up storage in the Firebase console before testing. First, click the **Storage** tab and then the **Get started** button, which opens the popup window shown in Figure 5-21. Then, click the **Next** button.

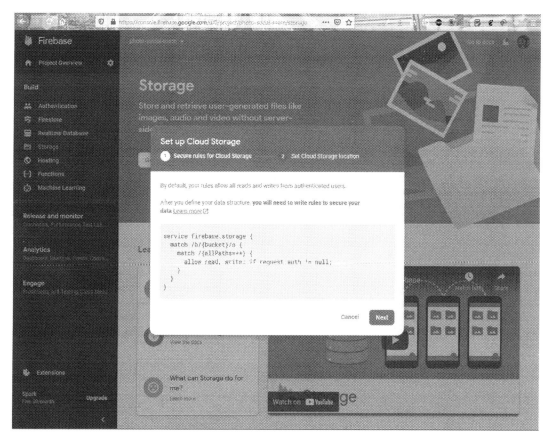

Figure 5-21. *Firebase storage*

On the next screen, click the **Done** button, as shown in Figure 5-22.

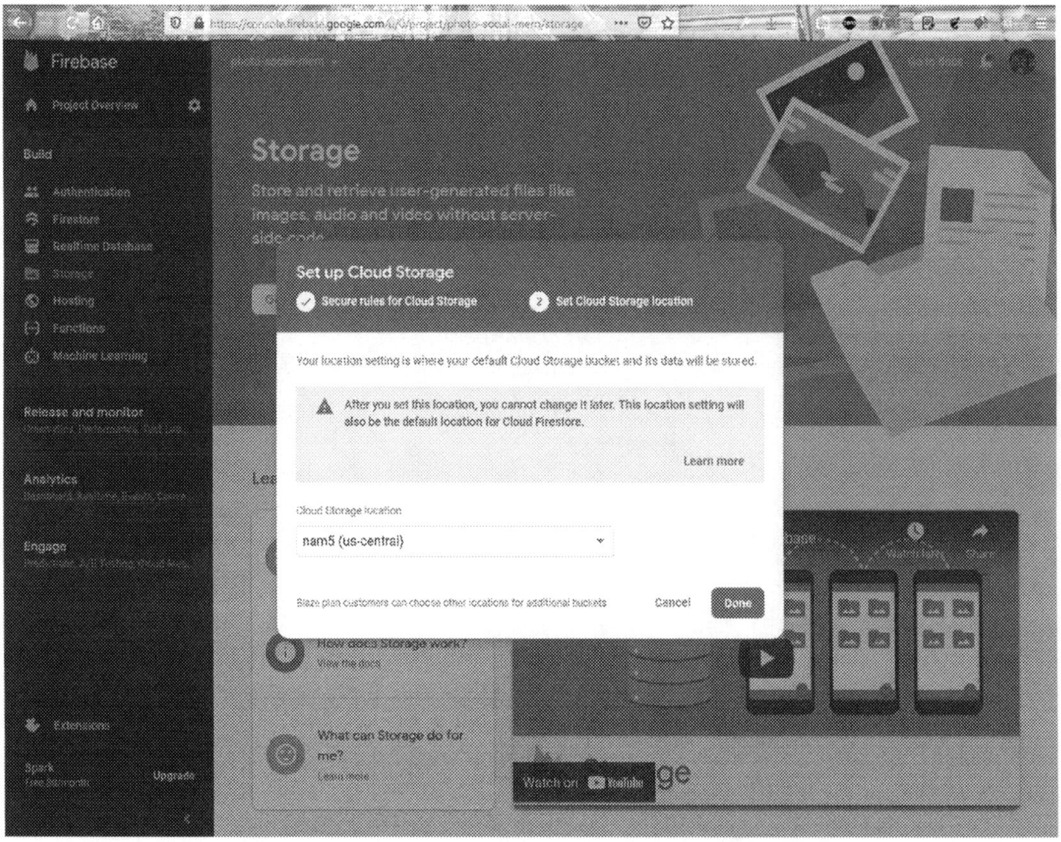

Figure 5-22. *Cloud storage*

Go to localhost, upload any images, enter captions, and hit the **Upload** button. You can see the post being saved to MongoDB (see Figure 5-23).

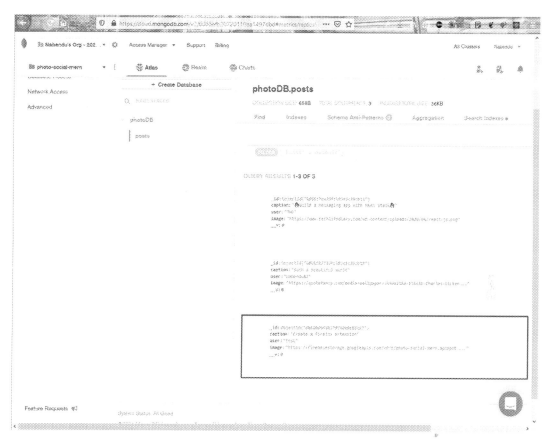

Figure 5-23. *MongoDB save*

In App.js, you need to fetch the posts from MongoDB. First, import the local axios. Then create a new useEffect hook and make the GET request to the /sync endpoint.

Next, update App.js with the data you received from MongoDB.

The updated code is marked in bold.

```
...
import axios from './axios'
...
function App() {
  ...
  const fetchPosts = async () => {
    await axios.get("/sync").then(response => setPosts(response.data))
  }
```

```
useEffect(() => {
  fetchPosts()
},[])
...
return (
  <div className="app">
      ...
      <div className="app__posts">
        {posts.map(post => (
          <Post
            key={post._id}
            username={post.user}
            caption={post.caption}
            imageUrl={post.image}
          />
        ))}
      </div>
      ...
  </div>
  );
}

export default App;
```

Figure 5-24 shows the post from the MongoDB database on localhost.

Figure 5-24. *Post from MongoDB*

Configuring Pusher

Since MongoDB is not a real-time database, it's time to add a pusher to the app to get real-time data. Since you already did the setup in Chapter 4, follow the same instructions, and create an app named **photo-social-mern**.

Adding Pusher to the Back End

Again, you need to stop the server and install Pusher. In the photo-social-backend folder, install it with the following command.

```
npm i pusher
```

In the server.js file, import it and then use the Pusher initialization code. Get the initialization code from the Pusher website (https://pusher.com). To add the code, open a database connection with db.once. Then watch the message collection from MongoDB with watch().

Inside changeStream, if operationType is inserted, you insert the data in the pusher. The updated code is marked in bold.

```
...
import Pusher from 'pusher'
...
//App Config
...
const pusher = new Pusher({
    appId: "11xxxx",
    key: "9exxxxxxxxxxxxx",
    secret: "b7xxxxxxxxxxxxxxx",
    cluster: "ap2",
    useTLS: true
});
//API Endpoints
mongoose.connect(connection_url, {  ...})

mongoose.connection.once('open', () => {
    console.log('DB Connected')
    const changeStream = mongoose.connection.collection('posts').watch()
    changeStream.on('change', change => {
        console.log(change)
        if(change.operationType === "insert") {
            console.log('Trigerring Pusher')
            pusher.trigger('posts','inserted', {
                change: change
            })
        } else {
            console.log('Error trigerring Pusher')
        }
    })
})
```

```
app.get("/", (req, res) => res.status(200).send("Hello TheWebDev"))
...
//Listener
app.listen(port, () => console.log(`Listening on localhost: ${port}`))
```

To test this, you need to upload a new image from the front end. At the same time, you need to be in the **Debug console** in Pusher.

Figure 5-25 shows the message displayed in the Debug console log.

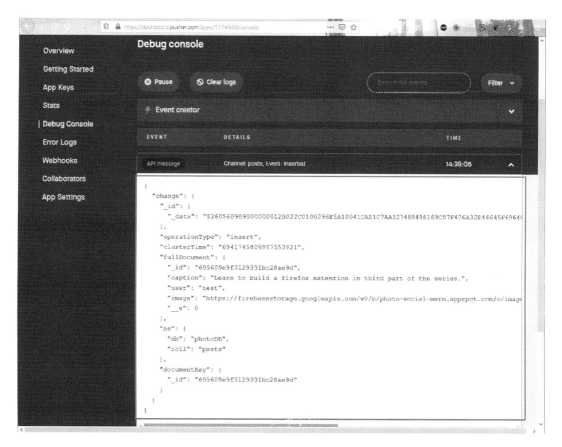

Figure 5-25. *Pusher log*

Adding Pusher to the Front End

It's time to move to the front end and use Pusher. First, you need to install the pusher-js package in the photo-social-frontend folder.

```
npm i pusher-js
```

Get the code from www.pusher.com to put in the front end of the app. Import Pusher and then use the code in the App.js file, where you have a new useEffect() hook for Pusher. The updated content is marked in bold.

```
...
import Pusher from 'pusher-js'

const pusher = new Pusher('56xxxxxxxxxxxxxxxx', {
  cluster: 'ap2'
});
function App() {
  ...
  const fetchPosts = async () => {
    await axios.get("/sync").then(response => setPosts(response.data))
  }

  useEffect(() => {
    const channel = pusher.subscribe('posts');
    channel.bind('inserted', (data) => {
      fetchPosts()
    });
  }, [])

  useEffect(() => {
    fetchPosts()
  },[])
  ...
  return (
    <div className="app">
      ...
    </div>
  );
}

export default App;
```

Go to Postman and send another POST request. You see the data from the console log on localhost. The app is complete. Whenever you post something, it is shown in real time.

Hiding Secrets

You can hide the secrets before deploying the app to Heroku or pushing it to GitHub, which is a best practice. Install dotenv in the photo-social-backend folder using the following command.

```
npm i dotenv
```

Then create an .env file in the photo-social-backend folder and add all secrets to it.

```
DB_CONN='mongodb+srv://admin:<password>@cluster0.giruc.mongodb.net/photoDB?
retryWrites=true&w=majority'
PUSHER_ID="11xxxx"
PUSHER_KEY="56xxxxxxxxxxxxxxxxxx"
PUSHER_SECRET="90xxxxxxxxxxxxxxxxxxx"
```

In server.js, import dotenv and then use the values from it in place of all secrets.

```
...
import Posts from './postModel.js'
import dotenv from 'dotenv';

//App Config
dotenv.config()
const app = express()
const port = process.env.PORT || 9000
const connection_url = process.env.DB_CONN

const pusher = new Pusher({
    appId: process.env.PUSHER_ID,
    key: process.env.PUSHER_KEY,
    secret: process.env.PUSHER_SECRET,
    cluster: "ap2",
    useTLS: true
});

//Middleware
...
```

Add the .env file in the .gitignore file in the back end. The updated content is marked in bold.

node_modules

.env

Deploying the Back End to Heroku

Go to www.heroku.com to deploy the back end. Follow the same procedure that you did Chapter 1 and create an app named **photo-social-backend**.

Since you have environment variables this time, you must add them in **Settings ➤ Config Vars**. Note that you don't put any quotes around the keys, as seen in Figure 5-26.

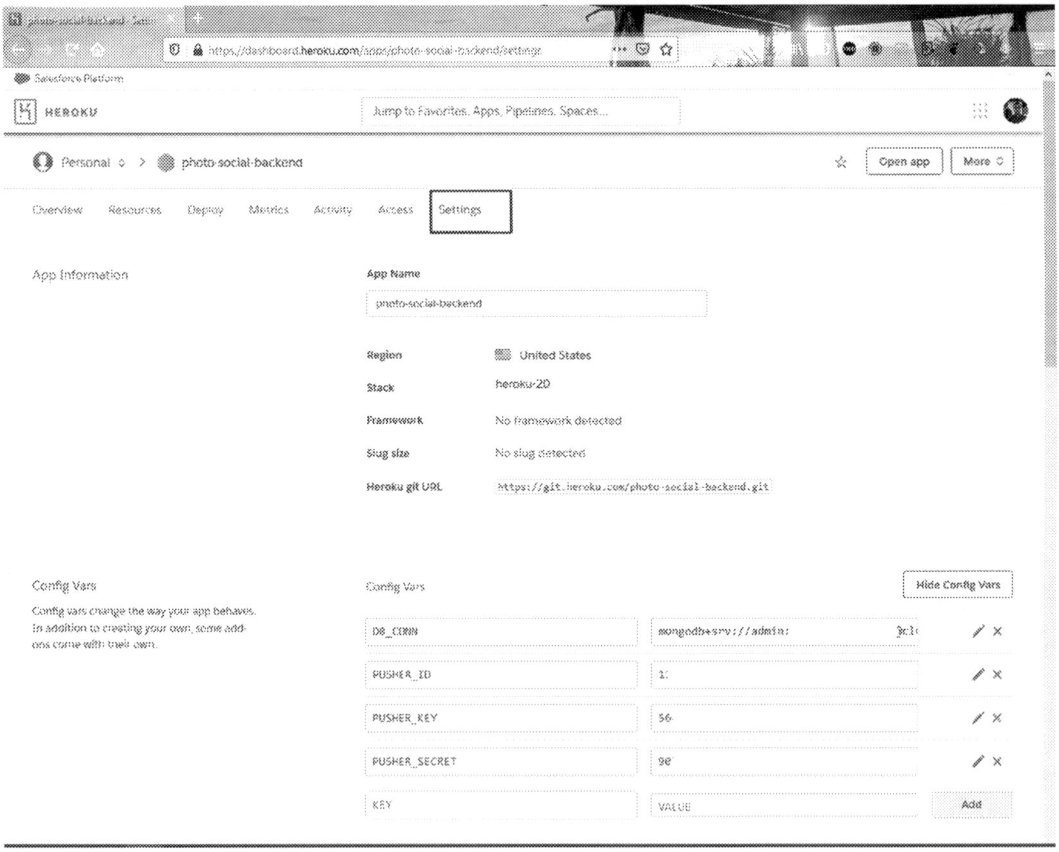

Figure 5-26. *Environment variables in Heroku*

After successfully deploying, go to https://photo-social-backend.herokuapp.com. Figure 5-27 shows the correct text.

Figure 5-27. *Back end deployed*

Go to axios.js and change the endpoint to https://photo-social-backend. herokuapp.com. If everything is working fine, your app should run.

```
import axios from 'axios'
const instance = axios.create({
    baseURL: " https://photo-social-backend.herokuapp.com "
})

export default instance
```

Deploying the Front End to Firebase

It's time to deploy the front end in Firebase. Follow the same procedure that you did in Chapter 1. After this process, the site should be live and working properly, as seen in Figure 5-28.

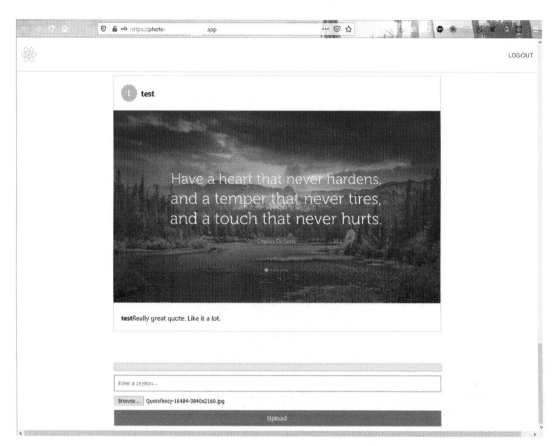

Figure 5-28. *Final app*

Summary

In this chapter, you created a simple but functional photo-based social network. Firebase hosted it on the Internet. You learned to add email authentication, by which you can log in with email. You also learned how to store images in Firebase and store links to images and posts in a MongoDB database with API routes created using Node.js.

CHAPTER 6

Build a Popular Social Network with MERN

Welcome to the final MERN project, where you build an awesome popular social network using the MERN framework. The back end is hosted in Heroku, and the front-end site is hosted in Firebase. Firebase also handles the authentication functionality. Material-UI provides the icons in this project. You also use styled components and CSS.

Pusher is used since MongoDB is not a real-time database like Firebase, and you want the posts to reflect the moment someone hits the submit.

In this project, you build a social media app that has Google authentication. The app's look and feel are similar to a popular social network. In it, you can post an image along with descriptive text. The final hosted app is shown in Figure 6-1.

© Nabendu Biswas 2021
N. Biswas, *MERN Projects for Beginners*, https://doi.org/10.1007/978-1-4842-7138-4_6

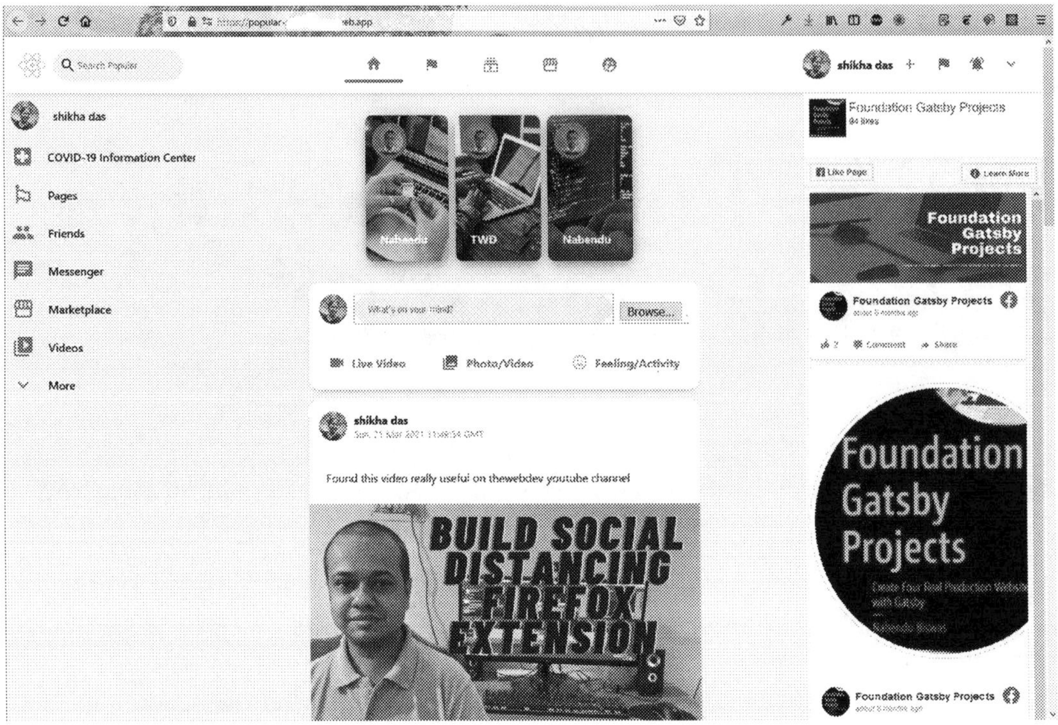

Figure 6-1. *Final app*

Go to your terminal and create a `popular-social-mern` folder. Inside it, use **create-react-app** to create a new app called **popular-social-frontend**. The commands are as follows.

```
mkdir popular-social-mern
cd popular-social-mern
npx create-react-app popular-social-frontend
```

Firebase Hosting Initial Setup

Since the front-end site is hosted through Firebase, you can create the basic setting while create-react-app creates the React app. Following the setup instructions from Chapter 1, I created **popular-social-mern** in the Firebase console.

Since you also are using authentication functionality, you need to do the additional configuration mentioned in Chapter 4 and get `firebaseConfig`, which you need to copy.

Open the code in Visual Studio Code (VSCode) and create a `firebase.js` file inside the `src` folder and paste the config content there.

```
const firebaseConfig = {
    apiKey: "AIxxxxxxxxxxxxxxxxxxxxxxxxxxxxxxxxxY",
    authDomain: "popular-xxxxxxxxxxxxxxxxxxxxxxx.com",
    projectId: "popular-xxxxxxxxxxx",
    storageBucket: "popular-xxxxxxxxxxx",
    messagingSenderId: "19xxxxxxx",
    appId: "1:59xxxxxxxxxxxxxxxxxxxxxxxxxxxxxxxx"
};
```

React Basic Setup

Go back to the React project and `cd` to the `popular-social-frontend` directory. Then, start the React app with `npm start`.

```
cd popular-social-frontend
npm start
```

The deleting of the files and basic setup in `index.js`, `App.js`, and `App.css` is like what was done in Chapter 2. Follow those instructions. Figure 6-2 shows how the app looks on localhost.

Figure 6-2. *Initial app*

Adding a Styled Component

You are going to use the famous CSS-in-JS library styled-components (`https://styled-components.com`) to style the project. This is one of the most popular alternative ways to use CSS in React projects. Open the integrated terminal and install it in the `popular-social-frontend` folder.

```
npm i styled-components
```

Then, import the styled components in the `App.js` file. In place of the div, there is the `AppWrapper` component. You style `AppWrapper` after the function. The updated content is marked in bold.

```
import styled from 'styled-components'

function App() {
  return (
    <AppWrapper>
      <h1>Popular Social Network MERN</h1>
    </AppWrapper >
  );
}

const AppWrapper = styled.div`
  background-color: #f1f2f5;
`

export default App;
```

Creating a Header Component

Let's create a component that displays a nice header in the app. To do this, create a `components` folder inside the `src` folder, and then create a `Header.js` file inside the `components` folder.

The icons are from Material-UI (`https://material-ui.com`). You need to do two npm installs, and then install the core and the icons in the `popular-social-frontend` folder.

```
npm i @material-ui/core @material-ui/icons
```

A lot of code is placed in `Header.js`, but it is mainly static code and uses Material UI icons. Note that styled components are used in all the files.

The styled components are like SCSS, where you can nest the internal div inside the parent element. For example, the `HeaderCenter` styled component contains styles for the header__option div. Also, note that pseudo-elements like hover are given by `&:hover`.

```jsx
import React from 'react'
import styled from 'styled-components'
import SearchIcon from '@material-ui/icons/Search'
import HomeIcon from '@material-ui/icons/Home'
import FlagIcon from '@material-ui/icons/Flag'
import SubscriptionsOutlinedIcon from '@material-ui/icons/
SubscriptionsOutlined'
import StorefrontOutlinedIcon from '@material-ui/icons/StorefrontOutlined'
import SupervisedUserCircleIcon from '@material-ui/icons/
SupervisedUserCircle'
import { Avatar, IconButton } from '@material-ui/core'
import AddIcon from '@material-ui/icons/Add'
import ForumIcon from '@material-ui/icons/Flag'
import NotificationsActiveIcon from '@material-ui/icons/
NotificationsActive'
import ExpandMoreIcon from '@material-ui/icons/ExpandMore'

const Header = () => {
    return (
        <HeaderWrapper>
            <HeaderLeft>
                <img src="logo192.png" alt="Popular" />
            </HeaderLeft>
            <HeaderInput>
                <SearchIcon />
                <input placeholder="Search Popular" type="text" />
            </HeaderInput>
            <HeaderCenter>
                <div className="header__option header__option--active">
                    <HomeIcon fontsize="large" />
                </div>
                <div className="header__option">
                    <FlagIcon fontsize="large" />
                </div>
                <div className="header__option">
                    <SubscriptionsOutlinedIcon fontsize="large" />
                </div>
```

```jsx
                <div className="header__option">
                    <StorefrontOutlinedIcon fontsize="large" />
                </div>
                <div className="header__option">
                    <SupervisedUserCircleIcon fontsize="large" />
                </div>
            </HeaderCenter>
            <HeaderRight>
                <div className="header__info">
                    <Avatar src="https://pbs.twimg.com/profile_
                    images/1020939891457241088/fcbu814K_400x400.jpg " />
                    <h4>Nabendu</h4>
                </div>
                <IconButton>
                    <AddIcon />
                </IconButton>
                <IconButton>
                    <ForumIcon />
                </IconButton>
                <IconButton>
                    <NotificationsActiveIcon />
                </IconButton>
                <IconButton>
                    <ExpandMoreIcon />
                </IconButton>
            </HeaderRight>
        </HeaderWrapper>
    )
}

const HeaderWrapper = styled.div`
        display: flex;
        padding: 15px 20px;
        justify-content: space-between;
        align-items: center;
        position: sticky;
```

```
        background-color: white;
        z-index: 100;
        top: 0;
        box-shadow: 0px 5px 8px -9px rgba(0, 0, 0, 0.75);
`

const HeaderLeft = styled.div`
        display: flex;
        justify-content: space-evenly;
        img {
            height: 40px;
        }
`

const HeaderInput = styled.div`
        display: flex;
        align-items: center;
        background-color: #eff2f5;
        padding: 10px;
        margin-left: 10px;
        border-radius: 33px;
        input {
            border: none;
            background-color: transparent;
            outline-width: 0;
        }
`

const HeaderCenter = styled.div`
        display: flex;
        flex: 1;
        justify-content: center;
        .header__option{
            display: flex;
            align-items: center;
            padding: 10px 30px;
            cursor: pointer;
```

```
            .MuiSvgIcon-root{
                color: gray;
            }
            &:hover{
                background-color: #eff2f5;
                border-radius: 10px;
                align-items: center;
                padding: 0 30px;
                border-bottom: none;
                .MuiSvgIcon-root{
                    color: #2e81f4;
                }
            }
        }

        .header__option--active{
            border-bottom: 4px solid #2e81f4;
            .MuiSvgIcon-root{
                color: #2e81f4;
            }
        }
    }

const HeaderRight = styled.div`
        display: flex;
        .header__info {
            display: flex;
            align-items: center;
            h4 {
                margin-left: 10px;
            }
        }
    }

export default Header
```

Include the Header component in the App.js file. The updated content is marked in bold.

```
import styled from 'styled-components'
import Header from './components/Header'

function App() {
  return (
    <AppWrapper>
      <Header />
    </AppWrapper >
  );
}

const AppWrapper = styled.div`
  background-color: #f1f2f5;
`

export default App;
```

Figure 6-3 shows that the header looks awesome on localhost.

Figure 6-3. *Beautiful header*

Creating Sidebar Components

Let's create the components to show a nice left sidebar containing the user avatar and some static information. Create a Sidebar.js file inside the components folder and put the following content in it. The content is static and mainly contains Material-UI icons passed to another SidebarRow component.

```
import React from 'react'
import SidebarRow from './SidebarRow'
import LocalHospitalIcon from '@material-ui/icons/LocalHospital'
```

```
import EmojiFlagsIcon from '@material-ui/icons/EmojiFlags'
import PeopleIcon from '@material-ui/icons/People'
import ChatIcon from '@material-ui/icons/Chat'
import StorefrontIcon from '@material-ui/icons/Storefront'
import VideoLibraryIcon from '@material-ui/icons/VideoLibrary'
import ExpandMoreOutlined from '@material-ui/icons/ExpandMoreOutlined'
import styled from 'styled-components'

const Sidebar = () => {
    return (
        <SidebarWrapper>
            <SidebarRow src="https://pbs.twimg.com/profile_images/
            1020939891457241088/fcbu814K_400x400.jpg" title="Nabendu" />
            <SidebarRow Icon={LocalHospitalIcon} title="COVID-19
            Information Center" />
            <SidebarRow Icon={EmojiFlagsIcon} title="Pages" />
            <SidebarRow Icon={PeopleIcon} title="Friends" />
            <SidebarRow Icon={ChatIcon} title="Messenger" />
            <SidebarRow Icon={StorefrontIcon} title="Marketplace" />
            <SidebarRow Icon={VideoLibraryIcon} title="Videos" />
            <SidebarRow Icon={ExpandMoreOutlined} title="More" />
        </SidebarWrapper>
    )
}

const SidebarWrapper = styled.div``

export default Sidebar
```

Create a SidebarRow.js file inside the components folder. Note that the MuiSvgIcon-root class is on every Material-UI. You are targeting it to add custom styles.

```
import React from 'react'
import { Avatar } from '@material-ui/core'
import styled from 'styled-components'
const SidebarRow = ({ src, Icon, title }) => {
    return (
        <SidebarRowWrapper>
```

```
            {src && <Avatar src={src} />}
            {Icon && <Icon />}
            <p>{title}</p>
        </SidebarRowWrapper>
    )
}
const SidebarRowWrapper = styled.div`
    display: flex;
    align-items: center;
    padding: 10px;
    cursor: pointer;
    &:hover {
        background-color: lightgray;
        border-radius: 10px;
    }
    p{
        margin-left:20px;
        font-weight: 600;
    }
    .MuiSvgIcon-root{
        font-size:xx-large;
        color: #2e81f4;
    }`

export default SidebarRow
```

In the App.js file, add a sidebar component within an app__body div and add styles for it in styled components. The updated content is marked in bold.

```
import styled from 'styled-components'
import Header from './components/Header'
import Sidebar from './components/Sidebar'

function App() {
  return (
    <AppWrapper>
      <Header />
```

```
      <div className="app__body">
        <Sidebar />
      </div>
    </AppWrapper >
  );
}

const AppWrapper = styled.div`
  background-color: #f1f2f5;
  .app__body {
    display: flex;
  }
`

export default App;
```

Figure 6-4 shows the sidebar on localhost.

Figure 6-4. *Nice sidebar*

Creating a Feed Component

Let's look at the middle part in the app, which adds and shows all the posts. Create a Feed.js file inside the components folder. Put the following content in it. A FeedWrapper styled component is wrapping a Stories component.

```
import React from 'react'
import Stories from './Stories'
import styled from 'styled-components'
const Feed = () => {
    return (
        <FeedWrapper>
            <Stories />
        </FeedWrapper>
    )
}
const FeedWrapper = styled.div`
    flex: 1;
    padding: 30px 150px;
    display: flex;
    flex-direction: column;
    align-items: center;

`

export default Feed
```

Next, create a Stories.js file inside the components folder. Here, you are passing image, profileSrc, and title to the Story component.

```
import React from 'react'
import Story from './Story'
import styled from 'styled-components'
const Stories = () => {
    return (
        <StoriesWrapper>
            <Story
image="https://images.unsplash.com/photo-1602524206684-fdf6393c7d89?ixid=MX
wxMjA3fDF8MHxwaG90by1wYWdlfHx8fGVufDB8fHw%3D&ixlib=rb-1.2.1&auto=format&fit
=crop&w=1350&q=80"
profileSrc="https://pbs.twimg.com/profile_images/1020939891457241088/
fcbu814K_400x400.jpg"
                title="Nabendu"
            />
```

```
                <Story
                    image="https://images.unsplash.com/photo-1602526430780-
782d6b1783fa?ixid=MXwxMjA3fDF8MHxwaG90by1wYWdlfHx8fGVufDB8fHw%3D&ixlib=rb-
1.2.1&auto=format&fit=crop&w=1350&q=80"
profileSrc="https://pbs.twimg.com/profile_images/1020939891457241088/
fcbu814K_400x400.jpg"
                    title="TWD"
                />
                <Story
                    image="https://www.jonesday.com/-/media/files/
publications/2019/05/when-coding-is-criminal/when-coding-is-criminal.jpg?
h=800&w=1600&la=en&hash=5522AA91198A168017C511FCBE77E201"
profileSrc="https://pbs.twimg.com/profile_images/1020939891457241088/
fcbu814K_400x400.jpg"
                    title="Nabendu"
                />
        </StoriesWrapper>
    )
}

const StoriesWrapper = styled.div`
    display: flex;
`

export default Stories
```

Next, create the Story.js file inside the components folder. Here, you show the props. Note that the StoryWrapper is using props in the background image, which shows the power of styled components. A ternary operator is used to show an image if the image is passed in props.

```
import { Avatar } from '@material-ui/core'
import React from 'react'
import styled from 'styled-components'
const Story = ({ image, profileSrc, title }) => {
    return (
        <StoryWrapper imageUrl={`${image}`}>
```

```
            <Avatar src={profileSrc} className='story__avatar' />
            <h4>{title}</h4>
        </StoryWrapper>
    )
}

const StoryWrapper = styled.div`
    background-image: url(${props => props.imageUrl ? props.imageUrl : ''});
    position: relative;
    background-position: center center;
    background-size: cover;
    background-repeat: no-repeat;
    width: 120px;
    height: 200px;
    box-shadow: 0px 5px 17px -7px rgba(0,0,0,0.75);
    border-radius: 10px;
    margin-right: 10px;
    cursor: pointer;
    transition: transform 100ms ease-in;
    &:hover {
        transform: scale(1.07);
    }
    .story__avatar {
        margin: 10px;
        border: 5px solid #2e81f4;
    }
    h4 {
        position: absolute;
        bottom: 20px;
        left: 20px;

        color: white;
    }
`

export default Story
```

In the App.js file, include the Feed component. The updated content is marked in bold.

```
import styled from 'styled-components'
import Header from './components/Header'
import Sidebar from './components/Sidebar'
import Feed from './components/Feed'

function App() {
  return (
    <AppWrapper>
      <Header />
      <div className="app__body">
        <Sidebar />
        <Feed />
      </div>
    </AppWrapper >
  );
}

const AppWrapper = styled.div`
 ...
`

export default App;
```

Figure 6-5 shows that the stories look great on localhost.

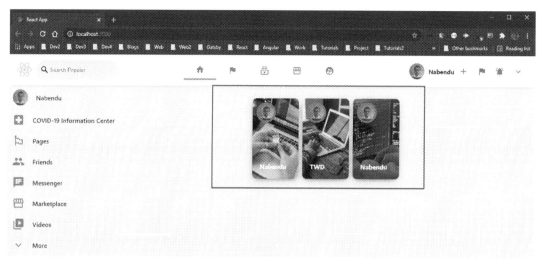

Figure 6-5. *Nice image*

Adding a Widget

Complete the front of the web app by adding a widget from the page plugin in Facebook. Add this in the right sidebar so that the app looks complete. Connect using a Facebook developer account (`https://developers.facebook.com/docs/plugins/page-plugin/`), so you can use it in any web app.

You need to give the Facebook page URL, width, and height, and then scroll down and click the **Get Code** button. I used my Gatsby cookbook page, as seen in Figure 6-6.

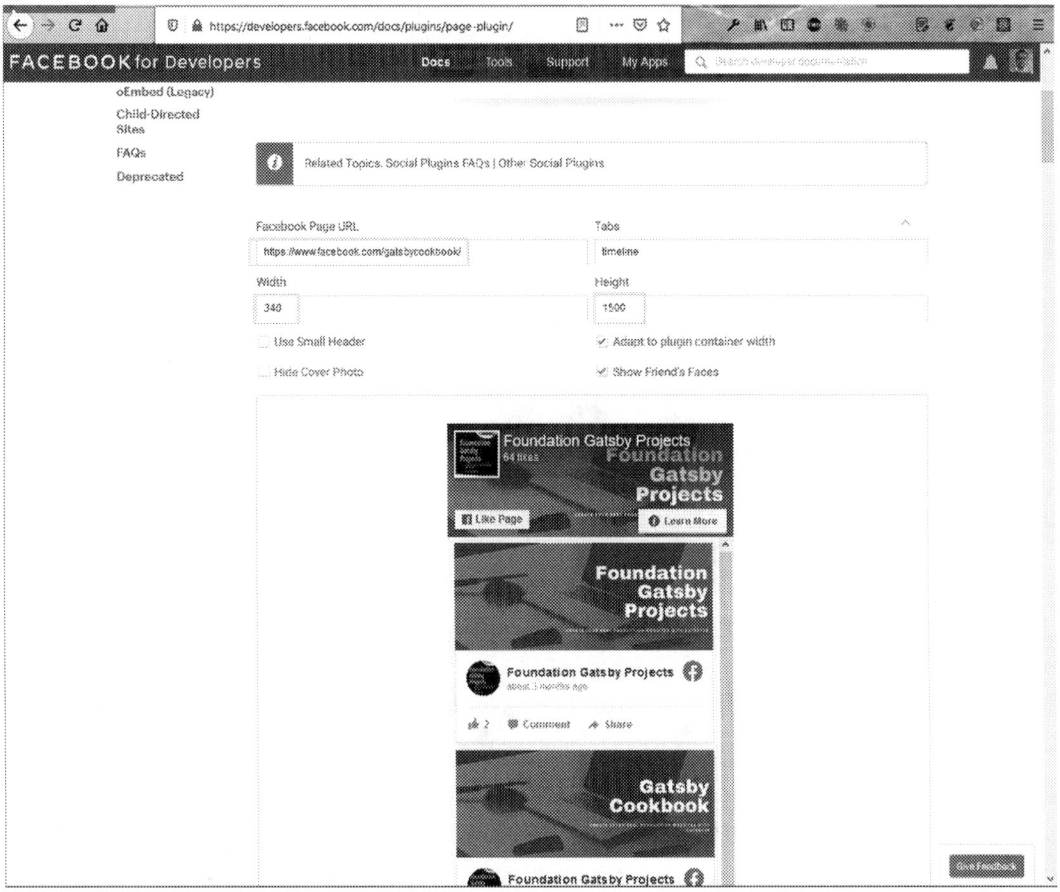

Figure 6-6. *Adding widget*

A popup window opens. You need to click the **iFrame** tab to get the code, as seen in Figure 6-7.

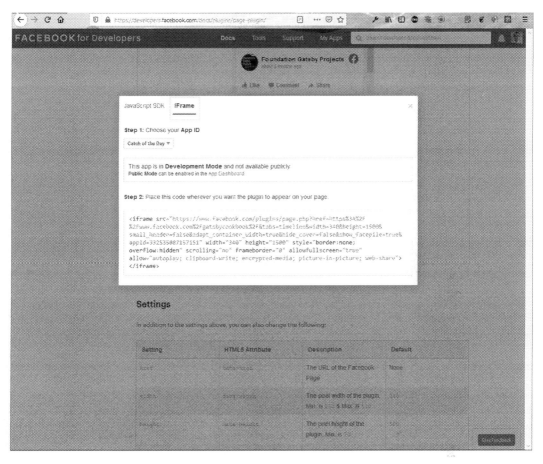

Figure 6-7. *Getting iFrame*

Create a `Widget.js` file inside the `components` folder. Include the IFrame from earlier but with slight modifications.

```
import styled from 'styled-components'
const Widget = () => {
    return (
        <WidgetWrapper>
        <iframe
src="https://www.facebook.com/plugins/page.php?href=https%3A%2F%2Fwww.
facebook.com%2Fgatsbycookbook%2F&tabs=timeline&width=340&height=1500&small_
header=false&adapt_container_width=true&hide_cover=true&show_facepile=true&
appId=332535087157151"
            width="340"
            height="1500"
```

```
            style={{ border: "none", overflow: "hidden" }}
            scrolling="no"
            frameborder="0"
            allow="encrypted-media"
            title="Facebook Widget"
        >
        </iframe>
        </WidgetWrapper>
    )
}

const WidgetWrapper = styled.div``

export default Widget
```

Figure 6-8 shows a nice widget on localhost.

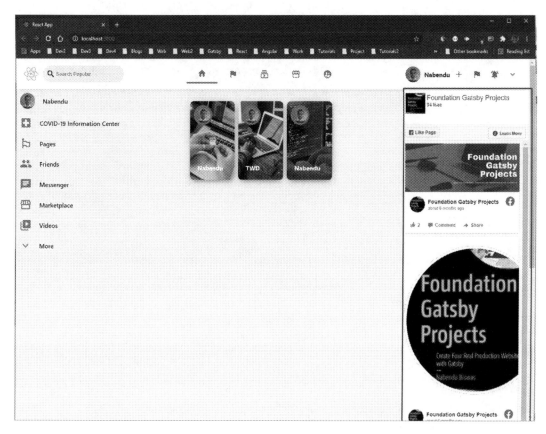

Figure 6-8. *Widget shown*

Creating a Messenger Component

Next, let's complete the Feed.js file by implementing the component through which the user can write a description for the post and upload an image. Two more components are added here. Create a new Messenger.js file in the components folder.

You include it first in the Feed.js file. The updated content is marked in bold.

```
import React from 'react'
import Stories from './Stories'
import styled from 'styled-components'
import Messenger from './Messenger'
const Feed = () => {
    rcturn (
        <FeedWrapper>
            <Stories />
            < Messenger />
        </FeedWrapper>
    )
}

const FeedWrapper = styled.div`
  ...
`

export default Feed
```

Let's create the Messenger.js file. Here, you mainly have the MessengerTop and MessengerBottom components. In MessengerTop, you mainly have a text box, a file, and a button. You make the button invisible with display: none in its CSS. Most of the functionality is in it once you set the back end.

The MessengerBottom component is mainly a static component that shows the icons.

```
import React, { useState } from 'react'
import { Avatar, Input } from '@material-ui/core'
import VideocamIcon from '@material-ui/icons/Videocam'
import PhotoLibraryIcon from '@material-ui/icons/PhotoLibrary'
import InsertEmoticonIcon from '@material-ui/icons/InsertEmoticon'
import styled from 'styled-components'
```

```
const Messenger = () => {
    const [input, setInput] = useState('')

    const [image, setImage] = useState(null)
    const handleChange = e => {
        if(e.target.files[0])
            setImage(e.target.files[0])
    }

    const handleSubmit = e => {
        e.preventDefault()
    }

return (
        <MessengerWrapper>
            <MessengerTop>
                <Avatar src=" https://pbs.twimg.com/profile_images/
                1020939891457241088/fcbu814K_400x400.jpg " />
            <form>
                    <input
                        type="text"
                        className="messenger__input"
                        placeholder="What's on your mind?"
                        value={input}
                        onChange={e => setInput(e.target.value)}
                    />
                    <Input
                        type="file"
                        className="messenger__fileSelector"
                        onChange={handleChange}
                    />
                    <button onClick={handleSubmit} type="submit">Hidden</
                    button>
                </form>
            </MessengerTop>
            <MessengerBottom>
                <div className="messenger__option">
```

```
                    <VideocamIcon style={{ color: 'red' }} />
                    <h3>Live Video</h3>
                </div>
                <div className="messenger__option">
                    <PhotoLibraryIcon style={{ color: 'green' }} />
                    <h3>Photo/Video</h3>
                </div>
                <div className="messenger__option">
                    <InsertEmoticonIcon style={{ color: 'orange' }} />
                    <h3>Feeling/Activity</h3>
                </div>
            </MessengerBottom>
        </MessengerWrapper>
    )
}

const MessengerWrapper = styled.div`
    display: flex;
    margin-top: 30px;
    flex-direction: column;
    background-color: white;
    border-radius: 15px;
    box-shadow: 0px 5px 7px -7px rgba(0,0,0,0.75);
    width: 100%;
`

const MessengerTop = styled.div`
    display: flex;
    border-bottom: 1px solid #eff2f5;
    padding: 15px;
    form {
        flex: 1;
        display: flex;
        .messenger__input {
            flex: 1;
            outline-width: 0;
            border: none;
            padding: 5px 20px;
```

```
            margin: 0 10px;
            border-radius: 999px;
            background-color: #eff2f5;
        }
        .messenger__fileSelector{
            width: 20%;
        }
        button {
            display: none;
        }
    }
`

const MessengerBottom = styled.div`
    display: flex;
    justify-content: space-evenly;
    .messenger__option{
        padding: 20px;
        display: flex;
        align-items: center;
        color: gray;
        margin: 5px;
        h3{
            font-size: medium;
            margin-left: 10px;
        }
        &:hover{
            background-color: #eff2f5;
            border-radius: 20px;
            cursor: pointer;
        }
    }
`

export default Messenger
```

The localhost is almost complete, and the Messenger component is showing correctly (see Figure 6-9).

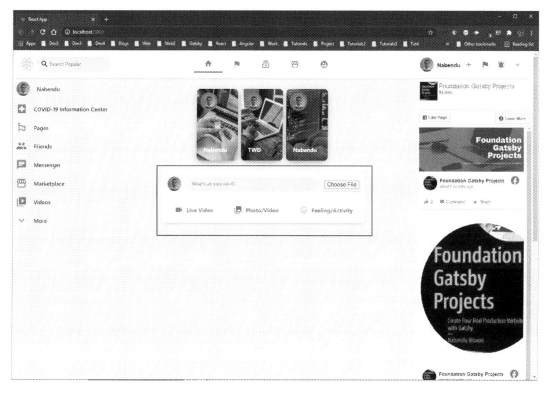

Figure 6-9. *Messenger component*

Creating a Post Component

Next, let's show posts in the web app. The Post component is in the Feed.js file. It is hard-coded now but comes from the back end soon.

The updated content is marked in bold.

```
...
import Post from './Post'

const Feed = () => {
    return (
        <FeedWrapper>
            <Stories />
            < Messenger />
```

```
        <Post         profilePic="https://pbs.twimg.com/profile_
        images/1020939891457241088/fcbu814K_400x400.jpg"
        message="Awesome post on CSS Animation. Loved it"
        timestamp="1609512232424"
        imgName="https://res.cloudinary.com/dxkxvfo2o/image/upload/
        v1598295332/CSS_Animation_xrvhai.png"
        username="Nabendu"
        />
        <Post                    profilePic="https://pbs.twimg.com/profile_
        images/1020939891457241088/fcbu814K_400x400.jpg"
        message="BookList app in Vanilla JavaScript"
        timestamp="1509512232424"
        imgName="https://res.cloudinary.com/dxkxvfo2o/image/upload/
        v1609138312/Booklist-es6_sawxbc.png"
        username="TWD"
        />
    </FeedWrapper>
  )
}

const FeedWrapper = styled.div`
  ...
`

export default Feed
```

Create a new Post.js file inside the components folder. Here, the PostTop section shows the avatar, username, and time. PostBottom shows the message and an image.

Next, show the icons in PostOptions.

```
import { Avatar } from '@material-ui/core'
import React from 'react'
import styled from 'styled-components'
import ThumbUpIcon from '@material-ui/icons/ThumbUp'
import ChatBubbleOutlineIcon from '@material-ui/icons/ChatBubbleOutline'
import NearMeIcon from '@material-ui/icons/NearMe'
import AccountCircleIcon from '@material-ui/icons/AccountCircle'
import ExpandMoreOutlined from '@material-ui/icons/ExpandMoreOutlined'
```

```
const Post = ({ profilePic, message, timestamp, imgName, username }) => {
    return (
        <PostWrapper>
            <PostTop>
                <Avatar src={profilePic} className="post__avatar" />
                <div className="post__topInfo">
                    <h3>{username}</h3>
                    <p>{new Date(parseInt(timestamp)).toUTCString()}</p>
                </div>
            </PostTop>
            <PostBottom>
                <p>{message}</p>
            </PostBottom>
            {
                imgName ? (
                    <div className="post__image">
                        <img src={imgName} alt="Posts" />
                    </div>
                ) : (
                        console.log('DEBUG >>> no image here')
                    )
            }
            <PostOptions>
                <div className="post__option">
                    <ThumbUpIcon />
                    <p>Like</p>
                </div>
                <div className="post__option">
                    <ChatBubbleOutlineIcon />
                    <p>Comment</p>
                </div>
                <div className="post__option">
                    <NearMeIcon />
                    <p>Share</p>
                </div>
                <div className="post__option">
                    <AccountCircleIcon />
```

```
                    <ExpandMoreOutlined />
                </div>
            </PostOptions>
        </PostWrapper>
    )
}

const PostWrapper = styled.div`
    width: 100%;
    margin-top: 15px;
    border-radius: 15px;
    background-color: white;
    box-shadow: 0px 5px 7px -7px rgba(0,0,0,0.75);
    .post__image{
        img{
            width: 100%
        }
    }
`

const PostTop = styled.div`
    display: flex;
    position: relative;
    align-items: center;
    padding: 15px;
    .post__avatar{
        margin-right: 10px;
    }
    .post__topInfo{
        h3{
            font-size: medium;
        }
        p{
            font-size: small;
            color: gray;
        }
    }
`
```

```
const PostBottom = styled.div`
    margin-top: 10px;
    margin-bottom:10px;
    padding: 15px 25px;
`

const PostOptions = styled.div`
    padding: 10px;
    border-top: 1px solid lightgray;
    display: flex;
    justify-content: space-evenly;
    font-size: medium;
    color: gray;
    cursor: pointer;
    padding: 15px;
    .post__option {
        display: flex;
        align-items: center;
        justify-content: center;
        padding: 5px;
        flex: 1;
        p {
            margin-left: 10px;
        }
        &:hover {
            background-color: #eff2f5;
            border-radius: 10px;
        }
    }
`

export default Post
```

Figure 6-10 shows the posts on localhost.

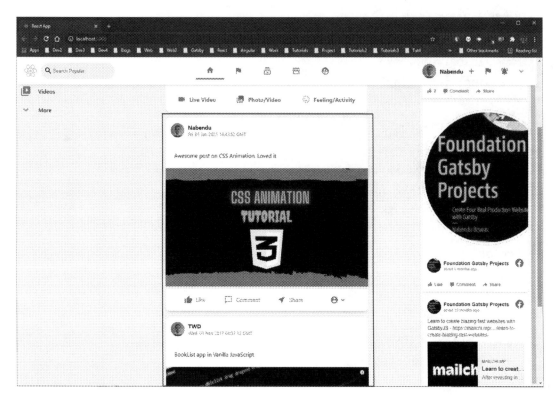

Figure 6-10. *Posts shown*

Google Authentication Setup

Let's work on the Google authentication, which allows you to log in to the app and post. Here, you use the process from Chapter 4 and add it to the Firebase console.

Inside the firebase.js file, initialize the app and use auth, provider and the database. The updated content is marked in bold.

```
import firebase from 'firebase'
const firebaseConfig = {
    ...
};
const firebaseApp = firebase.initializeApp(firebaseConfig)
const db = firebaseApp.firestore()
const auth = firebase.auth()
const provider = new firebase.auth.GoogleAuthProvider()
```

```
export { auth, provider }
export default db
```

You also need to install all dependencies for Firebase in the terminal. But make sure you are in the popular-social-frontend folder.

```
npm i firebase
```

Creating a Login Component

Let's create a Login.js file inside the components folder. The Login.js file is a simple, functional component showing a logo and a sign-in button. As before, you are using styled components.

```
import React from 'react'
import styled from 'styled-components'
import { Button } from '@material-ui/core'

const Login = () => {
    const signIn = () => {}
    return (
        <LoginWrapper>
            <div className="login__logo">
                <img src="logo512.png" alt="login" />
                <h1>Popular Social</h1>
            </div>
            <Button type='submit' className="login__btn"
            onClick={signIn}>Sign In</Button>
        </LoginWrapper>
    )
}

const LoginWrapper = styled.div`
    display: grid;
    place-items: center;
    height: 100vh;
    .login__logo {
        display: flex;
```

```
        flex-direction: column;
        img {
            object-fit: contain;
            height: 150px;
            max-width: 200px;
        }
    }
    .login__btn {
        width: 300px;
        background-color: #2e81f4;
        color: #eff2f5;
        font-weight: 800;
        &:hover {
            background-color: white;
            color: #2e81f4;
        }
    }
}
`

export default Login
```

Next, show the `Login` component if there is no current user. You create a temporary state variable to show it in the `App.js` file. The updated content is marked in bold.

```
...
import { useState } from 'react'
import Login from './components/Login'

function App() {
  const [user, setUser] = useState(null)

  return (
    <AppWrapper>
      {user ? (

          <Header />
          <div className="app__body">
            <Sidebar />
            <Feed />
```

```
        <Widget />
      </div>

  ) : (
      <Login />
  )}
  </AppWrapper>
  );
}
const AppWrapper = styled.div`...`

export default App;
```

Figure 6 11 shows the login screen on localhost.

Figure 6-11. *Login screen*

In the `Login.js` file, you need to import `auth`, `provider` from the local Firebase file. Then use a `signInWithPopup()` method to get the results. The updated content is marked in bold.

```
...
import { Button } from '@material-ui/core'
import { auth, provider } from '../firebase'

const Login = () => {
    const signIn = () => {
        auth.signInWithPopup(provider)
            .then(result => console.log(result))
            .catch(error => alert(error.message))
    }
    return (...)
}
const LoginWrapper = styled.div`...`

export default Login
```

Click the **SIGN IN** button on localhost, and a Gmail authentication window pops up. After clicking the Gmail username, you see all the logged-in user details in the console, as seen in Figure 6-12.

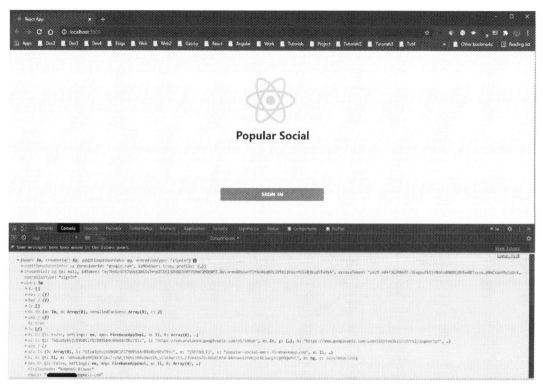

Figure 6-12. *Login details*

Using Redux and Context API

Let's dispatch the user data into the data layer, and here the Redux/Context API comes into play.

You want the user information to be stored in a global state. First, create a new StateProvider.js file. Use the useContext API to create a StateProvider function. The following is the content. Again, learn more about the useContext hook in my React hooks YouTube video at www.youtube.com/watch?v=oSqqs16RejM.

```
import React, { createContext, useContext, useReducer } from 'react'
export const StateContext = createContext()

export const StateProvider = ({ reducer, initialState, children }) => (
    <StateContext.Provider value={useReducer(reducer, initialState)}>
        {children}
    </StateContext.Provider>
)
export const useStateValue = () => useContext(StateContext)
```

Next, create a `Reducer.js` file inside the `src` folder. This is a concept similar to the reducer in a Redux component. Again, you can learn more about it at `www.youtube.com/watch?v=m0GOROTchDY`.

```
export const initialState = {
    user: null,
}

export const actionTypes = {
    SET_USER: 'SET_USER'
}

const reducer = (state, action) => {
    console.log(action)
    switch (action.type) {
        case actionTypes.SET_USER:
            return {
                ...state,
                user: action.user
            }
        default:
            return state
    }
}

export default reducer
```

In the `index.js` file, wrap the app component with the `StateProvider` component after importing the required files. The updated content is marked in bold.

```
...
import { StateProvider } from './StateProvider';
import reducer, { initialState } from './Reducer';

ReactDOM.render(
  <React.StrictMode>
    <StateProvider initialState={initialState} reducer={reducer}>
      <App />
    </StateProvider>
```

```
    </React.StrictMode>,
    document.getElementById('root')
);
```

In the `Login.js` file, when you get user data back from Google, you dispatch it to the reducer, and it is stored in the data layer.

Here, `useStateValue` is a custom hook. The updated content is marked in bold.

```
...
import { auth, provider } from '../firebase'
import { useStateValue } from '../StateProvider'
import { actionTypes } from '../Reducer'

const Login = () => {
    const [{}, dispatch] = useStateValue()

    const signIn = () => {
        auth.signInWithPopup(provider)
            .then(result => {
                console.log(result)
                dispatch({
                    type: actionTypes.SET_USER,
                    user: result.user
                })
            })
            .catch(error => alert(error.message))
    }

    return (...)
}
const LoginWrapper = styled.div`...`

export default Login
```

Return to the `App.js` file and use the `useStateValue` hook. Extract the global user from it and base it on your login. The updated content is marked in bold.

```
...
import { useStateValue } from './StateProvider';
```

```
function App() {
  const [{ user }, dispatch] = useStateValue()
  return (...);
}

const AppWrapper = styled.div`...`

export default App;
```

If you sign in on localhost, it takes you to the app, as seen in Figure 6-13.

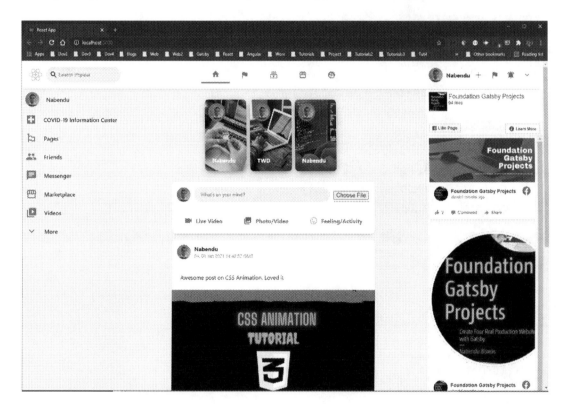

Figure 6-13. *Logged in*

Using Redux Data in Other Components

You have access to the user's data, so you can use it anywhere. Let's use the user's Google image as the avatar and the Google username instead of the hard-coded one in the Header.js file. The updated content is marked in bold.

```
...
import { useStateValue } from '../StateProvider'

const Header = () => {
    const [{ user }, dispatch] = useStateValue()

    return (
        <HeaderWrapper>
            ...
            <HeaderCenter>
            ...
            </HeaderCenter>
            <HeaderRight>
                <div className="header__info">
                    <Avatar src={user.photoURL} />
                    <h4>{user.displayName}</h4>
                </div>
            ...
            </HeaderRight>
        </HeaderWrapper>
    )
}

const HeaderWrapper = styled.div`...`

export default Header
```

Also, use the user's Google image as the avatar in the Messenger.js file.

```
...
import { useStateValue } from '../StateProvider'

const Messenger = () => {
    const [input, setInput] = useState('')
    const [image, setImage] = useState(null)
    const [{ user }, dispatch] = useStateValue()
        ...
    return (
        <MessengerWrapper>
            <MessengerTop>
```

```
                <Avatar src={user.photoURL} />
                <form>
        ...
                </form>
            </MessengerTop>
            <MessengerBottom>
        ...
            </MessengerBottom>
        </MessengerWrapper>
    )
}

const MessengerWrapper = styled.div`...`

export default Messenger
```

The Sidebar.js file includes the user's username and an avatar.

```
...
import { useStateValue } from '../StateProvider'

const Sidebar = () => {
    const [{ user }, dispatch] = useStateValue()

    return (
        <SidebarWrapper>
            <SidebarRow src={user.photoURL} title={user.displayName} />
            <SidebarRow Icon={LocalHospitalIcon} title="COVID-19
            Information Center" />
                ...
        </SidebarWrapper>
    )
}

const SidebarWrapper = styled.div`
`

export default Sidebar
```

Figure 6-14 shows the user's Google image and username in all the correct places on localhost.

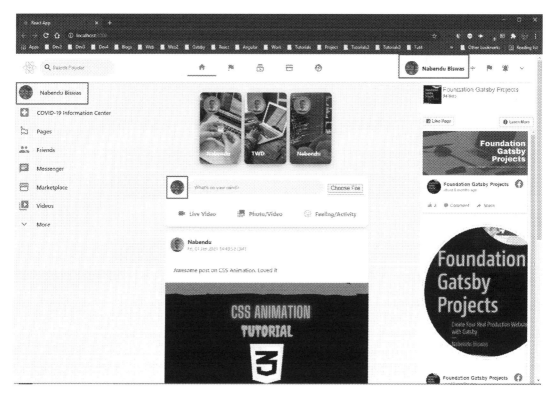

Figure 6-14. *Login details*

Initial Back End Setup

Let's move to the back end, starting with the Node.js code. Open a new terminal window and create a new photo-social-backend folder in the root directory. After moving to the photo-social-backend directory, enter the git init command, which is required for Heroku later.

```
mkdir popular-social-backend
cd popular-social-backend
git init
```

Next, create the package.json file by entering the npm init command in the terminal. You are asked a bunch of questions; for most of them, simply press the Enter key. You can provide the **description** and the **author**, but they are not mandatory. You generally make the entry point at server.js, which is standard (see Figure 6-15).

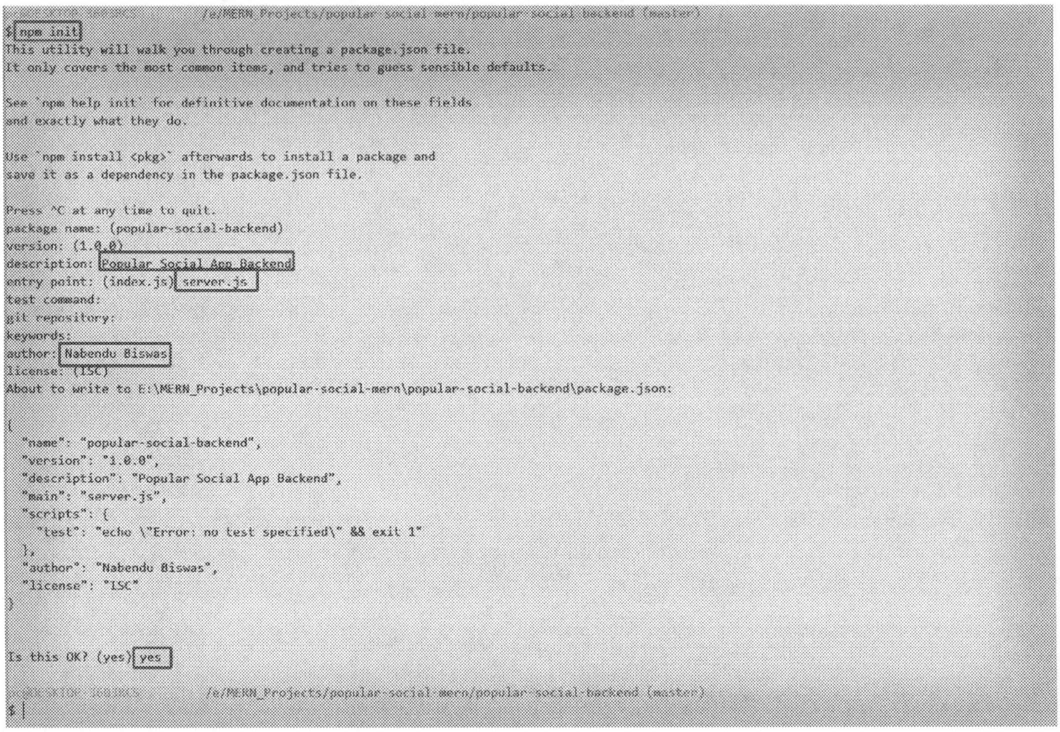

Figure 6-15. *Initial back-end setup*

Once package.json is created, you need to create the .gitignore file with node_
modules in it since you don't want to push node_modules to Heroku later. The following
is the .gitignore file content.

```
node_modules
```

Next, open package.json. The line "type": "module is required to have React-like
imports enabled in Node.js. Include a start script to run the server.js file. The updated
content is marked in bold.

```
{
  "name": "popular-social-backend",
  "version": "1.0.0",
  "description": "Popular Social App Backend",
  "main": "server.js",
  "type": "module",
  "scripts": {
    "test": "echo \"Error: no test specified\" && exit 1",
```

```
    "start": "node server.js"
  },
  "author": "Nabendu Biswas",
  "license": "ISC"
}
```

You need to install some packages before starting. Open the terminal and install cors, express, gridfs-stream, mongoose, multer, multer-gridfs-storage, nodemon, path, body-parser, and pusher in the popular-social-backend folder.

```
npm i body-parser cors express gridfs-stream mongoose multer multer-gridfs-
storage nodemon path pusher
```

MongoDB Setup

The MongoDB setup is the same as explained in Chapter 1. Follow those instructions and create a new project named **popular-social-mern**.

Initial Route Setup

Create a server.js file in the photo-social-backend folder. Here, you import the Express and Mongoose packages. Then use Express to create a port variable to run on port 9000.

The first API endpoint is a simple GET request created by app.get(), which shows the text **Hello TheWebDev** if successful.

Then listen on port 9000 with app.listen().

```
//imports
import express from 'express'
import mongoose from 'mongoose'
import cors from 'cors'
import multer from 'multer'
import GridFsStorage from 'multer-gridfs-storage'
import Grid from 'gridfs-stream'
import bodyParser from 'body-parser'
import path from 'path'
import Pusher from 'pusher'
```

```
//app config
Grid.mongo = mongoose.mongo
const app = express()
const port = process.env.PORT || 9000

//middleware
app.use(bodyParser.json())
app.use(cors())

//DB Config

//api routes
app.get("/", (req, res) => res.status(200).send("Hello TheWebDev"))

//listen
app.listen(port, () => console.log(`Listening on localhost: ${port}`))
```

In the terminal, type **nodemon server.js** to see the **Listening on localhost: 9000** console log. To check that the route is working correctly, go to `http://localhost:9000/` to see the endpoint text, as seen in Figure 6-16.

Hello TheWebDev

Figure 6-16. *Route test*

Database User and Network Access

In MongoDB, you need to create a database user and give network access. The process is the same as explained in Chapter 1. Follow those instructions, and then get the user credentials and connection URL.

In the `server.js` file, create a `connection_url` variable and paste the URL within the string from MongoDB. You need to provide the password that you saved earlier and a database name.

The updated code is marked in bold.

```
//imports
...
```

```
//app config
Grid.mongo = mongoose.mongo
const app = express()
const port = process.env.PORT || 9000
const connection_url = 'mongodb+srv://admin:<password>@cluster0.quof7.
mongodb.net/myFirstDatabase?retryWrites=true&w=majority'

//middleware
...
```

Storing Images in MongoDB

You are using GridFS to store the images. You installed it earlier through the `multer-gridfs-storage` package. The `gridfs-stream` package is responsible for reading and rendering to the user's stream.

Two connections are used in the project. The first one is for image upload, and the second one does other GET and POSTs. The updated code in `server.js` is marked in bold.

```
...
//middleware
app.use(bodyParser.json())
app.use(cors())

//DB Config
const connection = mongoose.createConnection(connection_url, {
    useNewUrlParser: true,
    useCreateIndex: true,
    useUnifiedTopology: true
})

mongoose.connect(connection_url, {
    useNewUrlParser: true,
    useCreateIndex: true,
    useUnifiedTopology: true
})

//api routes
...
```

Complete the code to upload the image. First, create a gfs variable, and then use the conn variable to connect to the database. Next, use Grid to connect to the database and then create a collection of images to store the pics.

Next, create the storage variable, which calls a GridFsStorage function with an object. Here, the connection_url variable is used. Inside a promise, create a unique filename by appending the current date to it. Create a fileInfo object containing the **filename** and the **bucketName** as the earlier create collection images.

Use the multer package to upload the image by passing the variable created earlier.

Build the endpoint to upload the image using POST requests, and upload the variable created earlier. The updated code in server.js is marked in bold.

```
...
//DB Config
const connection = mongoose.createConnection(connection_url, {
...
})

let gfs

connection.once('open', () => {
    console.log('DB Connected')
    gfs = Grid(connection.db, mongoose.mongo)
    gfs.collection('images')
})

const storage = new GridFsStorage({
    url: connection_url,
    file: (req, file) => {
        return new Promise((resolve, reject) => {
            const filename = `image-${Date.now()}${path.extname(file.
            originalname)}`
            const fileInfo = {
                filename: filename,
                bucketName: 'images'
            }
            resolve(fileInfo)
        })
    }
})
```

```
const upload = multer({ storage })

mongoose.connect(connection_url, {
  ...
})

//api routes
app.get("/", (req, res) => res.status(200).send("Hello TheWebDev"))

app.post('/upload/image', upload.single('file'),(req, res) => {
    res.status(201).send(req.file)
})

//listen
...
```

Check the endpoint in Postman. Open a POST request to `http://localhost:9000/upload/image`.

Select **Body** and then **form-data**. Next, select a file from the File drop-down menu and then click **Select Files**. This opens a popup window in which you must choose an image file (see Figure 6-17).

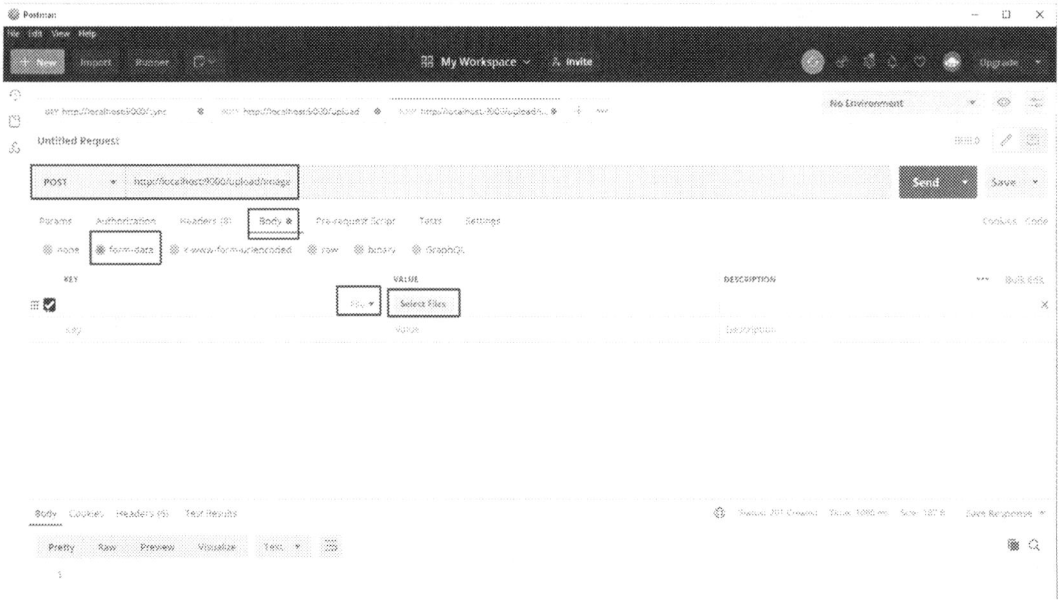

Figure 6-17. *POST request*

Click the **Send** button. If everything is successful, you see the image details in Postman, as shown in Figure 6-18.

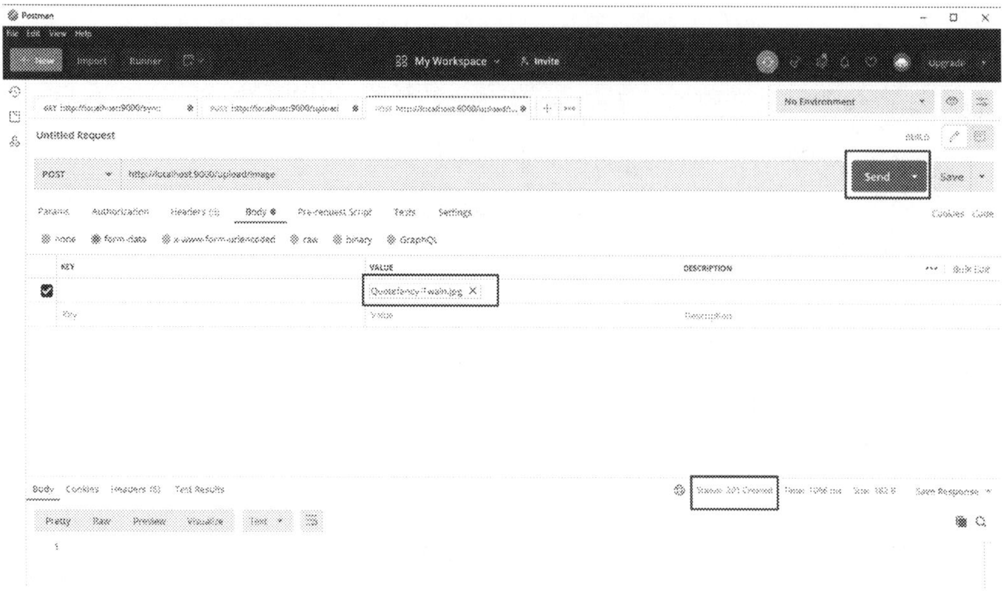

Figure 6-18.   *Post image*

You can also check in MongoDB, where the image is saved as `images.chunks` and the details are in `images.files`, as seen in Figure 6-19.

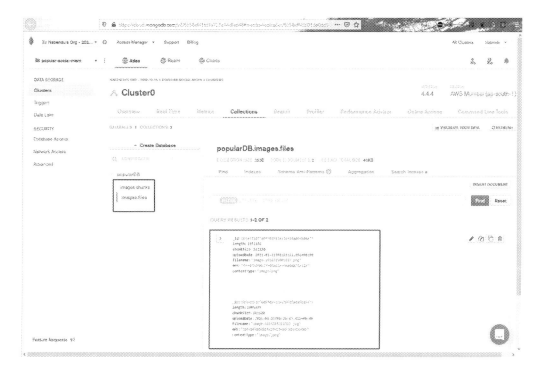

Figure 6-19. *Image chunk*

Create the route to get the file. To do this, create a /images/single GET route, which takes a parameter filename. Then use the findOne method to find the file.

If the file is present, use the gfs.createReadStream() to read the file. Then pass the res to this read stream using a pipe. The updated code in server.js is marked in bold.

```
...
//api routes
app.get("/", (req, res) => res.status(200).send("Hello TheWebDev"))

app.post('/upload/image', upload.any('file'),(req, res) => {
    res.status(201).send(req.file)
})

app.get('/images/single',(req, res) => {
    gfs.files.findOne({ filename: req.query.name }, (err, file) => {
        if(err) {
            res.status(500).send(err)
        } else {
            if(!file || file.length === 0) {
```

```
                res.status(404).json({ err: 'file not found' })
            } else {
                const readstream = gfs.createReadStream(file.filename)
                readstream.pipe(res)
            }
        }
    })
})
//listen
...
```

Next, let's test the GET route to receive an image in Postman.

In Postman, open a GET request to `http://localhost:9000/images/single`. Under Params, the **KEY** is **name** and the **VALUE** is the image from the MongoDB record. Once you hit the **Send** button, the image is returned (see Figure 6-20).

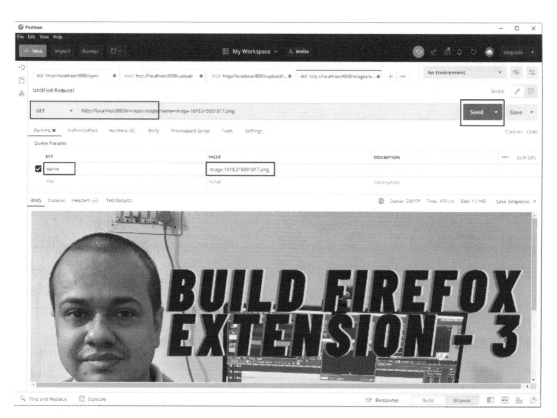

Figure 6-20. *GET request*

MongoDB Schema and Routes

Until now, the process was to get the image and save it in MongoDB. Now that you have the image details, you can save it in MongoDB with other post details.

To do this, you need to create the route to save the post. First, create the model for the post. Then create a `postModel.js` file inside the `popular-social-backend` folder.

Here, you create a schema with the required parameters to be passed and then export it.

```
import mongoose from 'mongoose'

const postsModel = mongoose.Schema({
    user: String,
    imgName: String,
    text: String,
    avatar: String,
    timestamp: String
})

export default mongoose.model('posts', postsModel)
```

You now use the schema to create the endpoint that adds data to the database.

In `server.js`, create a POST request to the `/upload` endpoint. The load is in `req.body` to MongoDB. Then use `create()` to send `dbPost`. If it's a success, you receive status 201; otherwise, you receive status 500.

Next, create the GET endpoint to `/sync` to get the data from the database. You are using `find()` here. You receive status 200 if successful (otherwise, status 500). A timestamp sorts the posts.

The updated code is marked in bold.

```
...
import Posts from './postModel.js'
...
app.post('/upload/post', (req, res) => {
    const dbPost = req.body
    Posts.create(dbPost, (err, data) => {
        if(err)
            res.status(500).send(err)
```

```
        else
            res.status(201).send(data)
    })
})

app.get('/posts', (req, res) => {
    Posts.find((err, data) => {
        if(err) {
            res.status(500).send(err)
        } else {
            data.sort((b,a) => a.timestamp - b.timestamp)
            res.status(200).send(data)
        }
    })
})

//listen
app.listen(port, () => console.log(`Listening on localhost: ${port}`))
```

Integrating the Back End with the Front End

You want to get all the messages when the app initially loads and then push the messages. You need to hit the GET endpoint, and for that you need Axios. Open the photo-social-frontend folder and install it.

```
npm i axios
```

Next, create a new axios.js file inside the src folder and create an instance of axios. The base URL is http://localhost:9000.

```
import axios from 'axios'

const instance = axios.create({
    baseURL: "http://localhost:9000"
})

export default instance
```

Do the necessary imports in the Feed.js file. After that, you have a postsData state variable. Next, call a syncFeed function from useEffect once.

The syncFeed function does the GET call to the posts endpoint and sets postsData with the res.data with setPostsData.

```
...
import React, { useEffect, useState } from 'react'
import axios from '../axios'

const Feed = () => {
    const [postsData, setPostsData] = useState([])
    const syncFeed = () => {
        axios.get('/posts')
            .then(res => {
                console.log(res.data)
                setPostsData(res.data)
            })
    }

    useEffect(() => {
        syncFeed()
    }, [])

    return (
        <FeedWrapper>
            <Stories />
            <Messenger />
            {
                postsData.map(entry => (
                    <Post
                        profilePic={entry.avatar}
                        message={entry.text}
                        timestamp={entry.timestamp}
                        imgName={entry.imgName}
                        username={entry.user}
                    />
                ))
            }
```

```
        </FeedWrapper>
    )
}

const FeedWrapper = styled.div`...`

export default Feed
```

In `Messenger.js,` add the imports for `axios` and `FormData`, which append the new image.

Update `handleSubmit()`. Here, check for the image that you already uploaded—and then append the image and the image name in the form.

Use `axios.post` to send the image to the `/upload/image` endpoint. In the then part, create a `postData` object to take the text from the user-entered input. `imgName` contains the name of the image from `res.data.filename`. The **user** and **avatar** are taken from the Firebase data and the **timestamp** is from `Date.now()`.

Call the `savePost()` with the `postData` object. Note that there is an `else`, where you are not sending the image to `savePost()`. This is for cases where the user creates a post without any image.

In `savePost()`, you take `postData` and do a POST call to the `/upload/post` endpoint. The updated content is marked in bold.

```
...
import axios from '../axios'
import FormData from 'form-data'

const Messenger = () => {
    ...
    const handleSubmit = e => {
        e.preventDefault()
        if(image) {
            const imgForm = new FormData()
            imgForm.append('file',image, image.name)
            axios.post('/upload/image', imgForm, {
                headers: {
                    'accept': 'application/json',
                    'Accept-Language': 'en-US,en;q=0.8',
```

```
                    'Content-Type': `multipart/form-data;
                    boundary=${imgForm._boundary}`
                }
            }).then(res => {
                const postData = {
                    text: input,
                    imgName: res.data.filename,
                    user: user.displayName,
                    avatar: user.photoURL,
                    timestamp: Date.now()
                }
                savePost(postData)
            })
        } else {
            const postData = {
                text: input,
                user: user.displayName,
                avatar: user.photoURL,
                timestamp: Date.now()
            }
            savePost(postData)
        }
        setInput('')
        setImage(null)
    }

    const savePost = async postData => {
        await axios.post('/upload/post', postData)
            .then(res => {
                console.log(res)
            })
    }
return (...)
}

const MessengerWrapper = styled.div`...`

export default Messenger
```

The next change is in the Post.js file, where you show the image you get from the http://localhost:9000/images/single endpoint by passing the image name as a parameter. The updated content in the Post.js file is marked in bold.

```
...
const Post = ({ profilePic, message, timestamp, imgName, username }) => {
    return (
            ...
        {
            imgName ? (
                <div className="post__image">
                    <img src={`http://localhost:9000/images/
                    single?name=${imgName}`} alt="Posts" />
                </div>
            ) : (
                    console.log('DEBUG >>> no image here')
                )
        }
        ...
        </PostWrapper>
    )
}
...
```

You now have a working application in which you can upload an image and post messages. It is stored in MongoDB and shown on the homepage. But you have a problem, and the posts are not reflected in real time. You must refresh the app (see Figure 6-21).

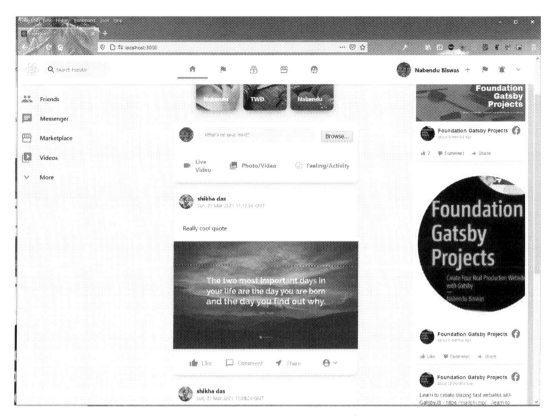

Figure 6-21. Problem

Configuring Pusher

Since MongoDB is not a real-time database, it's time to add a pusher to the app for real-time data. Since you already did the setup in Chapter 4, follow the same instructions, and create an app named **photo-social-mern**.

Adding Pusher to the Back End

Since Pusher is already installed on the back end, you just need to add the code for it in the server.js file. Use the Pusher initialization code, which you get from the Pusher website. You use it by creating a new Mongoose connection in server.js. Here, you use changeStream to monitor all changes in the posts. If there is any change, trigger a pusher.

```
...
//App Config
...
const pusher = new Pusher({
    appId: "11xxxx",
    key: "9exxxxxxxxxxxxxx",
    secret: "b7xxxxxxxxxxxxxxx",
    cluster: "ap2",
    useTLS: true
});

//API Endpoints
mongoose.connect(connection_url, {  ...})

mongoose.connection.once('open', () => {
    console.log('DB Connected for pusher')
    const changeStream = mongoose.connection.collection('posts').watch()
    changeStream.on('change', change => {
        console.log(change)
        if(change.operationType === "insert") {
            console.log('Trigerring Pusher')
            pusher.trigger('posts','inserted', {
                change: change
            })
        } else {
            console.log('Error trigerring Pusher')
        }
    })
})

app.get("/", (req, res) => res.status(200).send("Hello TheWebDev"))
...
//Listener
app.listen(port, () => console.log(`Listening on localhost: ${port}`))
```

Adding Pusher to the Front End

It's time to move to the front end and use Pusher. First, you need to install the pusher-js package in the photo-social-frontend folder.

npm i pusher-js

Import Pusher into Feed.js and then use the unique code. Then use useEffect to subscribe to the posts. If it changes, call syncFeed(), which gets all the posts again from the /posts endpoint. The updated code is marked in bold.

```
...
import Pusher from 'pusher-js'

const pusher = new Pusher('e6xxxxxxxxxxxxxxx', {
    cluster: 'ap2'
});

const Feed = () => {
    const [postsData, setPostsData] = useState([])

    const syncFeed = () => {
        axios.get('/posts')
            .then(res => {
                console.log(res.data)
                setPostsData(res.data)
            })
    }

    useEffect(() => {
        const channel = pusher.subscribe('posts');
        channel.bind('inserted', (data) => {
            syncFeed()
        });
    },[])
    useEffect(() => {
        syncFeed()
    }, [])
```

```
    return (...)
}
```

```
const FeedWrapper = styled.div`...`
```

```
export default Feed
```

And now back in the app, you can post anything in real time.

Deploying the Back End to Heroku

Go to www.heroku.com to deploy the back end. Follow the same procedure that you did Chapter 1 and create an app named **popular-social-backend**.

After successfully deploying, go to https://popular-social-backend.herokuapp. com. Figure 6-22 shows the correct text.

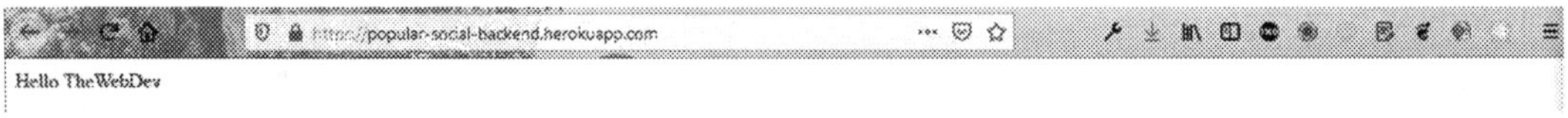

Figure 6-22. *Back end deployed*

Go back to axios.js and change the endpoint to https://popular-social-backend.herokuapp.com. If everything is working fine, your app should run.

```
import axios from 'axios'
const instance = axios.create({
    baseURL: "https://popular-social-backend.herokuapp.com"
})

export default instance
```

Deploying the Front End to Firebase

It's time to deploy the front end in Firebase. Follow the same procedure that you did in Chapter 1.

You need to update the Post.js file. The updated content is marked in bold.

```
...
        {
            imgName ? (
                <div className="post__image">
                    <img src={` https://popular-social-backend.
                    herokuapp.com/images/single?name=${imgName}`}
                    alt="Posts" />
                </div>
            ) : (
                    console.log('DEBUG >>> no image here')
                )
        }
...
```

After this process, the site is live and working properly.

Deploying the Front End to Firebase

It's time to deploy the front end in Firebase. Follow the same procedure that you did in Chapter 1. After this process, the site should be live and working properly, as seen in Figure 6-23.

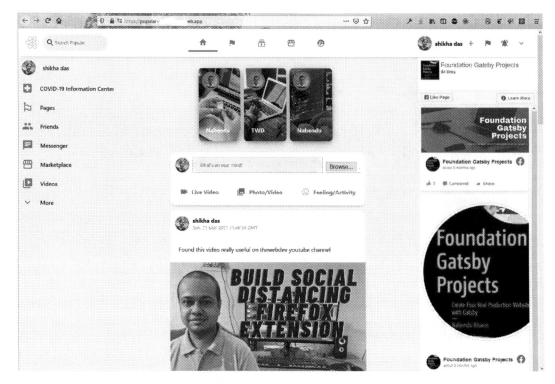

Figure 6-23. *Final deployed site*

Summary

In this chapter, you created a simple but functional social network. Firebase hosted it on the Internet. You learned to add Google authentication, by which you can log in with the Google account. You also learned how to store images in MongoDB and to give real-time capabilities to MongoDB using Pusher.

Index

A, B

Axios package, 56, 90

C

Components dynamic, 78–81, 177–179

D, E

Database user, 12–16, 50–51, 84–85,
    120–121, 200–201, 264–265
DatingCards.css file, 39, 41, 42
Document Object Model (DOM), 67

F

Firebase
    build, 25
    configuration, 24
    correct project, 24
    deploy front end, 59
    existing project, 24
    front end, 94, 167
    hosting, 143
    login, 23
Firebase hosting initial setup, 34
    add project, 3
    app name, 4
    console caption, 2
    project creation, 4, 5

G

Gmail authentication, 154, 254
Google authentication, 141, 151–155,
    250–251
Google image, 159, 160, 258, 260

H, I, J, K

HandleVideoPress function, 67
Heroku
    app name, 18
    back end, 93
    close popup, 21, 22
    command, 22
    instructions, 18, 19
    login credentials, 16, 17, 20, 21
    open back-end app, 23

L

Login.css content, 148, 149

M

MERN
    back-end setup, 47–49, 117, 118
    chat component, 108, 111
    chat messages, 114
    dating cards component, 39
    deployed version, 62

R

S, T, U

V, W, X, Y, Z

Printed in the United States
by Baker & Taylor Publisher Services